101

COLLEGE

Interpreting Death

WITHDRAWN FROM
THE LIBRARY

UNIVERSITY OF
WINCHESTER

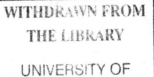

2 0 JAN 2000

D0317418

Other books by the editors:
Peter C. Jupp and Glennys Howarth (eds)
Contemporary Issues in the Sociology of Death, Dying and Disposal
The Changing Face of Death: Historical Accounts of Death and Disposal

Peter C. Jupp and Kieran Flanagan (eds)
Postmodernity, Sociology and Religion

Peter C. Jupp is also co-editor with Glennys Howarth of the journal
Mortality

Interpreting Death

Christian Theology and Pastoral Practice

———

Edited by
Peter C. Jupp and Tony Rogers

on behalf of
The Churches' Group on Funeral Services
at Cemeteries and Crematoria

Foreword by Michael Henshall

CASSELL
London and Washington

Cassell
Wellington House, 125 Strand, London WC2R 0BB
PO Box 605, Herndon, VA 20172, USA

© Peter C. Jupp, Tony Rogers and the contributors 1997

All rights reserved. No part of this publication may be reproduced or transmitted in any form or by any means, electronic or mechanical including photocopying, recording or any information storage or retrieval system, without prior permission in writing from the publishers.

First published 1997

British Library Cataloguing-in-Publication Data
A catalogue record for this book is available from the British Library.

ISBN 0–304–33784–6

Typeset by York House Typographic Ltd, London
Printed and bound in Great Britain by Biddles Ltd, Guildford and King's Lynn

KING ALFRED'S COLLEGE
WINCHESTER

OWL

02148250 236·1
JUP

Contents

Notes on the contributors

Hazel Addy is a minister in the United Reformed Church, formerly a university chaplain and the URC's National AIDS Advisor, and now working as a healthcare chaplain in Manchester. She hates putting pen to paper but has managed to contribute to *Life Cycles: Women and Pastoral Care* and *Silence in Heaven: A Book of Women's Preaching*. She also co-produced *A Gift Wrapped in Thorns*, a resource pack for church people concerned about HIV/AIDS.

Douglas Davies is a Professor of theology and the Principal of the College of St Hild and St Bede at Durham University. Before that, he was Professor of religious studies at Nottingham University. He is an anthropologist and theologian and an Anglican priest. He has written *Meaning and Salvation in Religious Studies* (1984), *Studies in Pastoral Theology and Social Anthropology* (1986), *Mormon Spirituality* (1987), *Cremation Today and Tomorrow* (1990), *F. B. Jevons* (1991), *Church and Religion in Rural England* (1991, with Watkins and Winter), *Reusing Old Graves* (1995, with A. Shaw), *British Crematoria in Public Profile* (1995), *Mormon Identities in Transition* (1996 edn) and *Death, Ritual and Belief* (1997).

Paul Denyer was born in 1946, the son of a Methodist minister, in Nassau, Bahamas. He was a librarian before Anglican ordination in 1974. He served as curate, team vicar and incumbent in the Bristol diocese for eighteen years before becoming Director of Ordinands in 1995. He is particularly concerned that the Church of England priesthood should retain and develop its role of representing God on behalf of the whole community, as opposed to offering chaplaincy or management for the committed.

David Forrester, educated at Keble College, Oxford, and the English College in Rome, is presently the Roman Catholic Chaplain and a teacher of history at Eton, having previously been the Roman Catholic Chaplain to Oxford University (1990–6) and a parish priest in Portsmouth. He is the author of *Young Doctor Pusey* (1989), a biography of the nineteenth-century Tractarian, and various books on spirituality and pastoral matters, particularly bereavement.

Anthony Gardiner is a full-time stipendiary minister in the United Reformed Church. He was ordained in 1972, having trained at Mansfield College, Oxford, and has previously served in churches in Castleford and Leeds. Since 1983 he has been minister of the URC in Havant, not far from Portsmouth.

Roger Grainger has worked as an actor, priest, counsellor and drama therapist and has carried out research into pastoral work, implicit religion and drama therapy. He has written extensively on these issues in both books and articles and was recently made Doctor of Divinity (University of London) for his work on rites of passage, liturgy and liturgical drama. His sixteen books include *The Language of the Rite* (1974) and *The Social Symbolism of Grief and Mourning* (1997). For eighteen years he was chaplain at Stanley Royd Hospital, Wakefield.

For twenty years **Michael Henshall** was Bishop of Warrington. He retired in November 1996. He has been described as a 'pioneering Chairman' of The Churches' Group on Funeral Services at Cemeteries and Crematoria. In the service of the group he has taken on everybody from cabinet minister to media shark. His deep concern for pastoral ministry in a changing society has served the group by extending its concerns and by encouraging the different members to contribute their own expertise. He is a deeply committed Anglican with an equally strong commitment to the Ecumenical Movement.

John Heywood Thomas, a United Reformed Church minister, is Emeritus Professor of the University of Nottingham and Honorary Professor of the University of Wales, Bangor. He has held posts in philosophy and theology at the universities of Durham and Manchester and in the USA. He has published works on nineteenth-century idealism, Kierkegaard and Paul Tillich, his main research interests. He is also occupied with issues in medical ethics and theological methodology.

Peter C. Jupp is a United Reformed Church minister, with pastorates at Thame, London University and Hampstead. He is currently Director of the National Funerals College. His special interest is the history of cremation. He was Convenor of the British Sociological Association's Sociology of Religion Study Group in 1991–4. He is the co-editor of *Contemporary Issues in the Sociology of Death and Dying* and *The Changing Face of Death* (both Macmillan) and the journal *Mortality* (Carfax).

John Lampard is Superintendent of the South London Mission. He was previously Secretary Responsible for Local Preachers in the Methodist Church Division of Ministries. He is a member of The Churches' Group on Funeral Services at Cemeteries and Crematoria, and of the Methodist Church Faith and Order Liturgical Committee. He has a special interest in liturgical and sociological aspects of funerals. Author of many booklets, articles and reviews, he was for nine years editor of the journal *Worship and Preaching*. He is currently engaged in a research degree on the history of funeral liturgies.

Derek Nuttall is Minister of the United Reformed Church in Windsor, Chaplain of the Thames Valley Hospice, Windsor, and Free Church Chaplain to the King Edward VII Hospital, Windsor. He was Director of Cruse-Bereavement Care in 1974–90. He did ministry and community work in Aberfan, South Wales, in 1967–74, following the 1966 disaster. He wrote *The Early Days of Grieving* (1991).

Ordained in 1976, **Michael Perham** has been Vice Dean and Precentor of Norwich Cathedral since 1992. Formerly Secretary of the Doctrine Commission, he has served with the Church of England Liturgical Commission since 1982, is a member of the General Synod, of the Cathedrals' Liturgy Group and until recently was Chairman of the Council of PRAXIS. Well known as a lecturer and author, his books include *Liturgy Pastoral and Parochial* (1984) and *Lively Sacrifice* (1992).

Tony Rogers is a priest of the Roman Catholic Diocese of East Anglia: currently parish priest in Cambridge and Secretary for Liturgy to the Bishops' Conference of England and Wales. He was involved in the recent adaptation for England, Wales and Scotland of *The Order of Christian Funerals* (1990) and has contributed articles in *Liturgy* magazine, *The Parish Funeral* (1990) and is currently working on *In Sure and Certain Hope: Rites and Prayers from the Order of Christian Funerals for the Use of Lay-Readers*.

Geoffrey Rowell has been Suffragan Bishop of Basingstoke since 1994 and is an Emeritus Fellow of Keble College, Oxford, where he was Chaplain and Tutor in theology from 1972. He has had a long-standing interest in Christian eschatology and is the author of *Hell and the Victorians* (1974) and *The Liturgy of Christian Burial* (1977). A member of the Church of England Liturgical Commission in 1981–91 and of the Doctrine Commission in 1991–6 (and a consultant to the present Doctrine Commission), he has recently been appointed as Chair of The Churches' Group on Funeral Services at Cemeteries and Crematoria. He is Visiting Professor at the Chichester Institute.

Margaret Saunders is the Anglican Chaplain to Milton Keynes Hospital and Community NHS Trusts. She trained with the St Albans Ministerial Training Scheme and has a postgraduate diploma in counselling. She has had previous experience at Stoke Mandeville and St John's Hospitals in Aylesbury. She has been greatly involved in helping to develop the hospital's response to peri-natal death.

Paul Sheppy is a Baptist minister in pastoral charge. His doctoral thesis was entitled *Liturgy and Death: An Examination of the Pastoral and Theological Issues Relating to Funerals, with Special Reference to Selected Funerary Rites* (1995). He has written a major review of Anglican funeral rites to be published by the University of Mainz, and other articles in the same field. He is Secretary of the Joint Liturgical Group of Great Britain and a member of the English Language Liturgical Consultation.

Peter Speck originally graduated in zoology and biochemistry. After parish life, he moved to full-time hospital chaplaincy in Sheffield, London and now Southampton University Hospitals NHS Trust. He was formerly Honorary Senior Lecturer (Medical Ethics) at the Royal Free Medical School, London. He is the author of several books and articles on pastoral care, palliative care, loss and bereavement. His research interest is in belief systems and the extent to which they influence outcome from life experiences.

Geoffrey Steel, a Roman Catholic priest, combines parish ministry in Preston, Lancashire, with various aspects of liturgical formation. For ten years he lectured in liturgy at Ushaw College, Durham, the regional seminary. He is a member of the liturgy committee of the Bishops' Conference of England and Wales, and is observer to the Church of England Liturgical

Commission. He also serves on the advisory committee of the Roman Catholic international commission, ICEL.

Tony Walter, who lives in Bath, is Reader in sociology at the University of Reading, where he is developing a new cross-disciplinary MA in Death and Society. Among his books are *Funerals and How to Improve Them* (1990), *The Revival of Death* (1994) and *The Eclipse of Eternity* (1995). He helped found the National Funerals College in 1992.

Penelope Wilcock is a Methodist minister and formerly Free Church Chaplain of St Michael's Hospice, Hastings. Her book *Spiritual Care of Dying and Bereaved People* was published by SPCK in 1996. She has extensive current involvement in crafting funerals which reflect the spirituality and life philosophy of the individuals concerned, both those bereaved and those deceased.

Acknowledgements

We wish to thank the following for permission to reprint copyright material. Although every effort has been made to contact the owners of the copyright material reproduced in this book, if any has been included without acknowledgement, apologies are offered to all concerned and we will happily include acknowledgement in any future editions.

W. B. Yeats, 'The Lover Tells of the Rose in His Heart', is reprinted with the permission of Simon & Schuster from *The Collected Works of W.B. Yeats*, vol. 1: *The Poems*, revised and edited by Richard J. Finneran. Copyright © 1983, 1989 by Anne Yeats. Also by permission of A.P. Watt Ltd on behalf of Michael Yeats. Text of 'Lord God, source and destiny' from the *Order of Christian Funerals*, © 1985, International Committee on English in the Liturgy, Inc. All rights reserved. Extracts from the *Salvation Army Ceremonies Book* are used by permission of The Salvation Army International Headquarters. Extracts from the *Methodist Service Book* © Trustees for Methodist Church purposes, used by permission of the Methodist Publishing House. Extracts from The Funeral Service from *The Alternative Service Book 1980* are copyright © The Central Board of Finance of the Church of England and are reproduced by permission. Draft texts by the Liturgical Commission of the Church of England are copyright © The Central Board of Finance of the Church of England and are reproduced by permission. These are not authorized for liturgical use.

We are grateful to St George's House, Windsor, for permission to reprint 'Confronting the abyss: the relationship between bereavement and faith' by Anthony Gardiner, which was first published in *St George's House, Windsor Castle: Annual Review 1990* (Windsor: St George's House, Windsor Castle, 1991).

Preface

We offer this book to all people involved in ministry to dying, dead or bereaved people. It is specifically written to help equip Christians both to face and to interpret mortality. Our conviction is that mortality is the gift of God, who therein provides clues both to his own character and purpose and to the human condition. Contributors to this book have recalled individuals whose deaths particularly affected them. We are also cautiously aware that our own faith here will only properly be tested when we become physically aware that our own deaths, if not imminent, are unavoidable.

The stimulus for the book came from our increasing awareness that, at the present time, funeral practice and bereavement support in our churches are insufficiently grounded in Christian teaching, or, put another way, they do not sufficiently inform each other. We were convinced that Christians needed greater resources to tackle the contemporary gaps between Christian doctrine, liturgical practice, funerary practices, popular beliefs and the needs of bereaved people.

Specifically, our concern came from a survey carried out by the Revd Dr John Hall, formerly Honorary Secretary of the Churches' Group on Funeral Services at Cemeteries and Crematoria. His report suggested that few colleges and courses were satisfied with the ministerial training they provided on three issues: the theology of death, the conduct of funerals, and support for dying and bereaved people. This book is one response made by the Churches' Group to this challenge.

We are grateful to members of Cassell who have seen this book through the press: Ruth McCurry, Gill Paterson, Liz Marsh, Leilah Nadir, Rachel Rogers, Michael Johnson and especially Helena Power. Their advice, patience and encouragement have continually helped us. We thank Clare

Gittings for guidance on the cover, and Katharine Riley for her secretarial assistance. We thank our authors for sharing their experience, wisdom and good-humoured patience.

We have also been conscious of the specific culture of the Christian churches to which we individually belong: hence the stimulus of working on funeral ministry with the ecumenical Churches' Group. Six years ago, one of the editors was being guided round a cemetery. The guide said, 'Look! This graveyard must have different sections for ten different denominations. Isn't that ridiculous?' 'Not necessarily,' was the reply, 'if my own church didn't offer a distinctive word to help me negotiate death, it wouldn't be a church worth joining.' The paradox of denominational loyalty is that, whilst, in a fallen world, such commitment is necessary to frame testable Christian convictions, our churches cannot separately provide the whole picture of God's world. Only after death may we be free to adopt a vantage point for that full perspective. In the interim, we trust with Charles Wesley,

> Love, like death, hath all destroyed,
> Rendered all distinctions void;
> Names and sects and parties fall:
> Thou, O Christ, art all in all.

Peter C. Jupp and Tony Rogers

Foreword

The state we live in often regards 'the last enemy' with dread, confusion, ignorance and self-inflicted blindness. For many people death has become an unspoken subject. Some years ago as a working bishop I received a serious complaint from an apparently intelligent lay person. The well-regarded local vicar had upset the congregation dreadfully by preaching a sermon on the forbidden subject. Would I rebuke him for an indelicate and insensitive address? Lest the sermon contain heavy heresy I requested a copy of the script. It was in fact a model discourse. It was biblically grounded. It was pastorally sensitive. It was even spiritually uplifting. It invited the listeners (not always to be equated with the hearers) to reflect on an inevitable occurrence and to prepare for that inevitability. There were one or two sharp comments on judgement – but what is a good sermon if it lacks a certain sharpness? But it was death not judgement that lay at the heart of the complaint.

I would have been glad to see that splendid sermon included in this significant volume, for like it these various essays are designed to help a consumer-dominated society reflect on those issues that gather round the journey to that other country; a journey that some deny, others doubt, but one on which Christian faith offers a hopeful signpost. I commend very warmly indeed the sensitive, balanced, supportive and informative con-tributions to this book. I know most of the contributors personally. I know that from long and careful study in a difficult field that all have wisdom above the average and significant thoughts to share.

It is likely that some will find the subjects discussed difficult, even painful. They are! But to consider death is for Christian people to consider life. At the heart of the matter is the firm Christian conviction that God raised Jesus Christ from the dead. All else is derived from that pivotal assertion ...

assurance, hope, resurrection, eternal life. The backcloth to any Christian book on death must be the total saving work of Christ. Behind the delicate task of supporting the bereaved glows the face of the compassionate Christ. Behind the spoken words of a funeral is a God who numbers the hairs and counts the sparrows. All these essays are woven around a golden thread. It is that certainty that while we do not know what the future holds, we do know who holds that future.

The paradox of our present age is that while not wishing to tangle with death many are significantly curious about it. A society that fails to reflect on the last things (heaven, hell, death, judgement) earns and deserves the label superficial. I hope that this volume will lead many out of the tangle and beyond the curious. Life is enriched not by seeking bolt holes in materialism, but by asking questions about what life is ultimately concerned to offer.

This book is promoted and inspired by The Churches' Group on Funeral Services at Cemeteries and Crematoria. Such a heavy title hides a dedicated, national, ecumenical group of scholarly and caring people. It has been my privilege to chair the group for some six years. I hope that the wisdom here attempted and the insights offered will help many as they wrestle with the task of interpreting death and singing the Lord's song in a strange land.

✝Michael Henshall

Introduction

Tony Rogers

This book originated as a result of a number of study days and seminars organized by the Churches' Group on Funeral Services at Cemeteries and Crematoria. The Group, which began its life as a sub-committee of the General Synod of the Church of England to examine the question of burial fees, soon expanded into an ecumenical body whose main concern is the promotion of good funeral practices and effective liaison between the churches, funeral directors, cemetery and crematorium authorities. Papers from the study days had been put together in pamphlet form, but there was a strong sense that there was room for a substantial work, with a breadth of contributors, on the theology of death and disposal, the experience of bereavement and the role of faith in that experience, and a survey of the liturgical ties and practices of the major Christian churches in Britain, together with some material on the increasingly common non-standard funerals. The writers are drawn from a wealth of sources – academic and pastoral, parish clergy and hospital chaplains, lay people, Protestant and Catholic.

The book is divided into three parts. Chapters 1 to 6 are concerned with the theology of death and disposal; Chapters 7 to 12 deal with the experience of bereavement and the role of faith, and Chapters 13 to 17 explore liturgy and its context. Peter Jupp's widespread and detailed knowledge of funerary practices across the centuries qualifies him to set the scene, putting before the reader the issues which face all those involved in funeral and bereavement ministry today.

Geoffrey Rowell's chapter 'Changing patterns: Christian beliefs about death and the future life' is an historical survey of the changes in Christian doctrine and popular belief, from the scriptures and the early Church, through to the present day, culminating in the Church of England Doctrine

Commission's report 'The Mystery of Salvation'. He especially highlights that shift which came at the Reformation from funerals being a time when something was done for the departed to their being an opportunity for moral exhortation to the living. Rowell shows that, whatever the belief and practice, there has, in human history and culture, always been a fascination with death.

Roger Grainger's chapter, 'To be dead is not enough', lays the emphasis on Christ's redeeming death and resurrection, with a discussion of contemporary theological and popular understanding about the ultimate *location* of the dead, with special reference to concepts of heaven, hell, limbo and purgatory. With references to modern surveys, he points to the fact that, in today's society, heaven is a more acceptable concept than hell, and that the fear of nothingness after death is, in itself, what draws so many to at least a wish-fulfilment that whatever would follow is the very best something possible, however hidden or uncertain it is.

In the fourth chapter, 'Towards a theology of transition', Paul Sheppy examines the paschal nature of Christian death, by asking the questions 'What is the life to which God calls us?' and 'In what sense is the death of Jesus for us?' He affirms, as a minister who conducts funerals regularly, that the death and resurrection of Jesus transforms 'the repellence of death into a holy event'. The author addresses the issues of the immortality of the soul and the resurrection of the body, and in response to what he calls a 'unitary' rather than a dualistic approach to death, offers a liturgy of 'release' as an alternative to commendation and committal.

Chapter 5 moves from the theology of death to the theology of disposal. John Heywood Thomas has written on 'Life, death and paradise: the theology of the funeral'. He examines the purpose of a funeral and sets it in the context of a minister's normal preaching and leading of worship. In this setting the Church is called upon to 'offer a word of hope at a time of despair, and a word of comfort to the mourners'. He also examines the taboo which surrounds death in our society, and the way in which a minister can hold back from addressing fundamental issues about Christ's triumphant death in the face of bereavement. He stresses that the Christian proclamation about death is clear about Christ – his death is our hope.

The final chapter in the first part – Douglas Davies' first contribution 'Theologies of disposal' – focuses more particularly on the theology of cremation. Davies makes the point that the churches have, traditionally, had a theology of cremation which is really based on that of burial, but questions whether this is an adequate response to the liturgy of cremation. In view of the increasing preference for cremation, his own view is that it is not, and his paper offers alternative theologies for cremation centred on ashes rather than corpses. He also makes a distinction between the significance of cremation within a religious tradition, and in newly emerging secular traditions.

Derek Nuttall opens the second part with a chapter on 'The needs of bereaved people at the time of the funeral'. Here he addresses another factor in the purpose of a funeral, which he sets in the context of the grieving process – 'conducted sensitively, it can aid grieving, conducted badly, it can hinder it'. He examines the question of funerals as ritual acts in the face of a major event in human experience, set in a time of change and readjustment of assumptions, providing an opportunity for family and friends to acknowledge what has happened and giving them responsibility for the choice of a final resting place. The importance of the minister's role before and after the funeral would seem to be greater than ever, in view of the complexity of circumstances surrounding both the deceased and the bereaved.

Peter Speck's chapter 'Bereavement and belief: an Anglican perspective' examines the rather broader base from which Anglicans involved in pastoral care of the bereaved come, and of the issues involved in dealing with people who have no obvious Christian faith. Examining the issues at each of Van Gennep's three stages of mourning, he shows how the everyday business of preparing for and carrying out the funeral can 'enable the grief process to happen'. He also examines the extent to which current Anglican funeral rites meet the needs of the bereaved.

David Forrester writes on 'Loss and gain' and deals at some length with the stages and characteristics of bereavement, making the point that 'our responses are as different as our experiences' and that there is, consequently, no one pattern or sequence that everybody must go through in the grieving process. He speaks from the Catholic perspective, especially of the role of the whole church community in the care of the bereaved, not just at the time of death but in the months and years that follow. Ritual support is needed for mourners, and David Forrester makes reference to the prayer and sacramental life of the Catholic Church in this regard.

Anthony Gardiner tackles the paradox of the life-affirming nature of the Christian faith being challenged profoundly by the experience of personal bereavement in his chapter 'Confronting the abyss'. The experience of death, he asserts, is not only painful, but also undermines our self-assurance, since we have invested so much in relationships with those whom we love.

But he points to a way in which grief in bereavement can be lessened by affirming, rather than denying, the value of what has been lost. Confronting this abyss can raise possibilities of healing.

Douglas Davies' second contribution, 'Contemporary belief in life after death', provides the reader with fascinating results from a survey conducted very recently by Davies and Shaw which shows the wide spectrum of belief, not only among committed Christians but also among atheists and agnostics. While half the population has some belief in immortality, about a quarter has no belief, while the rest are unsure. Davies teases out the tension between the faith as perceived by the Church and the faith as perceived by the mourners at a funeral. He points to the need for sensitivity on the part of clergy, who may have a very clear framework of belief themselves but be quite unaware of the range among the bereaved.

Chapter 12 comprises three shorter papers. These address funerals following specific examples of contemporary bereavement. This is a chapter about 'non-standard' funerals, not by way of presenting them as being out of the ordinary, but rather to flag the rise of such ceremonies in modern Britain. Penelope Wilcock tackles the increasingly common phenomenon of the Christian minister who is invited to conduct the funeral service at which neither the deceased nor the mourners were or are believers. Margaret Saunders deals with another sensitive subject: miscarriages, stillborn and peri-natal deaths, and the challenge taken up by all Christian churches in recent years to make provision for ritualizing these deaths. Hazel Addy has written about the experience, not only of the funeral of an AIDS victim, but of her involvement with the man, his partner and his family before and after death.

Michael Perham opens the final part on 'Liturgy and its context' with a chapter entitled 'Anglican funeral rites today and tomorrow' – a frank analysis of the shortcomings of the ASB texts, which he describes as being 'light years away from where most mourners are' and of the positive developments which have been taken up in the Church of England's draft funeral texts, particularly in regard to ritual gestures, signs and symbols. He also traces the history of the Prayer Book Burial Service and discusses the problem that has existed in the Church of England over prayer for the departed.

Geoffrey Steel's 'Celebrating our journey into Christ: The Roman Catholic *Order of Christian Funerals*' is a guide to the contents of the current Catholic funeral liturgy and the thought behind it. The book is seen as a resource because, while many of the shorter forms of service will probably not be used frequently, they are available and may be adapted at will. The *Order of Christian Funerals* parallels something of the process of bereavement by providing a phased or staged funeral – not primarily in terms of where things happen, but rather *when* they happen. These different occasions, different in mood and formality, can facilitate bereavement and can, in different ways, involve members of the church community in the 'ministry of consolation'.

John Lampard's task, as a Methodist minister writing on 'Funeral Liturgies of the Free Churches', was not enviable. Nonetheless he has provided a comprehensive picture of funeral practices in Baptist, Methodist and United Reformed churches as well as the Salvation Army and the ever-increasing Black Majority churches. In the first three traditions he shows how liturgical reform in other churches has made an impact on the thinking and practice of these bodies, while he also gives us a clear insight to the particular traditions of the Black Majority churches and the distinctive witness of the Salvation Army.

If one theme of this book is about the meeting of the secular mind and the Christian Gospel, then Paul Denyer's contribution, 'Singing the Lord's song in a strange land', brings the issue into sharp relief. He writes of the dilemma faced by Christian ministers when asked – especially in a crematorium where the range of musical technology is often wide – for music that may not seem appropriate in the circumstances, and of the challenge they may face to 'Christen the secular'.

Tony Walter provides the final chapter in the book. 'Committal in the crematorium' addresses the specific issues raised by the replacement of the church and graveyard/cemetery as the traditional setting for a funeral by the crematorium. Churches are normally settings for many of life's events and funerals fitted into this pattern. Crematoria, on the other hand, are only associated with death. Walter addresses those things which are common to all funerals – coffins, flowers and leave-taking – and the implications of all three in the crematorium setting.

In conclusion, this collection of essays is by way of a tribute to Michael Henshall, former and retired Bishop of Warrington, who until 1996 chaired the Churches' Funerals Group for many years with skill, good humour and great encouragement. He was our spokesman on many occasions with the media, and it is in no small measure due to his own vision that this work has taken shape.

To the members, past and present,
of the Churches' Group on Funeral Services
at Cemeteries and Crematoria

1

The theology of death and disposal

The context of funeral ministry today

Peter C. Jupp

> We are bound to provide that the remains (of our brethren in Christ)
> ... should rest undisturbed and inviolate till the Great Doom; that in
> the same place where they lie down to rest, in the same place they shall
> arise to their sentence.

These words, from the Anglo-Catholic *Ecclesiologist* in 1851, indicate the
cusp of change in Christian funeral ministry in Britain. Written in 1851, they
expressed a traditional Christian view of burials which would soon be an
anachronism. The Burials Laws of 1850 and 1852 closed 5000 urban churchyards within eight years and transferred the responsibility for providing land
for the disposal of the dead to local (and secular) authorities, ending a
period of 1000 years' virtual monopoly by the Church.

The 1840s had been a period of great change in British funerals. A
campaign to close urban churchyards, revealed as wholly inadequate for the
number of burials even before the cholera crisis of 1847–8, succeeded in
opening a new era of cemeteries, owned, funded and operated by local
government. Undertakers, heavily battered by the reform movement, were
about to rationalize their activities. The vast majority of funerals were still
conducted by Anglican clergy according to Anglican rites, but Roman
Catholics and Protestant Dissenters were now receiving more equal attention in the new private cemeteries.

The loss of the churches' control of burial grounds coincided, in ways I
one day intend to correlate, with their loss of control of traditional Christian

doctrines about the future of people after death. The Reformation synthesis consigned the dead to the earth in the sure and certain hope of (1) the resurrection of the body for (2) reunion with the soul for (3) the judgement, followed by (4) heaven or hell. These theological developments are surveyed by Geoffrey Rowell in Chapter 2. During the later nineteenth century, the Christian churches began variously to reconsider the traditional doctrines of 'the four last things', death, judgement, heaven and hell, in ways that varied with and within each denomination but which were increasingly accommodative to evolving new public attitudes towards death, dying and disposal.

By the Burial Laws Amendment Act 1880, Nonconformists were finally permitted to conduct funerals according to their own rites in rural churchyards. The same Act permitted funerals to be conducted without Christian rites, promoting a secularizing shift hardly observed at the time. In 1884 cremation, despite Catholic and some Anglican opposition, was legalized and local government soon recognized cremation's advantages over burial in economies of space and financial subsidy. The doctrine of Christ's descent into hell enjoyed a short-lived revival in the 1870s, but the more widely held doctrines of bodily resurrection, judgement and hell were increasingly under attack. The First World War would accelerate their consignment to history (Wilkinson, 1978).

In 1900, Joseph Jacobs commented: 'Death as a motive is moribund. Perhaps the most distinctive note of the modern spirit is the practical disappearance of the thought of death as an influence bearing directly upon personal life . . .Death has lost its terrors' (Jacobs, 1900, p. 264). For Jacobs, death had lost its terrors through longevity, urban life and the conquest of disease. Ten years later, Canon Henry Scott Holland, in his sermon 'Death the King of Terrors', wrote that 'Death is nothing at all'. Our own contemporaries have torn these words wildly from their historical context: reflections on the death of Edward VII (Holland, 1924). However unrealistic or comforting we may regard these well known and well used words, his sermon as a whole reminds us of how popular attitudes to death and the afterlife are correlated closely with people's experience of death, their customs at funerals and the provisions made by the community for the disposal and memorialization of the dead.

This book surveys contemporary Christian positions about death and the hope beyond. It examines the liturgical, pastoral and interpretative tasks of the Church and relates them to the needs of bereaved people. Its purpose is to arm Christians, and thereby all to whom the Church ministers, with stronger resources for funeral ministry and the experience of bereavement. This chapter examines the changing context of this vocation.

The changing context of death

Change in population structure

In 1850, only one in twenty Britons was aged over 65. Today, 15 per cent of us survive this long. On average, men are expected to live until 73, and women to 78. In the 1990s, 2.5 million of us have passed our 80th birthday. Our century has seen huge advances in diet and healthcare provision. Infant and maternal mortality have been massively reduced. By consequence, it is the elderly who die. At the very time when we have to cope with the death and the funeral of a partner, we have less energy to deal with it. By contrast, the deaths of young people and babies are so uncommon they are very traumatic experiences (Ariès, 1986, p. 37; see also Stone, 1988). The last 30 years have seen a blossoming of bereavement support organizations, like Cruse-Bereavement Care and the National Association of Bereavement Services. Some have specifically developed to cope with premature deaths, like The Compassionate Friends, the Stillbirth and Neonatal Deaths Society, the Gay and Lesbian Bereavement Service and Road Peace.

Change in the nature of disease

Acute infectious diseases like smallpox, scarlet fever and tuberculosis, which so terrified parents and patients eighty years ago, have largely departed. Today human mortality is particularly accomplished by long-term chronic and degenerative conditions, particularly circulatory, respiratory or cancerous (Nuland, 1995). There are three consequences: first, the age of normal death is beyond retirement age; second, chronic and degenerative diseases have become major aspects of health care; third, death is much less likely to be sudden and unexpected and, instead, dying typically takes place over a relatively long period. On the one hand, these provide for the government ethical and economic dilemmas over the funding of health resources for the very elderly, and euthanasia proponents are increasingly active. On the other, the long drawn-out nature of the disease encourages anticipatory grieving and the increasing perception of a difference between social and biological death (Mulkay, 1993; Glaser and Strauss, 1965), when relatives and visitors to hospital beds are increasingly exhausted by their attentions, the death becomes the climax of the long process. After that release, the funeral must work hard if it is not to be experienced as an anticlimax.

Change in families and households

Modern families are far smaller. Social and occupational mobility means that family members can live at great distances from each other. Such mobility has contributed to a loosening of local ties which, allied with changes in belief about the form of life after death, have contributed to the popularity of cremation over burial. A recent television programme about the Stockport fire of 1928 showed film of 20,000 mourners attending the funeral of a fireman. Whilst such deaths are exceptional, and the funerals therefore well attended, the development of work and leisure patterns has meant that far fewer people are now free to attend funerals.

Employment patterns have affected the roles of both sexes. The rise of women's paid employment and the deferral of the age of child-bearing have resulted in a steady reduction of the availability of (traditionally female) family members to act as unpaid carers and mourners. The burden of mourning costume has traditionally fallen upon women. These responsibilities were severely loosened during the First World War (Taylor, 1982). Since 1945, mourning wear has almost entirely disappeared in England. The fact that bereavement has become less visible may make the rest of us feel more comfortable. The internal pain and constriction remains. Indeed, they may be even sharper because their invisibility cancels the old signals of need for special consideration.

The institutionalization of death

Until 1958, over half the people in England and Wales died in their beds at home. Thus, Leslie Weatherhead could write confidently in 1960, 'Most ministers have watched people die' (1960, p. 246). Today, 25 per cent of us die at home, 54 per cent in a hospital, 18 per cent in residential/nursing homes and 4 per cent in hospices. When institutions become the context for death, families experience a loss of control and participation in the dying of their relative. In a long perspective, this control has shifted away from dying

people, their family and neighbours, towards specialists and their institutions, the clergy, the medical profession, the funeral directing sector and the
managers of cemeteries and crematoria (Jupp, 1995b).

Secularization

Popular belief in life after death – at least in its Christian versions – has
steadily declined. Douglas Davies surveys this process in Chapter 11. This is
not to say that we are yet a secular society: whilst we are decreasingly a
church-going society, the extent of our secularity is vigorously debated
(Davie, 1994; Bruce, 1996). Certainly, the nature, content and forms of
religious commitment have changed. The relevance of this for beliefs about
death is indicated by Young and Cullen in their conversations with East
Londoners. They found little indication that people had gained their belief
in the afterlife from the Church:

> The general secularisation of society ... has ... been accompanied by
> a lay view of immortality ... it has also thinned down the beliefs that
> lay people have inherited from a long tradition, and left them to
> wander round ... with their own beliefs or lack of them ... their
> religion was family religion, since it was mostly a dead member of the
> family ... who was thought to be waiting for the family to be re-united
> or reformed. They did not have general ideas about resurrection. But
> they had a notion of heaven: it was a place where they would be united
> with those they loved who also loved them, in which there would
> presumably be no room for those who loved no-one. (Young and
> Cullen, 1996, pp. 174, 173)

Life beyond death may thus be understood as selecting and magnifying
the most satisfying relationships experienced before death. The East Londoners whose experiences sharpened Young and Cullen's book did not
indicate that they had derived their ideas of the afterlife from the motion
picture industry. Film plots, based on belief in exorcism, reincarnation and
varieties of ghostly activity, have continued to make plausible concepts
about the afterlife which have little basis in religious tradition or creed (*The
Economist*, 7 September, 1991). Those whose Christian ministry is to
comfort bereaved people in public or in private must take account of the
fact that, today, people's beliefs are unlikely to be traditional, and are far
more individualistic.

The changing context of funerals

Such changes in people's experience of death suggests that funerals now have to meet different needs among bereaved people, as many of the chapters in the second part below indicate. In an earlier era, premature death was a regular occurrence. In the early nineteenth century, as many marriages were sundered by early death as are today broken by divorce. Funerals were a common experience in the family. People died at home and were buried in their parish churchyard, which was small, accessible and essentially local. The growth of cities, with their peculiar patterns of mortality, led to the introduction of large cemeteries. This in turn promoted developments in more efficient funeral directing, particularly in the provision of transport to the more distant cemeteries. Just as in the eighteenth century, the role of the clergyman at deathbeds had been steadily taken over by the doctor (Porter, 1989), so the funeral director increasingly took over tasks previously performed by families, neighbours and local joiners. The work of families watching at the bedside and waking by the open coffin has similarly passed to nursing, undertaking or mortuary staff whose ward is not continuous. The effect of the First World War in simplifying funeral procedures is a book yet to be written (but see Gregory, 1994; Taylor, 1982; Wilkinson, 1978 and Winter, 1995).

The promotion of cremation in the 1930s by local government signalled a rising interest in more economic forms of disposal, which was encouraged by the Welfare State provisions of the Labour government of 1945–51 (Jupp, 1990, 1997). Its introduction of a range of benefits for widowed people and for funeral expenses symbolized a widely-held conviction that funerals merited far less expenditure of time and money. Some of the same arguments are being advanced today by the euthanasia lobby. Meanwhile, the needs of bereaved people – for emotional, physical and metaphysical support – remain, less visible but huge.

Funeral practices have changed in at least four significant ways, all of which affect the scope of the Church's ministry.

Municipalization

Until 1850, the vast majority of burial grounds were owned and managed by the Anglican Church. Among the exceptions, the private cemetery companies which had sprung up since 1820 had often been established by Nonconformists. Their management principles provided a model for the management of public cemeteries after 1850 (Rugg, 1992). Faced with the loss of their churchyards, Anglican clergy responded in a number of ways. They co-operated with such movements as that of the public gardens movement to transform closed urban cemeteries into public parks for leisure. They also discarded interest in public cemeteries. *The Times* commented of a clergyman's appointment of chairman of the Burial Board at the new Maidstone cemetery in 1874 how rare it had now become to find a clergyman concerned for public cemeteries.

The Burials Act 1900 enhanced the role of public cemeteries and brought to an end decades of feuding between Anglicans and Dissenters. Two years later, the Cremation Act laid new foundations for local authority economies in their still relatively recent responsibility for the disposal of the dead.

The salience of local government in burial provision brought about the greatest change in the disposal of the dead in England for over a thousand years. The new cemeteries were spacious, non-denominational, increasingly difficult to maintain and, above all for our purpose, secular (Jupp, 1990). It is far easier to form and develop doctrines about life after death when you control the rite, site and mode of disposal. With (secular) local government controlling burial and cremation, decisions about the disposal of the dead are increasingly taken in an economic climate. The Cemeteries Order (1977) permitted parochial church councils to entrust the maintenance of their closed churchyards to the public purse. Consequently, the local Christian community had less control over the churchyard as a setting for the church building and as a symbol for its gospel of resurrection (Healey, 1967).

Churchyards and cemeteries, whilst they share one common purpose, offer critically different forms of control and culture and community. The Freckleton Decision (1994), focusing on the propriety of gravestone inscriptions, highlighted the specific role of a Christian churchyard as opposed to a community cemetery (Diocese of Blackburn, 1994; Brian, 1995).

Seventy per cent of funerals currently involve cremation. Crematoria designs display particular constraints and opportunities of their own (see Walter's chapter below; Cope, 1970). Seven crematoria out of eight are owned by local authorities, whose budget priorities determine the hours of opening, the length of service and facilities for music, as well as the architectural design, the landscaping and the permitted forms of memorialization. From one perspective, crematorium management has more control over the mode of funeral than either clergy or funeral directors. Those conducting Christian funerals at crematoria still largely need to come to terms with the fact that they are visiting actors on a stage they do not own, enacting a traditional drama subject to contemporary restraints.

Commercialization

The British undertaking industry has an annual turnover of £500 million. Disbursements – burial and cremation fees, medical and registration fees, and clergy costs – add another third to this figure. Monumental masons offer yet a third direction for funeral expense. British funerals are very big business indeed. Their development, from part-time entrepreneurs to international chains, has been described by Litten (1991), Howarth (1996, 1997) and Parsons (1997). In the 1930s, the Co-operative Societies entered the funeral industry in a bid to reduce clients' costs. After 1945, many part-time funeral directors sold their businesses. The introduction of refrigeration techniques and the development of Chapels of Rest gave the funeral director an increasing measure of control over funeral decisions. This control was increased by the development of motor transport necessitated by the growing popularity of (distant) crematoria. In the 1970s, the Great Southern Group embarked upon a programme of acquisitions, a process expanded hugely by men like Howard Hodgson in the 1980s (Hodgson, 1992). A further series of acquisitions in 1994 led to the pattern of market shares in 1997: Co-ops 25 per cent, Service Corporation International 14 per cent and independents 61 per cent.

Two other developments have sought to extend this commercial activity. In July 1995, the Department of the Environment issued a Private Finance Initiative which encouraged local authorities to sell their crematoria to private companies. Funeral directing firms are best placed to afford these purchases. The DoE's decision flew in the face of the Report (May 1995) of the Department of Trade and Industry that the joint ownership of crematoria and funeral directing outlets by a common company threatened to become a monopoly situation, which was not in the best interests of bereaved people purchasing their funerals.

Secondly, systems of pre-paid funeral plans are rapidly developing across the funeral directing industry. Whilst these offer advantages to people planning for their funeral in advance, they are also designed to enhance funeral directing companies' market share. As Sloane has revealed, the great power of funeral directors in the United States rests upon their ownership of all the facilities successively required for a funeral: funeral home, cemetery and crematorium, memorial mason, florist and grave maintenance (Sloane, 1991). It is no longer a nightmare scenario to envisage complete commercial control of the funeral process by a company's additional acquisition of nursing homes and pre-paid plan schemes.

Christian ministry for the dead and for the bereaved has now to take account of this huge shift in power and control over funeral arrangements. Yet the churches are themselves part of this financial picture. According to the Church Commissioners' estimate, the Church of England, conducting 70 per cent of funerals in England, receives an annual income of at least £11 million. The standard of clergy performance in funeral ministry is increasingly under public and professional pressure to improve.

Consumerization

Despite the control of the public and commercial sectors, there are alternatives to the 'standard' British funeral. Within the industry, funeral directing trade associations have improved their codes of practice. The Institute of Burial and Cremation Administration (IBCA) has published its *Charter for the Bereaved* (1996) promoting the rights of bereaved people and laying down new minimum standards for cemeteries and crematoria.

Funeral reform groups have grown up outside the industry. The Natural Death Centre promotes greater family involvement in caring for dying people, especially at home. It has sponsored new ideas for funerals with an ecological concern, promoting woodland burial schemes and cardboard and biodegradable coffins. The National Funerals College has promoted *The Dead Citizens Charter* (1996) which makes recommendations for better funerals for both 'the dead and the bereaved'. The College was founded by Lord Young, the pioneer of the Consumers' Association. This Association has published a number of surveys of funeral directing practices. Their spokesman Colin Brown has argued:

> many people are totally in the hands of the funeral industry right through from the GP or hospital, police, maybe coroner, funeral directors, clergy, cremation or burial staff, monumental masons, the whole lot. The consumer feels totally in their hands ... [People don't] know what is standard practice ... A funeral is a distress purchase by distressed people who are not equipped for the task ... the industry ... colludes with this unique set of circumstances to restrict choice. (Brown, 1995, p. 165)

As *The Economist* added, 'the funeral industry thrives on the acumen of its managers, but also because of three peculiar features of the market: ignorance, sentiment and taboo. Without them, its profits would decompose even faster than its corpses' (*The Economist*, 4 January 1997, p. 75). Consumer awareness has promoted calls for price economy, cheaper coffins and DIY funerals. Reformers have lobbied for investigation of the pre-paid plan market and company take-overs and have provoked growing interest and response on the part of the Department of Trade and Industry and other ministries.

The rules of the market-place are always to be challenged by the economy of God. Christian ministers stand under the same judgement. There are still ministers whose funeral work is below standard. As Geoffrey Rowell wrote: 'No liturgy ought ever to be mechanical, skimped or dis-engaged' (Rowell, 1997, p. 19). *The Dead Citizens Charter* called for clergy always to make contact with families to prepare themselves for the funeral. All crematorium and cemetery staff know of clergy who conduct a succession of funerals, with the same text and the same lack of preparation. All dioceses and denominations know the identities of the 'crematorium cowboys' who preside at too many funerals of which they never inform local clergy (Churches' Group on Funerals, 1997; Forrest, 1995; Luby, 1995; Naylor, 1991).

Personalization

Paradoxically, it was a Humanist, John Pearce, who identified the critical role of clergy in the reform of funerals. Surveying a series of funeral seminars, he wrote: 'clergy are in the best position to respond flexibly to the differing needs of bereaved people. They are less hide-bound by the system within which they work.'

Humanists, lacking a belief in any forms of life after death, conduct services which are, *ipso facto*, designed to celebrate a life which has completely ended. They can reflect only upon a past, not a future. With no intercessions for the dead, they take time to concentrate upon the life, values and achievements of the occupant in the coffin. With no traditional liturgies, they are more free to compose their own, tailored to the needs of individual bereaved families, with whom they often prepare the ceremony. In a multicultural Britain, Humanists are not alone in providing funeral liturgies which take account of the particular religious faith of individual families. Cemeteries and crematoria co-operate here because it is their public duty to provide facilities for all – or at least major – faiths.

There is a historical dimension to the funeral's focus upon the needs of bereaved people. The Reformation in Britain outlawed prayers for the dead and the doctrine of Purgatory, closed chantries and made redundant chantry priests (Duffy, 1992). Intended to secure the role of God Himself in decisions about what was to follow death, it had tremendous effects on funerals. Clare Gittings writes: 'the ritual ties between the living and the dead were severed' (Gittings, 1984, p. 40). Keith Thomas added: 'Each generation could [now] be indifferent to the spiritual fate of its predecessor' (Thomas, 1973, p. 721). No-one would deny the advantages won to the Christian Church by the Reformation, but they must be set alongside the enormous cost. These costs involved the Protestant Church's ministry to the dead and bereaved. Henceforth, funerals were shaped and conducted for the benefit only of the survivors, not the departed. The Prayer Book service could only commit, not commend, the dead. Thus the effective focus of funerals became the benefit and consolation and caution for the living. In Scottish ceremonies, for a time, even sermons were banned, lest a good word might be said about the deceased and thus steal God's prerogative (Rowell, 1977).

Thus funerals affected and were affected by the developing spirit of individualism in Britain (Gittings, 1984; Jacobs, 1900). Post-funeral activities mushroomed: the growth in mourning-wear fashions, in gravestones and memorials. Yet these functioned to emphasize the social status of the bereaved, now that funerals could no longer focus upon the heavenly status of the deceased. The development is complex. There is as yet no British Ariès to systematize the broad sweep of changing attitudes to death in England as there was in France (Ariès, 1976, 1983, 1985). Major jigsaw pieces are now steadily being assembled, by increasing numbers of scholars from many disciplines.

The changes in theology and belief in the last 130 years have contributed, in this age of cremation and longevity, to the diminution of death as a subject for religious interpretation (see especially Walter, 1995), however much solace funerals provide at a death. Contemporary industrial societies have largely sought to marginalize death from the pages of the book of active life. The situation seemed to have gone so far that in 1969, the President of the Institute of Burial and Cremation Administration said: 'In these islands I feel we have the finest funeral system in the world, with the impact of death on the community not too apparent. I want it to stay that way' (*Observer*, 13 July 1969).

A quarter of a century later, *The Economist,* in an article on euthanasia, hoped that dying might: 'come to hold again the place it used to occupy in the midst of life: not a terror, but a mystery so deep that man would no more wish to cheat himself of it than cheat himself of life' (*The Economist,* 20 July 1991).

The 1990s have witnessed accelerating developments within British funeral practice. There has been an increased tendency for rituals to concentrate less upon the future but upon the past and the individuality of the dead person. The coffin of Sir Lawrence Olivier was decorated with symbols of his great stage roles and the service was full of his recorded speeches. For lesser lights, music is the preferred vehicle of individuality, for which Frank Sinatra's 'I did it my way' supplies the theme. Funerals are increasingly being sought (and marketed) as personalized or tailor-made. The choice of disposal may reflect ecological choice or the convenience of survivors. Coffins may be bought in the colours of football team favourites, family members be invited to draft or contribute to the funeral service. Douglas Davies has described the contemporary funeral as the retrospective fulfilment of identity (Davies, 1995).

Crematoria are having to respond to this choice by extending minimum service times, cemeteries by providing woodland and shroud burial. A wide range of memorials – both for bodies and for ashes – is now marketed. Funeral directors are responding to the call for more personalized funerals, and increasingly pre-paid plans include opportunities for choices in funeral plans. This book seeks to empower the Christian Church as it seeks to develop its resources to respond to contemporary needs in bereavement, both in experience and in reflection.

References

P. Ariès, trans. P. M. Ranum, *Western Attitudes Toward Death from the Middle Ages to the Present* (London: Marion Boyars, 1976).

P. Ariès, trans. H. Weaver, *The Hour of Our Death* (Harmondsworth: Penguin, 1983).

P. Ariès, trans. J. Lloyd, *Images of Man and Death* (Cambridge, Mass: Harvard University Press, 1985).

P. Ariès, *Centuries of Childhood* (Harmondsworth: Penguin, 1986).

S. F. Brian, *Reflections on the Freckleton Experience* (London: Association of Burial Authorities, 1995).

C. Brown, 'Funerals – The consumers' perspective', *Pharos,* vol. 61, no. 4, winter 1995.

S. Bruce, 'Religion in Britain at the close of the 20th century: A challenge to the silver lining perspective', *Journal of Contemporary Religion*, vol. 11, no. 3, October 1996.

The Churches' Group on Funeral Services at Cemeteries and Crematoria, *Guidelines for Best Practice of Clergy at Funerals* (London: The Churches' Group on Funeral Services at Cemeteries and Crematoria, 1997).

G. Cope (ed.), *Dying, Death and Disposal* (London: SPCK, 1970).

G. Davie, *Religion in Britain since 1945: Believing without Belonging* (Oxford: Blackwell, 1994).

D. J. Davies, 'The theology of cremation', in P. C. Jupp (ed.) (1995a).

Diocese of Blackburn: Judgement in the Consistory Court, 16 July 1994.

E. Duffy, *The Stripping of the Altars: Traditional Religion in England 1400–1580* (New Haven and London: Yale University Press, 1992).

The Ecclesiologist, 1851.

M. Forrest, 'The clergy responsibilities at crematorium funerals', in P. C. Jupp (ed.) (1995a).

C. Gittings, *Death, Burial and the Individual in Early Modern England* (Beckenham: Croom Helm, 1984).

B. G. Glaser and A. L. Strauss, *Awareness of Dying* (Chicago, IL: Aldine, 1965).

A. Gregory, *The Silence of Memory: Armistice Day 1919–1946* (Oxford: Berg, 1994).

K. Healey, *English Churchyard Memorials*. Lecture to the Royal Society of Arts, 11 January 1967.

H. Hodgson, *How to Become Dead Rich* (London: Pavilion Books, 1992).

H. S. Holland, 'The King of Terrors' [1910], in H. S. Holland, *Facts of the Faith* (London: Longmans, 1924).

G. Howarth, *Last Rites: The Work of the Modern Funeral Director* (Amityville, NY: Baywood, 1996).

G. Howarth, 'Professionalising the funeral industry in England, 1700–1960', in P. C. Jupp and G. Howarth (eds) *The Changing Face of Death: Historical Accounts of Death and Disposal* (Basingstoke: Macmillan, 1997).

Institute of Burial and Cremation Administration (IBCA), *Charter for the Bereaved* (1996).

J. Jacobs, 'The dying of death', *Fortnightly Review*, new series, LXXII, 1900.

P. C. Jupp, *From Dust to Ashes: The Replacement of Burial by Cremation in England 1840–1967* (London: The Congregational Memorial Hall Trust, 1990).

P. C. Jupp (ed.), *Clergy and Cremation Today* (London: The Churches' Group on Funeral Services at Cemeteries and Crematoria/The National Funerals College, 1995a).

P. C. Jupp, 'Whose funeral is it anyway?', in K. A. G. Elliott (ed.) *Report of the Joint Conference of Burial and Cremation Authorities* (Swansea: 1995b).

P. C. Jupp, 'Why was England the first country to popularize cremation?', in K. Charmaz, G. Howarth and A. Kellehear (eds) *The Unknown Country: Experiences of Death in Australia, Britain and the USA* (Basingstoke: Macmillan, 1997).

J. Litten, *The English Way of Death: The Common Funeral Since 1450* (London: Hale, 1991).

J. Luby, 'Clergy and crematoria: contemporary issues in the relationship between clergy and local authorities in the facilities for cremation', in P. C. Jupp (ed.) (1995a).

Monopolies and Mergers Commission, *Service Corporation International and Plantsbrook Group plc: A Report on the Merger Situation* (London: HMSO, 1995).

M. Mulkay, 'Social death in Britain', in D. Clark (ed.) *The Sociology of Death, Theory, Culture, Practice* (Oxford: Blackwell, 1993).

National Funerals College, *The Dead Citizens Charter* (London: 1996).

M. Naylor, 'Crossed wires, frustrations and conflicts in crematoria funerals', in The Churches' Group on Funeral Services at Cemeteries and Crematoria, *The Role of a Minister at a Funeral* (London: The Churches' Group on Funeral Services at Cemeteries and Crematoria, 1991).

S. B. Nuland, *How We Die: Reflections on Life's Final Chapter* (New York: Vintage Books, 1995).

B. Parsons, 'The making of the modern funeral director, 1960–1990' (unpublished PhD thesis, University of Westminster, 1997).

R. Porter, 'Death and the doctors in Georgian England', in R. Houlbrooke (ed.) *Death, Ritual and Bereavement* (London: Routledge, 1989).

G. Rowell, *The Liturgy of Christian Burial* (London: Alcuin Club/SPCK, 1977).

G. Rowell, 'The role of the clergy in funeral arrangements: options for change', in *The Future of Funerals: Options for Change* (London: The National Funerals College, 1997).

J. Rugg, 'The rise of cemetery companies in Britain 1820–53' (unpublished PhD thesis, University of Stirling, 1992).

D. C. Sloane, *The Last Great Necessity: Cemeteries in American History* (Baltimore: Johns Hopkins University Press, 1991).

L. Stone, *The Family, Sex and Marriage in England 1500–1800* (Harmondsworth: Penguin, 1988).

L. Taylor, *Mourning Dress: A Costume and Social History* (London: Allen and Unwin, 1982).

K. Thomas, *Religion and the Decline of Magic* (Harmondsworth: Penguin, 1973).

T. Walter, *The Eclipse of Eternity: A Sociology of the Afterlife* (Basingstoke: Macmillan, 1995).

L. D. Weatherhead, *Key Next Door and Other City Temple Sermons* (London: Hodder & Stoughton, 1960).

A. Wilkinson, *The Church of England and the First World War* (London: SPCK, 1978, reprinted 1996).

J. Winter, *Sites of Memory, Sites of Mourning: The Great War in European Cultural History* (Cambridge: Cambridge University Press, 1995).

M. Young and L. Cullen, *A Good Death: Conversations with East Londoners* (London: Routledge, 1996).

2

Changing patterns: Christian beliefs about death and the future life

Geoffrey Rowell

Our contemporary understanding of dying, death and disposal is one that has been powerfully shaped by what the Christian faith has had to say about death and the hope of a life beyond death. The embodiment of those beliefs in funeral liturgy has been and is powerful. If we would understand that pattern of belief we have first to recognize that it has had a complex evolution, and that Christian eschatology is by no means simple.

Hope of a life after death became part of the faith of Israel at a comparatively late period. Hope was focused on the continuation of the people of God rather than on the individual, whose future was seen as a wraith-like existence in the underworld of *She'ol*. Breath was life, and, as the psalmist said of all living creatures, including human beings: 'You turn your face away, they suffer, you stop their breath, they die, and revert to dust. You give breath, fresh life begins, you keep renewing the world' (Psalm 104.29–30). It was the death of the righteous that pressed hard on the question of divine justice. Would there be no vindication in the Day of the Lord for those who had died in faith and for faith? In particular would martyrs such as the Maccabees be vindicated, and their oppressors punished? From such concerns grew a faith that at the Last Day there would be a resurrection of the dead, for judgement of the wicked and for the vindication of the righteous. That resurrection hope was an act of new creation. The hope of a future life was not based on a belief in the intrinsic immortality of the soul, but on the purposes of God.

In the time of Jesus, that resurrection hope was characteristic of many, but not all, Jews. In the Gospels (Matthew 22.23–33; Mark 12.18–27; Luke 20.27–40), Jesus is challenged by the Sadducees, a Jewish group who did not believe in the resurrection of the dead, and in his reply Jesus aligns himself firmly with those who hold to a resurrection hope. In Luke's Gospel he replies to the Sadducees with the words: 'God is not a God of the dead but of the living, for all live to him' (Luke 20.38). In John's Gospel Jesus says to Martha, whose brother Lazarus has died; 'Your brother will rise again.' Martha replies, 'I know he will rise again at the resurrection at the last day' (John 11.23–24). The Christian conviction was that in the resurrection of Jesus that 'Last Day' had already come – and St Matthew's Gospel makes the point by telling of the bodies of many holy men being raised from the dead after the resurrection of Jesus (Matthew 27.52).

St Paul wrestles with the question of what this faith means for Christian believers. Christ is, he writes, the first-fruits of God's new creation, the first instance of the resurrection life of the last times. The resurrection of Jesus is the ground of Christian hope in the resurrection of Christians. The new and eternal life that God gives in that resurrection is an embodied and a transformed life; the resurrection body is *soma pneumatikon*, a 'body animated by the (Holy) Spirit' (1 Corinthians 15.44).

If that is to be the case at the end of time, at the Last Day – the time of the Parousia, or coming again of Jesus – what then of the fate of those who have died before that time? Although there is some evidence in the New Testament for believing that those who have died 'sleep', awaiting the resurrection at the Last Day, there is other evidence that stresses the present reality of the Christian's life in Christ. There is a present sharing in the eternal life that is God's gift in Christ, and those who have died were believed to be 'with Christ'. The picture of the worship of heaven in the Book of Revelation came to underlie a Christian understanding of the faithful departed, and especially the martyrs, sharing immediately at death in the life of heaven. And so Christian eschatology straddled uneasily a sense of immediate sharing after death in the worship of the heavenly places and a waiting for the fulfilment of resurrection at the end of time.

As the Christian faith spread into the Hellenistic and Roman world, into a context very different from its Jewish Semitic roots, it spread into a world which often believed strongly in an immortal soul. Greek mythology, like Egyptian mythology, had been fascinated by the journey of the soul into that mysterious realm beyond the grave. That realm was one in which all kinds of perils and dangers might be encountered, and was a journey for which all kinds of provision had to be made, hence the abundance of grave goods and the practice of mummification in Egyptian funerary ritual. In Greek mythology the ferryman, Charon, conveyed the soul of the departed across the Styx, the dark river of the underworld. Some of the oldest prayers in Christian funeral liturgy betray adaptations of these ancient themes. Death is a journey, a journey to the heavenly city, the dwelling place of God. But it is a perilous journey and the angels were seen as the guides who brought the souls of the departed safely through those dangers and perils. The martyrs, who were believed to have merited immediate heavenly reward by their death for the sake of Christ, were also associated with the angels in welcoming the departed. The anthem, *In Paradisum*, from the Western funeral liturgy, prays that the angels may lead the departed to paradise and that the martyrs may come to greet the departed with joy and bring him or her to the holy city, the heavenly Jerusalem (Rowell, 1977, pp. 16–17, 61). In some parts of the early Church the practice developed of placing the Sacrament (the *Viaticum*, or food for the journey) into the mouth of the corpse, as Greek custom had placed a coin in the mouth to pay the fee to Charon for crossing the Styx (*ibid.*, p. 14).

In accordance with Jewish practice, and Christian reverence for the body, Christians buried their dead. Cremation was associated with Roman pagan practice. Roman practice also frequently included funeral feasts, held on anniversary days at graves, some of which were elaborately constructed to include a room for such feasts or providing a means of pouring a libation into the sarcophagus containing the remains. Following the official recognition of Christianity by the Emperor Constantine, the Church attempted to control and regularize the frequent debauchery of these funeral feasts. Already a Christian practice had become established of celebrating the eucharist at the burial places of the martyrs, and this led both to the building of churches over a martyr's grave, and often to a funeral eucharist, the true Christian funeral feast, a Requiem commending the soul to God and praying for forgiveness of sin and deliverance from judgement. A theology was elaborated which spoke of a 'particular judgement' of each individual after death, which was uneasily related to the Last Judgement at the end of time, which, drawing on the parable of the sheep and the goats (Matthew 25. 31–46), characterized this Last Judgement as the judgement of the nations.

In the period of almost a thousand years that we conventionally call the Middle Ages, Western Christianity elaborated a conception of the world into which souls passed beyond death. The ultimate points of reference were heaven and hell – heaven the place of union and communion with God, hell the place of everlasting torment and condemnation, where the damned suffered the twin pains of the *poena damni* (the pain of the loss of God) and the *poena sensus* (the pain of the punishment of various kinds of torment, most particularly the fire, originally associated as an image of purification with judgement at the end of the world). Jacques Le Goff sums up the belief of Western Christendom in the following way:

> After the Last Judgement men will be grouped for all eternity into two classes, the saved and the damned. A man's fate will be determined by his behaviour in life: faith and good works militate in favour of salvation, impiety and criminal sins consign the soul to Hell. About the period between death and resurrection Church doctrine had little of a precise nature to say. According to some writers, after death the deceased would await determination of their fate by the Last Judgement, either in the grave or in some dark but neutral region, such as the *She'ol* of the Old Testament, which was not distinguished from the grave. Others, more numerous, believed that souls would reside in various dwelling places. Of these the most prominent was the bosom of Abraham, the abode of souls which, while waiting to be admitted to Heaven in the true sense of the word, bide their time in a place of refreshment and peace. Most believed ... that a final decision was handed down immediately after death in the case of two categories: first, those who are entirely good, martyrs and saints, the fully righteous, who go to Heaven at once and enjoy the ultimate reward, the sight of God, the beatific vision; and second, those who are entirely bad, who go directly to Hell. Between the two there were one or two indeterminate categories. (Le Goff, 1984, p. 133)

Le Goff maintains that 'most of those who believed in the existence of an intermediate category held that the dead awaiting admission to heaven would have to undergo some kind of purgation' (*ibid.*). For some this was at the Last Judgement, for others it was in an intermediate state preceding the Last Judgement. Following St Paul's reference in 1 Corinthians 3.13–15 that at the Last Day every man's work would be tested by fire and that the one who is saved 'will be as one who has gone through fire', the place or time of purgation was thought of as a purifying fire. Between the fourth and eleventh centuries the Christian custom of commending the dead and praying for them that they might pass through the perils of the world beyond the grave and be brought to the heavenly Jerusalem, became focused on this intermediate stage of purgation. Le Goff's careful and detailed study of the development of purgatory in Western Christian thought and devotion from the twelfth century onwards chronicles the growth of descriptions of purgatory and the associated practices of the multiplication of masses for the dead, and also the increasing role of the Church authorities in the regulation of the system of penance beyond death in the practice of indulgences, granting remission of time in purgatory in return for devotional exercises, including giving to the Church, or going on pilgrimage or crusade. In Dante's *Divine Comedy* the medieval geography of life after death is elaborated in the poet's journey through Hell and Purgatory to Paradise and the Vision of God. Although in many respects purgatory and hell resemble each other, purgatory for Dante was entered by a narrow gate (unlike the broad gate of hell) and strained towards paradise. In purgatory, despite the purifying fires, hope reigned supreme (Le Goff, 1984, pp. 347–9). As Le Goff notes, as early as the thirteenth century purgatory began to change the attitude of Christians towards the final moments of life on earth. 'Purgatory dramatized the end of earthly existence and charged it with an intensity compounded of mingled fear and hope. The essential choice between Heaven and Hell could still be played out at the last moment, since Purgatory was the ante-chamber of Paradise. The last instants of life became man's last chance' (*ibid.*, p. 358).

However, in England in the late fifteenth and early sixteenth centuries, purgatory was often viewed as an 'out-patient department of Hell' rather than a stage on the way to heaven. In parish churches prayers were bidden each week 'for all the saules that abydes the mercy of god in the paynes of purgatory' (Duffy, 1992, pp. 344, 346). It was an important duty of the next of kin to pray for their departed relatives in purgatory, and this piety was evidenced in bequests made to altars and shrines in parish churches. This cult of the dead meant that, as Duffy puts it,

> funerals in late medieval England ... were intensely concerned with the notion of community, a community in which living and the dead were not separated, in which the bonds of affection, duty, and blood continued to bind. The means of this transaction between the living and the dead was charity, maintained and expressed in prayer. The dead, whose names were recited week by week in the bede-roll at the parish Mass remained part of the communities they had once lived in, and the objects they left for use in the worship of that community preserved their names and evoked the gratitude of the living towards them. (*ibid.*, pp. 474–5)

The theology of the Reformers attacked the notion of purgatory as having no grounding in scripture and as appealing to a theology of salvation earned by good works, not faith in Christ. Prayer for the dead was seen as inextricably bound up with belief in purgatory and although it survived in the English Prayer Book of 1549 it had no place in the more Protestant book of 1552. Duffy comments perceptively on the 1552 Prayer Book burial service: 'the service was no longer a rite of intercession on behalf of the dead, but an exhortation to faith on the part of the living'. At the committal the minister turns away from the corpse to the congregation, 'the person is spoken not to, but about, as one no longer here, but precisely as departed: the boundaries of human community have been redrawn' (*ibid.*, p. 475).

All the Reformation orders for the burial of the dead were a severe simplification of the elaborate medieval funeral ceremonies. The focus was increasingly upon an exhortation to the living. Archbishop Hermann of Cologne, whose *Simple and Religious Consultation* (1547) was one of the influences on Archbishop Cranmer's English Prayer Books, urged an exhortation at funerals chiefly on 'the exceading greatnes of synne, and of the wrath of God, whereupon death ensued', and secondly on the 'singuler and inestimable benefite of the redemption of Christ ... And if there be anie notable proues of goddes goodnes declared towardes the deade person in his lyfe, or death, the ministre shall declare and prayse the same' (Rowell, 1977, p. 76). In the Calvinist tradition the emphasis is even starker. John Knox's Genevan Service Book of 1556 simply states that 'the corps is reuerently brought to the graue, accompagnied with the congregation withe owte any further ceremonies, which beyng buriede the minister goethe to the church, if it be not farre off, and maketh some comfortable exhortation to the people, touching deathe and resurrection' (*ibid.*, p. 82). The *Directory* of 1644, which largely reproduces a book of discipline compiled by the English Puritan divine, Walter Travers, in 1586, states:

> When any person departeth this life, let the dead body, upon the day of burial, be decently attended from the house to the place appointed for public burial, and there immediately interred, without any ceremony.
>
> And because the custom of kneeling down, and praying by or towards the dead corpse, and other such usages, in the place where it lies, before it be carried to burial, are superstitious; and for that praying, reading, and singing, both in going to and at the grave, have been grossly abused, are no way beneficial to the dead, and have proved many ways hurtful to the living; therefore, let all such things be laid aside. (*ibid.*, p. 83)

However, although religious ceremonies were curtailed, civic honours were allowed.

The effect of the Reformation abolition of prayer for the dead, requiem masses and belief in purgatory, was not only to move the centre of funeral liturgy from doing something for the departed to moral exhortation of the living, it also highlighted a stark contrast between the poles of heaven and hell as the destiny of the dying. The strongly predestinarian theology of Calvinism often seemed to sever the links between moral behaviour and salvation, making the God who saved or damned by divine decree an arbitrary despot. The government of the universe could then appear to be mechanistic and impersonal. Although Luther and Calvin attempted to recover the theological significance of the Last Day, Protestant orthodoxy increasingly emphasized the day of death as the decisive determining point of salvation (*ibid.*, pp. 26–8). A verse of Edward Caswall's hymn, 'Days and moments quickly flying' (1858), although written by a Catholic convert, captures well this individualism and the emphasis on judgement at the moment of death:

> As the tree falls,
> So must it lie;
> As the man lives,
> So will he die.
> As the man dies,
> Such must he be,
> All through the days
> Of Eternity.

This individualized and anthropocentric eschatology increasingly came to stress the immortality of the soul, rather than the resurrection of the body, and in the late seventeenth and early eighteenth centuries moral discipline was enforced as much by an appeal to the immortality of the soul as to the Last Judgement.

Although Protestantism repudiated purgatory there was a legacy of a time of purification, though the process of being fitted for heaven belonged to this world rather than to the next. Professor Richard Fenn, who has explored this notion, comments that 'it was with the doctrine of purgatory ... that time took on an added seriousness far beyond that of apocalyptic. Time in this world became continuous with the afterlife, since, in purgatory, clocks tick and the hours and days pass on exactly the same schedule as on earth' (Fenn, 1995, p. 16). The Enlightenment made of this world 'a secular purgatory' in which 'the disciplines of spiritual growth invested the experience and the passage of time with significance for the soul's "eternal welfare" '. Western society lives in a tyranny of time, in which 'the deadline is the pale shadow of purgatory' (*ibid.*, pp. 13–14).

The stark antithesis of heaven and hell, and the apparent arbitrariness of predestination, was one of the roots of growing criticism of the doctrine of eternal punishment which began to manifest itself in the seventeenth century. The eternal torments of hell seemed to compromise the goodness of God and to make a nonsense of the Christian teaching that the nature and the name of God was love. Yet the reality of eternal punishment seemed to be grounded in scripture, and many were nervous of the moral consequences of abandoning an eternal hell as an ethical sanction. Protestants did not have the option of purgatory as a way of resolving the fate of those who at their death seemed neither saints to be taken straight to heaven nor sinners so black that an eternal hell was their just deserts. The critique of hell, however, in the seventeenth century remained largely the property of sceptical thinkers and sectarians, and did not greatly disturb the more general belief of Christians (Walker, 1964). Enlightenment thinkers in the eighteenth century debated the nature of the soul, and its relation to the resurrection body, as well as wrestling with the fires of hell and the problem of universal salvation. Biblical themes were often in tension with an understanding derived from Platonism in which, as Almond puts it, there was:

> essentially a vertical universe of two levels: of the aethereal heavenly Kingdom where dwelt God, the saints, the angels, and the souls of the blessed; and an aerial Kingdom, to the higher levels of which evil could not penetrate, in the lowest levels of which in the cavities within the earth and in the air around the earth dwelt Satan, his minions, and the souls of the wicked, always threatening to forestall the return of souls to the divine. The earthly life was perched precariously both in time and space between the hopes of an eternal blessedness and the possibilities of torments severe, long-lasting if not eternal. (Almond, 1994, pp. 36–7)

Enlightenment thinkers tended to be deistic rather than atheist or agnostic. They might quarrel with the Christian plan of salvation and carp at the Christian scheme of judgement but 'natural religion' could still profess a belief in the immortality of the soul. The hope of a future life could consort well with a philosophical, optimistic, moralizing religion, whose flavour can be read from hundreds of eighteenth-century memorials celebrating the virtue of the departed and professing an assured faith in the hope of their immortality (cf. McManners, 1981). But although the eighteenth century may well be characterized as 'the age of reason', it was also an age of religious revival. Methodism and the larger Evangelical revival in the Church of England of which it was part were revivals whose kinship with continental Protestant pietism and continuity with earlier English Puritanism is increasingly recognized. This revivalist religion was biblicist in character, and was part of the seedbed of the wider movement of romanticism with its stress on emotion as revelatory of truth about the human condition. The death-bed was the place where last words, uttered as a testimony of faith, showed the departed to have been one of the elect. Books of death-bed scenes provided pious encouragement or stern warning. Evangelical handbooks could urge that children should be edified by being brought to the 'death-beds of departing saints' and impressed with the retributive justice of God by witnessing public executions. The medieval devotional tradition of *memento mori* found an Evangelical expression in works such as James Hervey's *Meditations Among the Tombs* (1746/7), and, in the following century, in a more utilitarian vein in the planning of new urban cemeteries as places for botanizing as well as sombre reflection on mortality. J. C. Loudon in 1843 maintained that the new burial grounds should reflect a dual purpose:

> The main object ... is the disposal of the remains of the dead in such a manner as that their decomposition and return to the earth from which they sprung should not prove injurious to the living ... A secondary object is, or ought to be, the improvement of the moral sentiments and general taste of all classes and especially of the great masses of society. (Loudon, *On the Laying-out, Planting and Managing of Cemeteries* (1843), cited in Cope, 1970, p. 54)

The religion of Victorian England was marked by what, on the face of it, can seem to be strongly contrasting religious movements – Evangelicalism and the revival of Catholicism, both Roman Catholic, and within the High Church tradition of the Church of England. There was equally a growing challenge to traditional Christian faith focused for many on a perceived clash between scientific and religious accounts of human origins, but also influenced by a growing awareness of different faiths and cultures, and historical challenges to scripture. Some of the most notable Victorian debates were centred on the moral difficulties posed by the doctrine of eternal punishment and, by the end of the century, Gladstone could write anxiously that the doctrine of hell was gradually being abandoned (cf. Rowell, 1974). The traditional imagery of heaven continued to be used, but there was a new emphasis on particular themes. Professor Michael Wheeler comments: 'the interest in the nineteenth century in guardian angels, the recognition of friends in heaven, and the singing of hymns in the heavenly choir reflect a longing for different *kinds* of continuity between this world and the next' (Wheeler, 1990, p. 122). The mid-century also saw the emergence of spiritualism, and the founding of the Society for Psychical Research, pursuing the aim of proving a life beyond death and investigating its character. There are interesting contemporary parallels in late twentieth-century interest in 'near-death experiences'.

The increased wealth of Victorian England and the revival of Gothic architecture as *the* Christian architecture had an impact on Victorian funeral customs and memorials, which manifested the elaboration characteristic of Victorian domestic and public décor in general. The 'Ecclesiologists' who propagated an elaborate code for the restoration and building of churches were also concerned to promote Christian funerals, and in their mind this often meant the revival of some medieval customs. The Catholic revival in the Church of England led to the revival of prayers for the dead and requiem masses, though it was the concern to meet the needs of the bereaved in the slaughter of the First Word War that finally overcame much English Protestant antagonism to prayer for the dead. In Westminster Abbey on All Saints' Day, 1919, William Temple declared in a sermon: 'Let us pray for those who we know and love who have passed on to the other life ... But do not be content to pray for them. Let us also ask them to pray for us.' Growth continued beyond the grave, and we pray for the dead not because we believe that God will otherwise neglect them, but because 'we claim the privilege of uniting our love for them with God's' (Wilkinson, 1978, p. 178). Four years earlier, Winnington-Ingram, the Bishop of London, had comforted the bereaved at the Canadian memorial service in St Paul's Cathedral with the words: 'the family circle is still complete ... Unseen hands uphold you; unseen spirits speak to yours; close by, though hidden by a veil, the real, lasting activities of the other world proceed apace. Death has been for them a great promotion' (*ibid.*, p. 181).

Nineteenth-century England had seen a massive growth and a movement from the countryside into the towns. One of the consequences of this population shift and growth was a crisis for burials. Town churchyards became inadequate to cope with the need to bury the dead, particularly when the dead were buried in coffins. In London and other large conurbations it became essential to open large new burial grounds, such as Highgate and Kensal Green. The inevitable result of this was the sundering of the ancient relationship between the church as the centre of the worshipping community and the departed members of that community. Those who controlled the new cemeteries were secular authorities rather than the Church. Even more was this the case with the beginnings of cremation which was legalized in England in 1884. The churches opposed cremation for a number of reasons – the long-standing tradition of burial from inherited Jewish custom onwards, the association of cremation with pagan funeral rites and, for some, belief in the resurrection of the body. The consequence was that cremation, and the crematoria which were built to provide for this way of disposing of the dead, developed with little reference to Christian belief and practice – even though crematoria chapels were provided with the accoutrements of 'an altar, cross and candlesticks', the 'altar' more often resembling a sideboard and never used for its central purpose, the celebration of the Eucharist.

The twentieth century has seen a continuing growth of cremation in Britain, and a waning of membership of institutional churches. Not only has British society been changed by the presence of those of other world faiths, but the subjectivism characteristic of 'post-modernism' has in the latter part of the century produced a variety of beliefs and non-beliefs about death and a future life even within the Christian churches. Within these churches also there are those whose hope is for a social and political transformation of this world, rather than beyond it, whose eschatology is realized rather than future. Scientific materialism has also eroded for some the hope of a life beyond death. Changing liturgies have tried in some instances to return to the resurrection emphasis on early Christian funerals, and this is notably true of the new Roman Catholic *Order of Christian Funerals* (Latin text 1970). All churches have found themselves constrained by the secular, urban context of most contemporary funerals, with the sundering of the link between the place of worship and the place of the funeral and the commemoration of the departed. Yet even in an age of secular agnosticism it is perhaps worthy of note that the 1996 report of the Doctrine Commission of the Church of England, *The Mystery of Salvation*, was commented on by the media almost entirely with reference to the few pages in that report which argued both for the reality of God's final judgement and suggested that hell might be better thought of in terms of the imagery of a second death of total non-being rather than of the imagery of flames. That same report speaks of the farewell of the Christian funeral as being a commendation of the soul of the departed into the hands of God, 'and in this context language about the soul indicates that living centre of human personality, which is no longer present in the dead body before us'. 'A commendation into the hands of God is a commendation into a deeper participation in the communion of God's love, which is God's being and so into the communion of saints' (Doctrine Commission, 1996, p. 197). In the end, Christian theology emphasizes, it is God who is the horizon both of our human life and our human death; the God whose eternal life is Easter gift and promise, who, in the words of the First Letter of Peter, 'gave us new birth into a living hope by the resurrection of Jesus Christ from the dead, the hope of an inheritance, reserved in heaven for you, which nothing can destroy or spoil or wither' (1 Peter 1. 3–4). It is that to which Christian funeral liturgies strive to give expression as well as trying increasingly to be pastorally sensitive to the needs of those of diverse personal faith who still look to the churches to offer consolation to the bereaved and commendation to those who have died and who seek for some meaning in the ultimate mysteries of human life and human death.

References

P. C. Almond, *Heaven and Hell in Enlightenment England* (Cambridge: Cambridge University Press, 1994).

G. Cope (ed.), *Dying, Death and Disposal* (London: SPCK, 1970).

Doctrine Commission of the Church of England, *The Mystery of Salvation* (London: Church House Publishing, 1996).

E. Duffy, *The Stripping of the Altars: Traditional Religion in England 1400–1580* (New Haven and London: Yale University Press, 1992).

R. K. Fenn, *The Persistence of Purgatory* (Cambridge: Cambridge University Press, 1995).

J. Le Goff, trans. A. Goldhammer, *The Birth of Purgatory* (London: Scholar, 1984).

J. McManners, *Death and the Enlightenment* (Oxford: Oxford University Press, 1981).

G. Rowell, *Hell and the Victorians: A Study of the Nineteenth Century Theological Controversies Concerning Eternal Punishment and the Future Life* (Oxford: Oxford University Press, 1974).

G. Rowell, *The Liturgy of Christian Burial* (London: Alcuin Club/SPCK, 1977).

D. P. Walker, *The Decline of Hell: Seventeenth-century Discussions of Eternal Torment* (London: Routledge and Kegan Paul, 1964).

M. Wheeler, *Death and the Future Life in Victorian Literature and Theology* (Cambridge: Cambridge University Press, 1990).

A. Wilkinson, *The Church of England and the First World War* (London: SPCK, 1978, reprinted 1996).

3

To be dead is not enough

Roger Grainger

Heaven

The wrong of unshapely things is a wrong too great to be told;
I hunger to build them anew and sit on a green knoll apart,
With the earth and the sky and the water, re-made, like a casket of gold
For my dreams of your image that blossoms a rose in the deeps of my heart.

W. B. Yeats, *The Lover Tells of the Rose in his Heart*

The idea of heaven is always and unavoidably linked with perfection. Heaven is seen as the world emerging in a new form, its real spiritual significance revealed as another way of interpreting life, and yet as its true meaning – the dream that lies outside our grasp. It is as if things were involved in a process of renewal from within, as the rose unfurls on its stem. The message of heaven is enshrined in many examples of perfection. Many works of art express balance, beauty and repose – the way we believe things would be if we could discipline ourselves to leave them alone. As it is, human effort plays as large a part in realizing our experience of the rose as it does in rituals which involve sojourning in the belly of the sea monster in order to draw nearer to holiness. The element of achievement consists in being able to stay in its presence. Whereas rites of passage aim at reaching a particular level of human society, one which usually signifies a more mature relationship with a god, the purpose of religion which contemplates divine perfection is to abandon consciousness of the world as long, and as often, as possible. From this point of view, rites of passage play a restricted role concerned with entry into, conditions in, and final departure from the ordinary world. The place of perfection we hope we are going to is one we would never choose to leave.

The vision of perfection acts upon conscious awareness at various levels, providing us with a source of *immediate* refreshment, one which is not restricted by membership of a particular religion. God's perfection refreshes mind and spirit in works of art which are intentionally religious, and in the perfection of those which are not. Popular forms of religious expression, enjoyed by many who do not regard themselves as particularly 'religious', mediate the vision of a transcendent wholeness to vast numbers of people. The imagery of perfection functions at a deeper level, however: according to Jung it is the most important component of mankind's unconscious mind. He draws attention to the archetypal symbolism of the mandala, 'A primordial image of psychic totality' (McGuire and Hull, 1978, pp. 327–8).

In Christian pictures of heaven, concentric circles of angels expand to lift the image of the Godhead out of the frame towards the spectator (McDannell and Lang, 1990). The whole thing is greater than itself. Our notions of what is perfect must take account of the creation of still more perfection, a more satisfactory balance, new kinds of completeness. To this extent the ideas of the *Gestalt* psychologists were incomplete: the closure we seek always contains an openness. Our 'personal construct systems' are continually modifying themselves in order to enable us to predict an unknown future, so that the confidence we feel is the result of openness, not finality. Patterns evolve spirally, seeking stability at every stage. This is reflected in myths and legends about heaven.

Throughout the world, the mandala of heaven exists to answer questions concerning a disharmony of human experience centering upon three kinds of existential problem. First of all, the world demands to be understood; secondly, its sufferings must be lessened; thirdly, the unfairness of the things that happen in it must be countered. Life is puzzling, painful and unjust (Geertz, 1966, p. 14). Religious teaching has found it hard to answer all three kinds of question with the same kind of reasoning. For example, knowledge about phenomena throws little light on the rightness of human or divine behaviour, while the problem of soothing agony with argument remains as intractable as ever. The idea of heaven solves these problems by means of a vision of divine beauty – a perfection of being that is able to take every problem up into itself, the reconciliation of differences.

Certainly, all this contains a powerful element of wish-fulfilment. Yet it cannot merely be dismissed as 'pie in the sky'. In fact, the idea of heaven would seem to be founded upon an experience of bliss, primal human bliss. The experience of rebirth, reproduced in rituals of change, involves both the chaos of dissolution and the joy of resurgence. The things that make up this experience are readily available outside the ritual metaphor. We feel the excitement and profundity of love, the sexual ecstasy that overpowers thought, the blessed psychological relief on the cessation of stress that has driven us to the edge of collapse, the kind of joy that pushes us to the far edge of what we conceive as our capacity as human beings. Memories like this give content to our idea of heaven as well as the longing for states of relationship that we have known and enjoyed for considerable periods in our lives – the omnipotence of life in the womb, the interchange of shared interests and the passionate mutuality of love. These are experiences of validation which provide the material for any ideas of heaven that we may entertain.

It should perhaps be noticed that these are experiences of relationship rather than of the simple satisfaction of instinctual urges. The fact remains that heaven, the image of perfect happiness and fulfilment, is unavoidably social (cf. Suttie, 1988). As the limiting condition of fulfilment, it reverses the hell of isolation imagined by such writers as Charles Williams and given scientific support by experiments in sensory deprivation. While we may not usually think of it as a place nowadays, we still think of it *as if it were* locatable; indeed it must be because there are so many people there. (The problem of locating purgatory was not solved until the twelfth century (Le Goff, 1984). Once men and women knew where it was, of course, they could pay due attention to its significance!) First, heaven is a place for meeting God, just as hell is his complete absence. This is the image of heaven presented by corporate ritual in which actions and words communicate the human intention to enable a public encounter with divinity to take place by clearing a space – an actual physical/temporal/geographical location. Those taking part in the ensuing ritual are involved in an event that is the apotheosis of encounter. In meeting God they encounter one another and themselves. This is the meaning and intention of the rite, the thing that it is contrived to symbolize.

Before anything else, ritual concerns meetings. In many cultures heaven is conceived of as a kind of extension of corporate ritual. The ritual 'movement' concerned is the post-liminal phase of the extended rite, Van Gennep's 'Rite of Incorporation' (Van Gennep, 1960). Incorporation refers to a new level of social or interpersonal belonging either in human or divine society – human with regard to birth rituals or puberty rites, marriages or initiations into various social bodies possessing restricted membership; divine with regard to funerals or rites carried out by the living to ensure the welfare of the dead (see Chapter 8 by Speck). In the *latter* case the *limen* to be crossed is the threshold of actual physical death as well as a poetic interpretation of the significance of passing from one stage of life to another.

Ritual and actual dying reinforce each other's meaning. The rite brings home the reality of death by giving it a significance which, to use Douglas Davies' distinction, can be either 'eschatological' or 'retrospective' or both (Davies, 1995), as we look forwards to a life which is to come and backwards at one already fulfilled. It does this first by the shape of the rite of passage, its identity as a real event, the locus of happenings which possess a recognizable significance and embody actual change in the way that those involved view the world they live in (Grainger, 1988a). Another way is by opening up the idea of an afterlife and giving it some of the emotional value attached to, and experienced in, the rite itself: particularly the transitional phase, the crucial 'chaos section'. The emotional effect of incorporation depends largely on an experience of deliverance from the agonies of the preceding phase.

This joy is communicated in the language of social relationships. Our heavens are full of those who have been reunited 'after great tribulation'. They are also inhabited by those who have been consciously and deliberately installed by their successors, 'handed on to glory' by the people they have left behind. Throughout the world men and women carry on a social relationship with their ancestors, either informally, by private arrangement, or publicly, officially, in terms of established religious belief and practice. The relationship between the living and the dead is at the heart of religion everywhere (Warner, 1959). It is the framework on which hangs the religious explanation of social and personal phenomena that constitutes knowledge of life and death.

Death and life together constitute a statement about final truth that in order to be expressed needs both partners. Heaven would seem to be an essential element in this transaction. Like the outer circle of the mandala, heaven binds us together. In a so-called primitive society the dead and the living are conceived as living in close partnership. R. E. Bradbury describes ghost-lore among the Edo:

> A primary division must first be made between what I may call the unincorporated dead (ghosts of several varieties) and those ghosts who have been assigned a 'constitutional' position vis à vis the living by a deliberate act of re-incorporation ... In psycho-social terms such an action may be described as one of re-establishment within communal – and hence individual – awareness in which the well-disposed dead are brought back home and the malevolent excluded in a direct and final way. (Bradbury, 1966, pp. 127–53)

The gateway between the two kinds of social belonging which correspond to the two principal spheres of reality as religion sees them – before and after death – is the funeral. It is the funeral that establishes the dead in heaven or hands them over to God for reward or punishment. From the point of view of the eternal balance of divine reality, hell has the same 'weight' as heaven. In so many religions, in their folklore or official religious teaching, funerals are held to be deeply involved in determining the destination of the dead. This remains so even when the religious authorities refuse to countenance such ideas. Heaven is not the reward of good behaviour on earth, but of ritually adequate funeralization.

Funerals are a clear assertion that death, like life, is in God's hands. As such they are messages to the dead themselves that, being now dead, they must preserve an appropriate relationship with the living – that is, a non-intrusive one. The funerals of many cultures send the departed on their way in a series of gestures, whose meaning is unmistakable: This way only! (Grainger, 1988b). Having arrived, their establishment in 'the land of the dead' is carried out with the same kind of firmness and finality. The dead are kept in their place by repeated 'rituals of re-incorporation'. Catholic Christianity prays for those in between the two kinds of life and frequently remembers the saints in heaven. An Austrian Catholic commented: 'There is a great sense of community between the living and the dead because the dead are still very much part of our way of life' (Habenstein and Lamers, 1963, p. 499). The Chinese commemorate the dead at three great yearly festivals: *Ching Ming* (Spring), 'The Feast of Hungry Ghosts' (Summer) and 'The Feast of the Tenth Month' (Autumn). These practices have survived the atheistic rigours of the present Communist regime.

This is not surprising. Practices concerned with the fate of people already dead can escape the attention of social reformers, or appear irrelevant to the more developed kinds of theology. However, they are basic to the religious view of the meaning and purpose of life. This meaning requires exclusions as well as inclusion. In order for heaven to be worth getting into it must be recognizable as heaven; in other words it must be something, or somewhere, so that you might have got into it even if you didn't. Of all special places heaven is the most special – which is why it must have rules of entry and membership. To a very great degree its perfection depends on the rite of passage that distinguishes it from the imperfections of this world. Such a distinction, occurring in every culture that disposes of its dead with cere- mony, undercuts cultural divisions and theological differences. Wherever there is a heaven it is assumed that some people will not go there. It should be stressed, however, that the perfection required in most cultures is ritual and therefore achievable. The qualifications for heaven are religious and the purpose of the funeral is to render the dead religiously acceptable. The principal psychological purpose of the funeral is that of containment. 'To neglect to allow death the significance of a completed process is to refuse to accept it as a happening at all. In the language of religious understanding, this is to give the dead person nowhere to go. Nowhere to go and nothing to be' (Grainger, 1988b, p. 71).

This is an important idea with regard to any consideration of the afterlife. Somehow it has to exist. No-one likes the idea of simply 'dropping into nothingness'. Not only ourselves; at these emotionally critical times it is our loved ones we want to protect. We want to hand them over to a greater love than they have known until now. Heaven is not simply perfection, it is necessary perfection: the obvious answer to the thought of nothingness as well as to traditional doctrines about hell and eternal punishment. Out of a hundred people I questioned about heaven only one brought up the subject of its traditional partner. Whatever it may be at an unconscious level, fear of death appears largely to be fear of nothingness. At least it does so in West Yorkshire; and if the alternative is to be something, wish fulfilment requires that it should be the very best something.[1]

The effect of such wishing is extremely important, despite the contempt that the faithful may feel about fantasy solutions instead of genuine reli- gious assurances. The funeral itself as well as the arrangements leading up to it are essentially social happenings. In fact, they are public declarations of social belonging whose significance is very widely recognized. This is private wish fulfilment made public fact, whether or not the wish is a religiously informed one. As we have seen, funerals throughout the world profess to move the dead 'forward' into an afterlife of completeness, harmony and fulfilment – and, we might add, well out of the way of the living. To long for such things is to associate oneself with a culture that is as wide as humanity itself. To perceive them as far off on the other side of pain and hardship is to be conformed to the shape reproduced both in the funeral ritual and within the experience of human grieving, as it moves from trauma through darkness and confusion into a new kind of light. This is the shape of real existential change; as such it is very far from being mere fantasy. Whatever the details – and they change from culture to culture, almost from person to person – the movement remains the same. It is expressed in its shape, proceeding from pre-liminality to post-liminality via a phase of liminal chaos in which the old is over and the new has not yet begun.

To be effective, a rite of passage must suggest heaven, even if it has to pass through hell on the way. At this level of personal change the three-fold images of stability and movement are compulsory; funerals which attempt to omit any one of the three motifs of separation, transition and incorporation run the risk of falling short of expressing themselves with the symbolism that would otherwise be theirs. No rite that avoids the suggestion of breakdown can possibly achieve the symbolism of unity. By eliding painful transitions we interfere with the realism of any picture of heaven we might be capable of; and with the ability to picture comes the power to hope. Of the hundred passers-by willing to answer my question in Wakefield city centre, 56 per cent claimed to 'believe in heaven'. Seventy-nine per cent of a Sunday morning congregation gave the same reply (see Appendix). In this secular age it seems that heaven is very important to people. It would be absurd to form conclusions on what statisticians would dismiss as a 'natural experiment'.[2] On the other hand there is evidence to suggest that the long reign of materialistic philosophies over the hearts and minds of men and women in the Western world is drawing to a close – or at least, that an ever-increasing number of people are beginning to trust their spiritual experience as a valuable source of genuine understanding. During the last five years the proliferation of groups concerned with various kinds of meditation, both Western and Eastern, Jungian archetypal analysis, psychosynthesis, *T'ai chi* and other spiritually aware approaches has been remarkable; there certainly seems to be a hunger for deeper meanings than those characterizing the social philosophy of the age we live in.

Chiefly hell

I have scarcely mentioned hell. Within the history of religions, hell is chiefly understood in terms of this defining opposition to heaven. This remains the case even when the medieval iconography of eternal torment has been very largely abandoned. A dialectical opposition dictates the idea's structure, even when the literal has been discredited, an opposition which establishes the polarities of the construct, clarifying them as absolute alternatives, not merging into each other: neither of which can be tied down by reference to the other. Heaven's only alternative is hell. In-between conditions do not qualify; nobody can be said to choose purgatory.

At the same time, even though its existence is required by heaven, hell's presence may be questioned doctrinally, on the grounds of its incompatibility with the loving omnipotence of God. The preferred way of coping with the dilemma of divine love that permits no opposition (and it is so hard to imagine realistically) is to suppose that the hell that heaven demands simply by being itself is the one that we create for ourselves, and impose upon eternity.[3] Thus, it is not the true metaphysical opposite of heaven, but a condition put together out of our own sinfulness in which we are totally contained, either after this life or actually during it. 'You make your own hell in this world' could mean either of these things. Heaven is given, hell is earned: traditional Christianity suggests the second alternative, popular mythology the first. According to Origen, 'The individual sinner kindles the flame of his personal fire' (in *De principiis*, II, x, 4).[4] Baron von Hugel described hell as 'rejecting everything that is not simply yourself'.[5] By the time I am given the choice of heaven or hell, I have made it impossible for me to choose heaven because, like everything else that I come into contact with, I experience it only as an extension of my own private hellish world. Developed for hell, my skills are no earthly use in heaven, in whose atmosphere my ability to survive has long since decayed through lack of use. If heaven is eternal love, hell is unredeemed self – an idea that seems to make sense to a generation that has demythologized hell even more drastically and effectively than it ever did heaven.

Geoffrey Rowell, in the previous chapter, has more to say about the origins of the Church's teachings. Christians still hold fast – officially, that is – to an idea of opposing states of reward and punishment which forms the moral underpinnings of human reality without actually existing within its dimensions. Hell and heaven have notional force in this life, where their actuality is given human form in terms of recognizable human experiences of exaltation and abasement. Both have suffered in credibility by attempts to be too literal about them: Jesus himself tends to speak of them within the story-telling mode more often than not (Strawson, 1970). Those who answered my questions about heaven most forcibly in the affirmative invariably vouched for the existence of hell as well, as if it were simply a test of religious orthodoxy; those who gave the matter more thought scarcely mentioned hell at all.

It could well be that, in a materialistic and reductionist society, the awareness of hell has been buried deep in the shadowlands of the individual psyche, where it is known but not understood, felt but not acknowledged (Blanchard, 1993). It can no longer be aimed for or avoided, as its unlocatability is the most outstanding thing about it. Instead of two vivid centres of transcending meaning, we have a vague dream of God's loving purpose for us, to be experienced more fully and satisfactorily than we experience it in this life, and an undefined area that we prefer not to think about, which nevertheless does not cease to exert its own influence upon our awareness. To paraphrase Samuel Beckett, to be dead is not enough.

There is conflict between the yearning for perfection (and the dread of its total extinguishment) and our twentieth-century hesitation to believe in an afterlife. However we deal with the first fact, we still have to take account of the second. And yet there is a need for something else – something which expresses a yearning that, I believe, precedes our religious categories as it does our theological objections, because it belongs to our identity as human beings. Our longing for perfection is the critical condition of the need to find meaning in things. It is for us as Duns Scotus says it is for God: 'Being is Making'. In creating we affirm ourselves, say who we are, establish the terms of our being in the world. 'Ah, but a man's reach should exceed his grasp ... ', Browning was right. This is what a heaven is for. If we have rejected the one we had, we shall have to invent another.

Appendix

Procedure

A 'natural experiment' was carried out in order to list the spontaneous reactions of two independent populations of people to the question: 'Do you believe in heaven?'. The first group of people consisted of an entire congregation assembled for Parish Communion in a middle-class, residential district of a city in the West Riding of Yorkshire. The second group was chosen at random by approaching passers-by in the centre of the same city. The first (church) group was aware that the questioner was a clergyman; the second (secular) group was not.

Results

	Church group	Secular group	Total
Number of people asked	73	111	184
Number of replies	62 (100%)	100 (100%)	162 (100%)
Yes	49 (80%)	56 (56%)	105 (65%)
No	4 (6%)	17 (17%)	21 (13%)
Not sure	9 (14%)	27 (27%)	36 (22%)

Discussion

The investigation was in the nature of a thumbnail sketch rather than a serious investigation into the beliefs of those questioned. For instance, it is unlikely that the second group was completely secular, containing no members of any religion. People were encouraged to respond without much thought and most of them did so. Only a minority refused to reply at all (11 church group, 11 secular group). I was expecting more resistance than this from both groups, particularly the secular one, so this was a surprising result. In fact, the results as a whole surprised me. Wishful thinking or not, there seems to be a lot of it about.

This is the conclusion reached by some more systematic surveys. The 1986 Gallup Investigation into 'Religious Activity and Belief in Western Europe' found that 40 per cent of the total population subscribed to a belief in heaven.[6]

Religious activity and belief in Western Europe: belief in heaven

Irish Republic	83%
Northern Ireland	81%
Great Britain	57%
Spain	50%
Italy	41%
Netherlands	39%
Belgium	33%
Germany	31%
France	27%
Denmark	17%
Average	40%

Leslie Francis asked 200 A-level students what it was that made someone a Christian: 50 per cent included 'believes he/she will enter heaven through Christ' among the criteria. Of these, 64 per cent were regular churchgoers (Francis *et al.*, 1992). The Christian Research Association asked 2000 church and school teenagers if they believed in heaven. One hundred per cent of churchgoing teenagers said they believed; of those who formerly attended church 88 per cent still held to a belief in heaven, as did 63 per cent of those who never went to church at all. The 1986 Gallup survey found belief in heaven among 46 per cent of this age range.

Notes

1. Cf. M. Hornsby-Smith, *Roman Catholic Beliefs in England: Customary Catholicism and Transformations of Religious Authority* (Cambridge: Cambridge University Press, 1991, p. 99), 'It seems that, for many ordinary Catholics, concepts such as eternal damnation or hell and the devil are uncomfortable, unpleasant and inconvenient.' Hornsby-Smith reports 'fairly widespread' evidence of non-Catholic ideas like reincarnation which seem to offer something tangible and tolerable to fill the gap made by the absence of life.
2. For a more systematic survey see D. Davies and A. Shaw, *Re-using Old Graves: a Report on Popular British Attitudes* (Crayford: Shaw & Sons, 1995).
3. In *The Great War and Modern Memory* (Oxford: Oxford University Press, 1975), Paul Fussell discusses the role of the 1914–18 War in promoting the idea of a 'hell we create for ourselves'.
4. In H. Bettenson (ed.) *The Early Christian Fathers* (Oxford: Oxford University Press, 1969), p. 258.
5. F. von Hugel, 'What do we mean by heaven and hell?', *Essays and Addresses on the Philosophy of Religion*, series 1, 1921; also C. S. Lewis, *The Problem of Pain* (London: Bles, 1940) and *The Great Divorce* (London: Bles, 1945).
6. By courtesy of Christian Research Association, Vision Building, 4 Footscray Road, Eltham, London SE9 2TZ.

References

J. Blanchard, *Whatever Happened to Hell?* (Darlington, Co. Durham: Evangelical Press, 1993).

R. E. Bradbury, 'Fathers, elders and ghosts in Edo religion', in M. Banton (ed.) *Anthropological Approaches to the Study of Religion* (London: Tavistock, 1966).

D. Davies, 'The theology of cremation', in P. C. Jupp (ed.) *Clergy and Cremation Today* (London: The Churches' Group on Funeral Services at Cemeteries and Crematoria/The National Funerals College, 1995).

L. J. Francis, C. Wilcox and J. Astley, 'What is a Christian? Investigating the understanding of 16–to–19 year-olds', in J. Astley and D. Day (eds) *The Contours of Christian Education* (Great Wakering: McCrimmon, 1992).

C. Geertz, 'Religion as a cultural system', in M. Banton (ed.) *Anthropological Approaches to the Study of Religion* (London: Tavistock, 1966).

R. Grainger, *The Message of the Rite* (Cambridge: Lutterworth, 1988a).

R. Grainger, *The Unburied* (Worthing: Churchman, 1988b).

R. M. Habenstein and W. M. Lamers, *Funeral Customs the World Over* (Milwaukee: Bulfin, 1963).

J. Le Goff, trans. A. Goldhammer, *The Birth of Purgatory* (London: Scholar, 1984).

C. McDannell and B. Lang, *Heaven: A History* (New Haven and London: Yale University Press, 1990).

W. McGuire and R. G. C. Hull (eds), *C. G. Jung Speaking* (London: Thames & Hudson, 1978).

W. Strawson, *Jesus and the Future Life* (London: Epworth, 1970).

I. D. Suttie, *The Origins of Love and Hate* (London: Free Association Books, 1988).

A. Van Gennep [1909], trans. M. B. Vizedom and G. L. Caffee, *The Rites of Passage* (London: Routledge and Kegan Paul, 1960).

W. L. Warner, *The Living and the Dead: A Study of the Symbolic Life of Americans* (New Haven: Yale, 1959).

4

Towards a theology of transition

Paul Sheppy

Introduction

'What are human beings that you are mindful of them' asks the Psalmist, 'mortals that you care for them?' 'What are human beings, that you make so much of them' echoes Job, 'that you set your mind upon them, visit them every morning, test them every moment?' (Psalm 8.4; Job 7.17–18).

Questions about death and life beyond death raise questions about what it is to be human, to be mortal. For Christians these questions can never be satisfactorily resolved without reference to God, the creator and sustainer of life, and to the life, death and resurrection of Jesus. This chapter proposes an account of death which attempts to address the question 'What happens when I die?' by attending to the further questions 'What is the life to which God calls us?' and 'In what sense is the death of Jesus *for* us?'

Body and soul

Traditional Christian language about death has frequently talked of the separation of the soul from the body (see Davies, Chapter 6 below). A common illustration has been of the envelope and the letter. When we die, it is suggested, our body is like the envelope – it has served its purpose – but the soul ('the letter') survives. So long as we accept a body–soul dualism, this illustration is useful. However, what if we are not letter and envelope, but postcard? What then?

To ask these questions is to suggest an anthropological stance which is unitary rather than dualist. The revolt in some theological circles against body–soul language has not been unanimous. There is still a significant weight of opinion urging traditional language. A recent opponent has been Richard Swinburne who argues for traditional categories in his language about both God and personal anthropology. Swinburne acknowledges that dualism as an explanation of human existence and experience is 'not a popular philosophical position today'; nonetheless he finds it 'inescapable' (1996, p. 77). However, it is not clear that he is able to locate the soul in anything other than the quality of consciousness, which he denies to the body. In reducing the notion of body to materiality, he attaches consciousness to the soul (*ibid.*, p. 69). Inevitably, Swinburne is drawn into the notorious debate about whether mental events can be distinguished from brain events. Despite his own certainty that they can, the matter is still in dispute. It may be that among other difficulties the body–soul paradigm leaves us unable to resolve the issue simply by the oppositions it implies.

A unitary anthropology may offer us another approach. To be sure, it will reveal its own inadequacies; but equally it may afford us a way of speaking about human existence and experience which offers considerable illumination. Such a stance is not new to religious thought; indeed, there is a very strong tradition within the Hebrew scriptures which speaks in these terms.[1] Death in earliest Judaism meant a descent into a land of shades (*She'ol*) in which the praise of God fell silent. It is only later, as questions of theodicy begin to be addressed, that life beyond death emerges as a consideration. Inevitably, a theory needed to be developed which allowed the dead person to survive death beyond the corruption of the body. Such an anthropology was conveniently to hand – the immortal soul.[2]

Despite the attraction of this notion, there are problems. Theological affirmation of the material universe is imperilled, and with that devaluation the doctrine of the incarnation is threatened. In such a case the death of Jesus is denigrated by the kind of assertion that it was only the body of Jesus which suffered while the eternal Word was unscathed. From this there follow implications for the doctrine of the atonement, since as the Fathers argued 'what has not been assumed cannot be saved'.[3] A bipartite anthropology demands too high a price for the initial benefit it offers.[4]

A unitary view

If we revert to a unitary view, we may begin with the proposition that a human person is an ordered self. This ordering is effected by God's breathing into us and by social relationships as well as by centred conscious awareness. I gain knowledge of whom I am by my own self-awareness, by the awareness and recognition which others accord to me, and by the awareness and recognition granted to me by God.

At its most trivial and commonplace such external recognition may be accorded to me when I am asleep. More seriously, it may be granted to me when I am in a trauma – either of a physiological or psychological kind. I am still me, even if I have lost arms and legs or have collapsed after an accident or operation into a coma. I am equally still me if I have lost all recollection of who I am. The 'me' in such a trauma is obviously diminished, but I remain the one whom God called into being and whose history makes me who I am. This holds good in the realm of human development. In the early stages there is a growing self-awareness; yet before the infant 'I' knows who I am, I am known by others.

This fact of external recognition is crucial counter-evidence against those who end up by giving my psychological history a distinct ontology from 'me'. Even though those who recognize me may only do so with difficulty, even though they may say 'He's not himself any longer' or 'He's not who he was', there is yet a recognition that the 'he' of whom they speak is related to the previous 'he' whom they remember as me. There is change and alteration; but there is also continuity.

These external identifications are important. They confirm who I am when I cannot identify myself. They are not, however, exclusive or incontrovertibly accurate or complete. My own self-awareness is not necessarily false. Moreover, we are more than merely the recognition we receive. In relationship with others there is formation and growth into personhood. Our personhood is ordered by its self-awareness, its relationship to others and its calling into existence by God. This ordered being we call the self. However distorted or diminished it may become, it is the self. This self is characterized by life both as origin (*bios*) and goal (*zoe*).[5]

Bios and zoe[6]

Bios is that which the self organizes in order to be a living being. If the self, as we at present experience it, is embodied, then *bios* is the energy which the self embodies. This *bios* may be thought of as the breath which made Adam from the dust. In everyday speech it is 'life'. When we speak of being alive it is with *bios* that we are concerned. The important thing to observe here is that this language does not separate *bios* from the religious or spiritual sphere. *Bios* is the gift of God; and this way of speaking reminds us that our everyday living is dependent upon God. All life is given, and cannot be compartmentalized into those areas which belong to God and those which do not.

Zoe is our response to the call by God to live teleologically. It is not separate from *bios*, nor is *bios* separate from *zoe*. *Zoe* is the God-ward orientation of *bios*; it is *bios* lived to a 'zoetic' end. To live zoetically is to live with a self in which *bios* and *zoe* are in harmony.[7] Sin is both the failure to order *bios* zoetically and the state in which that failure occurs. Just as *bios* is inclusive of all our living so also is *zoe*. There are no areas of existence which fall outside the teleological purposes of God.

To summarize, the self is the way in which *bios* is organized, and this organization is both individual and social. A self which organizes that God-given *bios* to fulfil the purposes of God expresses itself in *zoe*. By speaking in this way, we avoid a dualism which allows the body to decay in death while asserting that an immortal soul escapes. And it is to death that we now must turn.

Whatever model we use to describe human existence, no amount of argument can disguise the fact that we die. Indeed, Heidegger described it as *Sein-zum-Tode* ('being-unto-death'). For my theological position, death is a total event. Nothing escapes. As Barth puts it: 'When we die, all things and we ourselves come to an end' (1960, p. 588). Karl Rahner sees the resurrection of the body and the immortality of the soul as parallel statements arising from different ways of speaking of the human (1966, p. 352). He is unwilling to allow that death can be adequately described as separation of soul and body, saying that 'death puts an end to the *whole* man' (*ibid.*, p. 347).[8]

The totality of death is a crucial tenet of the theology of this chapter. Since I want to describe human personhood and life in unitary terms, I am committed to a similar stance in relation to death. When we die, our *bios* ends and our self loses its organizational control.[9]

This accords with the findings of medical science;[10] and while I am unwilling to grant to medicine a metaphysical competence, a theology of death which ignores what we know of *bios* is to my mind perverse. Since my life in response to God's calling (*zoe*) is given to me as a self, it too ceases without self and *bios*. It is the purpose, to which we are called by God, which continues; and it continues independently of the existence of those who are summoned to its consummation.

Resurrection thus retains its place as a gracious act of God in which *bios* and *zoe* are restored to a re-ordered self. This self is differently organized beyond death. If we speak of an embodiment, a resurrection of the body, then that body will be the 'spiritual body' of which St Paul speaks in 1 Corinthians 15. Resurrection is a new creation in which the *bios*, which the self organized before death in embodied form, is now reconstituted and organized in the self beyond death. The *zoe* of God, our life in response to God's teleological claim, is now lived by the self in freedom. Resurrection is not simply the same old thing beyond death. It is life in a radically new dimension of eschatological liberty.[11] Rahner puts it thus: 'We do not mean that "things go on" after death, as though we only changed horses, as Feuerbach puts it, and rode on ... Eternity is not an immeasurably long-lasting mode of pure time, but a mode of the spirit and freedom ... ' (Rahner, 1966, pp. 347, 348).

The importance of such an understanding of death and resurrection for funeral liturgies lies in the challenge it brings to the body–soul anthropology which is so commonly assumed. Language which speaks of commending the soul to God and the body to the elements loses its place. The whole person is dead and all must be released to God. Resurrection is different from immortality, and the anthropology which I propose affirms resurrection as an act of God in response to the totality of death.

However, there is a further liturgical consideration. An increasing importance is being given to the funeral service as a celebration of the Paschal Mystery. I believe this to be a correct emphasis, since it addresses the transcendental questions about God which death poses. It is, therefore, to the life, death and resurrection of Jesus that I now wish to apply my theological anthropology of self, *bios* and *zoe*.

Jesus as normative

I have indicated earlier that I have reservations about the two nature theory. If, as I have argued, human nature may be described satisfactorily in terms of our relationship to God without recourse to a body–soul anthropology, then the two nature theory is redundant for Christology. Jesus was a self. His uniqueness consists in his ability to harmonize *bios* and *zoe*. 'He became obedient to the point of death', runs the *Carmen Christi*; 'Son though he was he learnt obedience' declares the writer to the Hebrews (Philippians 2.8; Hebrews 5.8). It is in this obedience to God that he demonstrates normative humanity in which *zoe* and *bios* are at one. This is what it means to be human (a self), to live life (*bios*) in obedience to the calling of God (*zoe*).

The death of Jesus exemplifies his loving obedience to God. This is the thrust both of the *Carmen Christi* (Philippians 2.6–11) and of Hebrews 5.8. When Jesus gives up his spirit (Luke 23.46), it is the breath which gives life (*bios*) to his self which he returns to God. The docetic hypothesis that Jesus' death is incomplete (or even feigned) is impossible in my reading, since the suggestion depends upon the two nature theory. The death of Jesus is total, as is our death. The sense of abandonment which Jesus feels is a recognition that death is 'a return to non-being'.[12] The dead go down to *She'ol* where there is no praise of God, no communion with the source of all life who calls us into being. To this descent I shall return later, for Jesus' descent to the dead is a crucial sign of hope in which the death of death is worked.

The resurrection of Jesus is the mighty act of God in which the *bios* of Jesus is reconstituted and finds itself newly organized in a resurrection self. The *zoe* of Jesus is the bringing to glory of the children of God. This is accomplished in the ministry he exercised in life and in death, and which by the resurrection he exercises yet. This resurrection is the expression of Christian hope for the creation, which groans for its freedom (Romans 8.19–25). This, too, is normative.

When we speak of the dead at the funeral, we speak by reference to Christ the firstborn from the dead (Colossians 1.18). The funeral rite which fails to make this connection is not, in my judgement, Christian. It fails to establish Christ as our representative. The death of Christ for us is an act primarily of representation rather than of substitution.[13] It is not so much that Christ dies instead of me, since I would then not have to die at all. It is that his death represents mine, and so my death is caught up into his. St Paul's language of being 'in Christ' reflects just such a representative view of the atonement.

An exegesis of death which does not relate all human dying to the death of Christ shifts the burden of the pastoral agenda which the funeral rites seek to address. It leads to the comment often made by ministers that they find 'non-Christian funerals' hard to do. I find them impossible, but for a different reason. From my theological stance all the funerals I conduct are Christian, since their liturgical thrust is precisely to relate the particular death we are marking to the death of Christ. If I am offering nothing more than a formalized farewell, I am not acting as a Christian minister. There is a cosmic implication to the descent of Christ to the dead which ought to be expressed in the funeral liturgy. Where Christ has gone before to proclaim his victory over death, all may follow in safety.[14]

The liturgical agenda

One of the tasks of Christian liturgy is to provide an ordering of rites by means of which those present are enabled to actualize the connection of 'secular' and 'sacred'. In funeral rites, this means transforming the repellence of death into a holy event. Theologically we do this by reference to the death and resurrection of Jesus, but how is liturgy to fashion this connection for those at the funeral?

At the beginning of the twentieth century, Arnold Van Gennep (1960, p. 11) identified three stages which he described as shaping what he called 'rites of passage'. He talked of a doorway (*limen*) through which those enacting a rite passed. They approached the doorway in a pre-liminal phase, they passed through the door in a liminal stage and emerged into a post-liminal situation. These phases were marked in turn by separation from one state, transition through an intermediate phase and incorporation into a new status.[15]

In using Van Gennep's language of transition, the primary thought here will be of personal rather than social anthropology, and it is from his work on rites of passage that we may make a useful liturgical beginning. If we accept the categories of separation, transition, and incorporation, we can describe the task of the funeral rites to lead us from death to life.

The separation which death brings is two-fold. It separates the deceased from us and it separates us from the deceased. This is mirrored in the events of Good Friday, where Jesus is separated not simply from his family and his friends, but even from God (cf. Mark 15.34). Not least of the things, incidentally, that we can say at funerals from this passage is that God is to be numbered among the bereaved.

The transition in which we move through the chaos of bereavement grief is parallelled by a transition in which the dead move from life in this world to life in God. The ancient church tradition which turned the civic funeral procession into a signifier of the journey of the soul to God made this very clear.[16] The Holy Saturday story of Christ's descent to the dead, which is told in 1 Peter 3.18–4.6 and which is hinted at in John 5.25, is suggestive of the redemption of death as a process rather than the instantaneous victory which resurrection is often taken to imply. I understand the Petrine text to be a preaching of the gospel to the dead, not simply a re-assurance of the

Old Testament saints that their salvation is assured. The reference to Noah is a reminder that in Jewish thought the people of the Flood were the most wicked of all time – for them there was no hope. Peter calls these hopeless cases into evidence here as signs of the power at work in the death of Christ who himself brings hope to those who have none. This accords well with Jesus' own words about the people of Sodom and Gomorrah on the day of judgement for whom there was indeed hope (Matthew 10.15; 11.23–24).[17] At the funeral, we have the opportunity to affirm this hope and to reiterate what St Paul says – that not even death can separate us from God's love (cf. Romans 8.38, 39).[18]

The incorporation which funerals signify is the new life which is available not only to the dead, but also to the bereaved. Grief-counselling is sometimes seen as an activity in which people are enabled to 'get back to normal'. If this is indeed the goal, then we may ask whether it is not a mistaken one. There is no return to what was before; that is the finality of death. There is a gateway to new life; that is the promise of resurrection. The gospel call is always to new life rather than to revisions of the old life.[19] It is this resurrection for the living and the dead which makes the Christian funeral a gospel event.

How officiants achieve this ritual agenda in funeral liturgies is beyond the scope of this chapter.[20] Nonetheless, one final observation should be made. If a unitary anthropology is adopted, a new liturgical strategy is required. We must briefly address it.

Release: an alternative to commendation and committal

Where body and soul are not used as descriptive categories of human existence, the tradition of commending the soul to God and committing the body to the elements becomes inappropriate. In its place comes a language of release.

The release of the person to God fulfils two ritual functions. It declares that the living have no further claim on the dead, and that the dead have no further claim on the living. We leave the past and our judgement of it to the mercy of God; we commit ourselves and the one we mourn to the continuing love of God in Christ. All of what we have been, all of what we are, and all of what we shall be is placed with God our creator and saviour.

As an example of what a liturgy of release might mean I have devised the following formulae:

At a burial:

> From the dust you made us, O God;
> to the dust we return.
> Awaken your *daughter N.*,
> whom we release to you,
> from the sleep of death,
> and feed *her* at your table with life eternal.[21]

At a cremation:

> Purge me as gold and silver
> that I may be an offering to the Lord.
> Receive *N.*,
> whom we release to you, our God,
> and bring *her* to life eternal.[22]

At a burial at sea:

> Deep speaks to deep
> at the thunder of God.
> Bring *N.*,
> whom we release to you, O God,
> through the waters of death,
> and may the trumpets sound for *her* on the other side.[23]

Ministerial practice

If ministers officiating at funerals adopt the unitary anthropology and the theological and liturgical approach to the Paschal Mystery urged in this chapter, they will need new rites and liturgies. They will need to find ways of speaking about death which do not allow life beyond death to appear like an act of Houdini but which root resurrection in God's action in Christ. We do not escape; we are delivered.

They will need to relate every human death far more closely to the death of Christ, and to recover the processional nature of the Paschal Mystery in liturgical forms which lead mourners from death and despair to new life and hope.

Where possible, they will need to share with those who mourn strategies for undertaking grief's journey. For example, the remembrance of anniversaries and the use of the Feast of All Saints may be useful stepping-stones through the flood.

They will need to be less diffident about the kerygmatic implications of death. If Jesus preached to the dead, and if 'the dead will hear the voice of the Son of God, and those who hear will live' (John 5.25), then the permissive subjunctive of the rubric *A sermon may be preached* must give way to a more robust formula.

Of course, there is no one system which the minister can slide into when the telephone rings and the voice says: 'I'm sorry to tell you that N. has died. Will you do her funeral?' What counts beyond all else at such a moment is our ability to see Jesus abandoned and Mary desolate and to stand with them on death's margin. Words too soon, words before tears, are noisy gongs and clanging cymbals. But later we must speak, we must declare the gospel. Part of the task of the officiant is to articulate the sorrows, the fears and the hopes of the liturgical assembly. The Christian hope is in Christ who died for us and was raised for us. Can the pastor, who is a disciple of the Good Shepherd, be silent about this?

Conclusion

This chapter has sought to find a new way of speaking of death which remains true to Christian tradition and to the insights of those medical and scientific descriptions of human existence which resist dualism. It has resisted a rigid reductionism and has proposed a theological approach to funerals which relates all human death to the death of Christ. In much of its expression it is likely to prove controversial, but it is offered as a contribution in the search and struggle for understanding. Contention is not bad where we contend for the truth and where we wrestle with God whom we will not leave without a blessing.

Notes

1. H. W. Robinson (1911) and Hans Walter Wolff (1974) both describe this anthropological stance in books which have become classics.
2. Most commentators, cf. for example, Simon Tugwell's extended discussion (1990), refer to the Greek tradition with which inter-testamental Judaism would have been familiar. It is also quite likely that the religious categories of Egypt and Persia would have had some influence.

3. This particular formulation of the argument was that of Gregory of Nazianzus (Epistles 101.7) in the controversy with Apollinarius.
4. Geoffrey Rowell (1974, pp. 18–31) traces the historical development of these two theologies in the field of Christian eschatology, showing their importance for the nineteenth-century debate.
5. For further discussion of this issue of personal identity, see the contributions of Alistair McFadyen (1990), Karen Grandstrand Gervais (1986), and Fred Feldman (1992).
6. My use of *bios* and *zoe* in this essay is my own development. It arises from a discussion with Alistair McFadyen at the University of Leeds. At the time he was my PhD supervisor and he invited me to look at the problem of describing a resurrection in non-dualist terms which accounted and allowed for both continuity and non-continuity. The strategy I adopted was to consider human existence both in its origin and its goal. Since our life is one of creaturely dependence, its origins and goals find their meaning in the same reliance upon God. God calls us to being-with-God. My choice of the language of being comes from my reading of John Macquarrie (1966) when I was an undergraduate.
7. The hymn writer John Hunter spoke of this call to harmonization and its fulfilment in Christ:

    Dear Master, in whose life I see
    All that I long, but fail to be,
    Let thy clear light for ever shine,
    To shame and guide this life of mine.
    Though what I dream and what I do
    In my poor days are always two,
    Help me, oppressed by things undone,
    O Thou, whose deeds and dreams were one.
    The Baptist Hymn Book, no. 465 (London: Psalms and Hymns Trust, 1962)

8. The stress is Rahner's.
9. The dead are described as *rephaim* ('powerless') in the Old Testament. This corresponds to my description of a self losing *bios*.
10. Sherwin Nuland (1994) gives a physician's detailed account of death with clarity and honesty. Nuland's candour spurns a sentimental reaction, but it reveals and evokes a sensitivity to the enormity of death.
11. Frances Young (1990) tells the story of her handicapped son Arthur and reflects as mother and as theologian on what Arthur's experience means for our understanding both of personhood and of God. She concludes that resurrection cannot mean a 'making perfect' which would erase both the suffering and joy of Arthur's life by making him 'normal'. To deny his handicapped experience in such a way would be to suggest that he is sub-human. Professor Young has no easy answer to the questions about the darkness of God. Her intellectual rigour applied to her family life is certainly profoundly moving. I believe that my anthropology is open to what she has written. I would certainly want it no other way.

12. Barth describes death in this way when he speaks of death as a sure sign of judgement (1960, pp. 595ff.).
13. See D. Sölle (1967), who distinguishes between a substitute, whose actions cannot be appropriated by the one substituted, and a representative, whose actions are designed to be appropriated by those represented. See also J. A. T. Robinson (1987), chapter entitled 'What future for a unique Christ?'
14. See W. Pannenberg (1972), also P. Sheppy (1992) where I discuss in greater detail the missiological significance of Jesus' descent to the dead. A brief indication of the argument follows in the main text of this chapter when I refer to the text of 1 Peter 3.18–4.6.
15. Some recent commentators (R. A. Williams, 1990; E. A. Hallam, 1996) have questioned whether the tripartite pattern is as universally observable as most have suggested. Most scholars, however, have accepted Van Gennep's analysis. They have been convinced by its descriptive quality rather than any prescriptive powers. See Peter Speck, Chapter 8 in this volume.
16. The Christian funeral was not simply an adoption of the cultural norm. It strove to be counter-cultural by its witness to death not as a finality but as a gateway to life eternal. Cyprian, Chrysostom and Augustine – among others – all urged upon their listeners and readers the importance of grief being redeemed by the hope of the resurrection. Joy was to be the keynote rather than weeping. Cf. Geoffrey Rowell (1977, pp. 22, 32–52) for a detailed discussion of the processional nature of early Christian funerals – especially in the East.

    We may feel that grief can be short-circuited or even repressed – and with damaging consequences – by too quick a move from separation to incorporation. However, this may be to apply unsympathetically post-enlightenment understandings of life and death in exclusively individualistic terms to those whose conceptual and cultural frameworks are far removed from ours.
17. Here I want to add to the emphasis John Heywood Thomas gives in Chapter 5. I agree that Jesus' descent into the dead implies his identification with our death, but I take it to be more. My exegesis of the 1 Peter text is frequently supported by systematic theologians; NT scholars are much less supportive! – but see Goppelt (1993).
18. Emil Brunner (1962, p. 344) wrote of Romans 8.38–39: 'The whole of Eschatology is contained in this one saying of Paul.' This text is not a sentimental expression, but a Christological statement at the conclusion of Paul's most fully argued theology of the Christian hope.
19. This is what Jesus means when he talks of the folly of patching up old clothes with new cloth (cf. Mark 2.21 and parallels).
20. The Joint Liturgical Group of Great Britain is at present preparing funeral liturgies which seek to address these issues, both traditional body-soul language and the anthropological concerns of the present chapter. See also my doctoral thesis (University of Leeds, 1995, pp. 230–72) where I discuss the liturgical agenda and make a number of general proposals accompanied by particular draft texts.

21. The reference is to the raising of Jairus's daughter (Mark 5.35–43). This avoids the colourful Greek *epitaphion* – with which British mourners probably could not cope! – 'May the earth which fed you now eat you.'
22. The image of fire in death is often that of hellfire. A more positive image of fire is of the tongues of flame at Pentecost; but the fire of the crematorium is the fire which consumes. It may therefore be best to use the language of purification and refinement as found in Malachi 3.2b–4. See Douglas Davies' discussion of precisely this issue in the section of Chapter 6 entitled 'Light, Spirit and Fire', and his reference to Teilhard de Chardin in the following section, 'Creative Fire'.
23. Psalm 42.7 and Bunyan's *The Pilgrim's Progress*.

References

K. Barth, *Church Dogmatics III.2 – The Doctrine of Creation* (Edinburgh: T. & T. Clark, 1960).

E. Brunner, *The Christian Doctrine of the Church, Faith and the Consummation: Dogmatics Vol. III* (London: Lutterworth Press, 1962).

F. Feldman, *Confrontations with the Reaper: A Philosophical Study of the Nature and Value of Death* (New Haven: Yale University Press, 1992).

K. G. Gervais, *Redefining Death* (New Haven: Yale University Press, 1986).

L. Goppelt, trans. J. E. Alsup, *A Commentary on 1 Peter* (Grand Rapids, Michigan: Wm B. Eerdmans, 1993).

E. A. Hallam, 'Turning the hourglass: gender relations at the deathbed in early modern Canterbury', *Mortality* I.1, pp. 61–82, 1996.

J. Macquarrie, *Principles of Christian Theology* (London: SCM Press, 1966).

A. I. McFadyen, *The Call to Personhood* (Cambridge: Cambridge University Press, 1990).

S. B. Nuland, *How We Die* (London: Chatto and Windus, 1994).

W. Pannenberg, *The Apostles' Creed in the Light of Today's Questions* (London: SCM Press, 1972).

K. Rahner, *Theological Investigations*, vol. 4 (London: Darton, Longman and Todd, 1966).

H. W. Robinson, *The Christian Doctrine of Man* (Edinburgh: T. & T. Clark, 1911).

J. A. T. Robinson (ed. E. James), *Where Three Ways Meet* (London: SCM Press, 1987).

G. Rowell, *Hell and the Victorians* (Oxford: Oxford University Press, 1974).

G. Rowell, *The Liturgy of Christian Burial* (London: Alcuin Club/SPCK, 1977).

P. P. J. Sheppy, 'He descended to the dead', *Theology Themes*, vol. 1 no. 2 (Manchester: Northern Baptist College, 1992).

P. P. J. Sheppy, 'Liturgy and death: an examination of the pastoral and theological issues relating to funerals, with special reference to selected funerary rites', unpublished, PhD thesis (Leeds: University of Leeds, 1995).

D. Sölle, *Christ the Representative: An Essay in Theology after the 'Death of God'* (London: SCM Press, 1967).

R. W. Swinburne, *Is there a God?* (Oxford: Oxford University Press, 1996).

S. Tugwell, *Human Immortality and the Redemption of Death* (London: SCM Press, 1990).

A. Van Gennep [1909], trans. M. B. Vizedom and G. L. Caffee, *The Rites of Passage* (London: Routledge and Kegan Paul, 1960).

R. A. Williams, *A Protestant Legacy: Attitudes to Death and Illness among Older Aberdonians* (Oxford: Oxford University Press, 1990).

H. W. Wolff, trans. M. Kohl, *Anthropology of the Old Testament* (London: SCM Press, 1974).

F. Young, *Face to Face: A Narrative Essay in the Theology of Suffering* (Edinburgh: T. & T. Clark, 1990).

5

Life, death and paradise: the theology of the funeral

John Heywood Thomas

Though death is clearly the focus of the funeral, the funeral is performed by the living for the dead. A funeral also reveals how death is related to various issues of life in this world and to notions about time and reality that are theologically interrelated. It celebrates a life and so involves the notion of the meaning of life – a specific life and life in general. The minister proclaims the message of life's meaning which is a word of hope at a time of despair and a word of comfort to mourners. In the funeral the deceased passes out of the context of our daily business and into history so that at the very heart of the funeral service there is the theological issue of the new status of the person remembered and commended. Finally, in the message to the bereaved there is the proposal of a policy of behaviour: we are encouraged to 'number our days and apply our hearts to wisdom' (Psalm 90, 12).

This, then, is how I want to consider the theology of the funeral. I speak of the *theology* of the funeral because the minister's message here is no different from his normal message. A vital part of preaching must be the Christian message about death. If death has become something about which we no longer speak it is all the more important that the minister should continually expound the message of hope to his regular congregation.

In our society for the most part we shuffle by death. In my own lifetime the process of the funeral service is something which has become much neater and more efficient. An unfortunate consequence of this is that all too often the funeral service is anonymous. Rarely do the bereaved protest against this. They are more likely to thank the parson for 'a nice funeral service'. All too often death is for many both comfortless and without fear, a non-event. Besides the psychological effects of such an ignoring of death there is the more important ethical consequence that we neither properly value the life that has ended nor incline our hearts to wisdom. It is thus a cliché that the subject of death is loaded with taboo; but, like many clichés, it is strangely illuminating. It illumines our embarrassment which has something to do with metaphysics, ethics and theology. Taboo was always in abundance in my childhood experience of death – the tiptoe approach to the house of the dead or the dying, the almost macabre interest in the coffin-cart, the funeral bier or the funeral carriage with its magnificent black horses. Part of that taboo was the respect which, as far as I can recall, was never taught. It was so much part of my way of life that to this day I cannot witness a funeral procession without showing respect. In contemporary reactions to an impending funeral I see something of a polarization of attitudes. On the one hand, there is the extreme logical development of the quest for efficiency in those guides to a DIY funeral, reminding us that neither a parson nor even an undertaker is legally required. On the other, there is the very different aesthetic development witnessed by the popularity of the revival of funeral processions – and of horse-drawn carriages.

This changed thought-world is the kind of phenomenon which has been discussed increasingly in recent years (Ariès, 1981; W. A. de Peter, 1984; Walter, 1994). Of greatest relevance to the present discussion is Frederick Hoffman (1972). Though it describes itself as an effort in 'the history of man's attempts to account for violence, to anticipate it and to adjust to its dislocations', it is in fact a rhetoric of death in a post-liberal ideology. It is an account of Western literature from Stendahl to Sartre. The rhetoric is afforded by the organization of this literature around three themes – grace, violence and self. Hoffman traces in some detail the secularization of grace. He relates this to what he regards as a normal but largely lost connection between life and death, that the inevitable event of death is something for which we can prepare in life. Leaving aside the relation of violence to death, what is his thesis? Deprived of a normal connection with death but faced with the inevitability of his own dying, modern man as revealed in this literature seeks new definitions of the self – in process, in a unique self-consciousness and in values derived from these two. This logical analysis of the history seems to me wrong. What our cultural history shows is a different thought-movement, namely the prior advent of these new kinds of self-definition and the waking appreciation of the consequences of such. To describe this as our history is to seek to escape our responsibility for these views and beliefs. Man himself is responsible for understanding what it means to die.

While there are many interesting philosophical problems involved in understanding the meaning of death, I turn at once to the theological issues and take the traditional doctrine which Milton encapsulated in the opening lines of *Paradise Lost* with his reference to 'man's disobedience and the fruit of that forbidden tree whose mortal taste brought death into our world'. Death is thus regarded as the consequence of and the punishment for the original sin of Adam in the Garden of Eden. In this complicated issue of Original Sin and the Fall of Adam, the question that concerns us is the relatively simple issue whether this doctrine is a proper explanation of death. It is interesting to see that Locke in his *Reasonableness of Christianity* rejects original sin and argues that Christ redeems mankind not from original sin but from the loss of immortality which was the consequence of the fall. By the fall Adam 'lost paradise, wherein was tranquillity and the tree of life, i.e. lost bliss and immortality . . . Death then entered, shewed his face which before was shut out and not known' (Locke, 1958, p. 26). For Locke it was perfectly clear that there is no sense in which sin can be culpable if it is not one's own – 'every one's sin is charged upon himself alone' (*ibid.*, p. 27). Not surprisingly Locke is given a chapter to himself by Richard K. Fenn (1995). Fenn is more concerned with *Some Thoughts concerning Education* than with *The Reasonableness of Christianity* but he emphasizes that for Locke penitence becomes the way of life for the Christian soul. To return to our theme, as Adam was ejected from paradise so for Locke all his posterity were born out of it. However, that is no punishment of the seed of Adam for Adam's sin – unless, says Locke, we call 'keeping one from what he has no right' a punishment and that is nonsense (Locke, 1958, p. 27). Mortal life is still God's gift to men – 'they could not claim it as their right, nor does he injure them when he takes it from them' (*ibid.*). Thinking of the history of mankind in any other way is for Locke 'foolish metaphysics' so that 'though all die in Adam, yet none are truly punished, but for their own deeds' (*ibid.*). From this estate of death Christ restores all men to life. This life 'is that life which they receive again at the Resurrection' (*ibid.*, p. 28).

Locke complicates the issue in a typically Puritan fashion when he insists that death is the just desserts of all men as sinners – 'an exclusion from paradise and the loss of immortality is the portion of sinners' (*ibid.*). Since all have sinned it follows that no-one could have eternal life and bliss. That would be the case 'if God had not found a way to justify some, i.e. so many as obeyed ... the law of faith' (*ibid.*, p. 29). It is clear that Locke had considerable difficulty in sorting out the various issues involved in talking of death and sin. Whilst anxious to remove any suggestion of necessity or biological heritage from our understanding of sin, he was not prepared to abandon the understanding of death as a penalty for sin. What he does in fact is something that characterizes much Protestant theology in succeeding generations – he asserts that the generality of the connection has to do with the universality of sin (*ibid.*). It is indeed interesting that he thus shows a characteristic reticence in defining the nature of Adam's legacy – how that which happened to Adam is a perpetual historical situation. Meanwhile, the most significant point is that he reinforces the view of death as the punishment for sin.

What we have been considering is the traditional view in both Protestant and Catholic theology. Of the former I mention but two examples. In his highly influential *Outlines of Theology*, A. A. Hodge says: 'The entire penalty of the law including all the spiritual, physical and eternal penal consequences of sin is called death in Scripture' (Hodge, 1972, p. 548). For E. A. Litton death 'is the consequence of that primal prevarication by which man fell' (Litton, 1960, p. 545). The Catholic position likewise is that death is a consequence of original sin (Denzinger, 1957, pp. 101, 109a, 175, 788f.; Denzinger and Schönmetzer, 1965, p. 413). Having made clear in his classic essay, *The Theology of Death* (1961), that he dissociates the possibility of death from Adam's sin, Karl Rahner has further clarified the complexity of the scriptural basis to our theology of death in *Foundations of Christian Faith* (1987):

> The biblical story about the sin of the first person or first persons in no way has to be understood as an historical, eyewitness report. The portrayal of the sin of the first man is rather an aetiological inference from the experience of man's existential situation in the history of salvation to what must have happened 'at the beginning' if the present situation of freedom actually is the way it is experienced and if is accepted as it is. (Rahner, 1987, p. 114)

With this comment we can begin to review the traditional doctrine; for his first sentence very gently points to the fundamental flaw. A critical understanding of Genesis will not allow us to regard it as historical evidence of any kind. Therefore *no* statement of a causal connection between the paradise story and the recorded history of man as mortal is possible. What is possible is indeed only the kind of thing that he goes on to mention, some strange kind of inference which is in fact the converse of the traditional doctrine's hermeneutic.

Understanding Scripture critically enables us to see something more profound. The point of there being a tree of the knowledge of good and evil in the garden is that the story shows the reality of man's capability of refusing the creation. Man can refuse the gift given by God. Man is placed in the garden, that is, in the area of God's first decision. But no animal he; he is called upon, of his own free will, to ratify God's decision. Luther's comment is very profound. He refers to the tree as a temple and points out that Satan tempts Adam not to kill, to fornicate or do anything such. That 'first sin' is not such and such an act but a fundamental attitude towards God. Regarding the traditional doctrine, then, I would emphasize two points. First, the mythological nature of the Genesis story demands a reading very different from the naive assumption that it is because Adam fell that mortality is the biological condition and existential situation of man. This is more than a simple rejection of the historicizing of the myth as a pre-history of the human race. Quite apart from this false reading of Scripture as quasi-science the traditional doctrine is a false reading of Scripture even as myth; its theme is broken relationship rather than crime and punishment.

Tillich's comments on the story reveal how the story is concerned with the nature of sin rather than its causal effects:

> It is the profoundest and richest expression of man's awareness of his existential estrangement and provides the scheme in which the transition from essence to existence can be treated. It points, first, to the possibility of the Fall; second, to its motives; third, to the event itself; and fourth, to its consequences. (Tillich, 1957, p. 35)

Tillich finds the very possibility of the Fall to be the distinguishing mark of man which enables him to serve the divine glory (*ibid.*, p. 37). He sees the 'event' itself arising from the anxiety which is man's state as the awareness of his finitude. Man's finite freedom makes possible the transition from essence to existence and his decision to reject the dreaming innocence of his essential being and to opt for self-actualization (*ibid.*, p. 41). This transition from essence to existence is a 'universal quality of finite being' (*ibid.*, p. 42). Tillich offers this avowedly mythological account as his doctrine of man's nature and situation. Creation and Fall coincide, he says; and there never was a time when created goodness was actualized – there never was an original Utopian paradise (*ibid.*, p. 50). While I would not follow Tillich's analysis in every respect his sensitive interpretation of the Genesis myth does clarify my point. It is not to some first sin that we look for the cause of mortality any more than for the cause of sin's universality. Consequently my first point is that in the traditional theology of death we have not been given the causal explanation it is assumed to provide.

The second point is perhaps the converse, namely that the original sinfulness of man is an important feature of the theology of death. I mean that any theological account of death must do more than simply note the philosophical error of talking in terms of a causal origin. Theology notes that, as a situation in man's relation with God, death like life finds man in sin. 'Original sin expresses nothing else but the historical origin of the present, universal and ineradicable situation as co-determined by guilt' (Rahner, 1987, p. 114). This means that the connection between sin and death is accidental. Reinhold Niebuhr expressed this important point in his famous paradox that sin is inevitable but not necessary (Niebuhr, 1941, p. 279). The whole tragedy of man is not that he should die but rather that he has mixed up with death's inevitability something which is not necessary, namely sin. Tillich's interpretation of original sin bravely attempts to spell out that paradox by showing the close relation between man's development of individuality and the process of alienation which is the essential nature of sin. Though Tillich sometimes blurs the distinction between the activity or action of sin and its cause, he is surely right when he says that the truth of the doctrine of original sin is that sin is fact before it is act (Tillich, 1957, cxiii–cxiv).

What I have argued so far is that man's mortality is wrongly conceived if we see it as in any sense a consequence of his sinful history. Mortality, I contend, is no accident of his creation but a necessary feature of it. That seems to me to be implied by the very finitude of the created world of which man is a part. It is very interesting that Barth (1958), for whom theology involves a real devotion to the exposition of Scripture, views the Genesis narrative as a picture of the created world as something finite. It is specific, limited, given a human definition and is there as and for a covenantal relation between God and man. All this must mean that to treat the story of Eden as immortal man's paradise is quite wrong, despite the way in which this interpretation unites such strange bed-fellows as Locke and A. A. Hodge. As I have tried to make clear, making Eden some kind of historical explanation of man's condition is futile precisely because it explains nothing. In his great essay *On the Theology of Death* (1961), one of Rahner's crucial points was that even if man had not sinned God would still have brought his life to a temporal end. This is illuminated by Tillich's comments about time as a category of existence. In his first volume of *Systematic Theology* Tillich gives the finest categorical analysis in all twentieth-century theology and possibly the most impressive such metaphysical effort since Kant's *Critique of Pure Reason* (Tillich, 1953, pp. 210ff.). 'The categories', he says, 'are forms of finitude' (*ibid.*, p. 211).

Tillich's analysis of time is profoundly helpful because he stresses its ambiguity. After pointing out the positive element in time he continues:

> On the other hand, it is impossible to overlook the fact that time 'swallows' what it has created, that the new becomes old and vanishes, and that creative evolution is accompanied in every moment by destructive disintegration ... The melancholy awareness of the trend of being toward non-being, a theme which fills the literature of all nations, is most actual in the anticipation of one's own death. What is significant here is not the fear of death, that is the moment of dying. It is anxiety about *having* to die which reveals the ontological character of time. (*ibid.*, p. 215)

Time is the central category for understanding man's finitude. It underlies all the other ways in which we spell out the difference between God's infinity and man's finitude. For our purposes the crucial point is that the onward march of time brings man closer to death. This time before death is when man is anxious that he has to die. Tillich reinforces Rahner when he says that this anxiety is as actual in Adam as it is in Christ (*ibid.*, p. 215). In other words, this is something that is ontologically true of man and the nature of salvation is something quite separate from this character of existence. This is why, whether or not one rejects a Wittgensteinian analysis of 'immortality' as meaning something other than life after death, it cannot be dismissed as nonsense. If death is natural so, as we have seen, is the fear of it. To be 'half in love with easeful death' is the attitude of Romanticism. Nevertheless Keats was too good a philosopher to describe himself as anything more than half in love and the young apothecary, knowing his own medical condition and remembering his brother's death, could be forgiven for desiring an easeful death. The man who does not fear death is either pretending or not thinking or is devoid of imagination. Barth says that the man who does not recoil at the thought of the open grave can have very little joy in life (1958, p. 153). It is to the man who is frightened by the prospect of death and fearful of approaching it that, says Barth, the meaning of resurrection is clear. That is why the story of Jesus approaching his death is not one of the simple confidence displayed by Socrates in Plato's account of the martyrdom. By contrast with Socrates Jesus agonizes in sheer terror and courageously submits.

One important feature of man's temporality is that it includes death. Contrary to Wittgenstein's claim, death is an event in life. This is indeed a paradox so that what Wittgenstein says is in one sense not only true but self-evidently true. Death is not lived through as an event of today that I will remember tomorrow. Death is the unique event that ends our state of pilgrimage. A great deal of literature tends to speak of that event as a consummation; but it is only in a somewhat mathematical sense that death is a consummation. It brings man's life of pilgrimage to an end in the way in which infinity brings to an end any mathematical progression. There is a finality about it which makes a man's life, whatever it may be, unalterable. Hence, 'Call no man happy until he is dead.' The basic decisions of a man's life here reach an end: they are made quite final. Time has another significance; for death makes a man's life obviously historical and unrepeatable. Tennyson's words express the point perfectly: 'the sound of a voice that is still'. Do I then deny that there is in death no consummation of decision? On the contrary, I do think that the character of death as dying is the totality of decision. I know that there are many moments of dying which come unexpected and even unknown. 'He died in his sleep – how nice for him', we say; or time and again the doctor will comfort the bereaved by saying 'He did not suffer anything. He did not know.' For myself – pain and suffering apart – it is better to know than not to know. It is better to know because I thus decide my life finally. This is surely one of the significant features of the Passion narrative, especially in that great classical drama, the Fourth Gospel. In the Garden Jesus makes his submission – 'Not my will but thine. For this I came into the world.' Then comes the glorious conclusion of the story – 'It is finished. Into thy hands ... ' This is the totality of the decision – no longer a decision about this or that or in favour of this rather than that but a decision about life and the world. I should stress that we can speak thus only because we do not regard death as the wages of sin. One implication of this totality of death is that we do not soften the notion of death by making it refer only to a body which is separate from the real person, the soul. Death is a cessation of life and that is why the Christian hope uses the language of totality and speaks of the resurrection of the body.

For Christian theology it is of paramount importance that Christ died our death, as Sheppy emphasizes (Chapter 3 above). What concerns me now is not the atonement and justification he thus achieved but simply his death. His death was not merely like ours in its external aspects: his death is the very same death as ours. So the Bible and the Creeds, in confessing his death, are not concerned to recite a historical fact, the datable event of the crucifixion 'under Pontius Pilate'. As the Creed goes on to say that he descended into hell so in the New Testament already there had been an anxiety to say that. Nor was there some anxiety about the pre-Christian era as is suggested by the 'Enoch' reading of the verse in 1 Peter as if this were Dante's *Paradiso*. It is quite simply that after the crucifixion he was a corpse and the two days in the tomb are days when he was not part of the spatio-temporal world. His descent into hell is an essential moment of death and it establishes the substantial identity of Christ's death with our own. If the deed of his death is important so too is the fact of the Resurrection. The interrelation of the two is precisely the point that both Tillich and Bultmann in different ways grasp. For Bultmann (Bartsch, 1953, pp. 38–9), who would make it a myth, the Resurrection is – it is true – not a problem any more than it is for those who would regard it as 'the best-attested fact in history'. Both these options seem to me to diminish the paradoxicality of the claim; for, even if we have the eye-witness accounts referred to by Paul, we do not have the peculiar event of which he speaks. As the Resurrection of Christ this was no mere event; and as the Resurrection of Christ it, even as an event, is one that is both in time and beyond time. The Resurrection belongs as much to eternity as it does to time, 'Christ dieth no more' and death has no more dominion over him. He lives; and the point of that claim is that this life is absolute and unconfined. So the Christian proclamation about death – as about everything else – is a claim about Christ. His self-oblation in death is the context of all our lives including our death. His death is thus our hope.

Clearly the funeral is an expression of the hope that is implied by this theology of death. We sometimes describe this life as an afterlife or immortality: but here it is important to understand the nature of religious language. Talking about the 'other side' of death as immortality is to use model language, taking as our model the mortality we know and saying 'Not that but its opposite'. This is the obvious and indeed the only kind of meaning we can give to the notion of immortality. It is impossible here to discuss the notion of the soul; but I would insist that thinking about the soul has been generated by the notion of immortality which is then cashed out by talk about the soul. The tendency to think of the soul as some shadowy substance which is a counterpart to the body has come under very proper philosophical attack. It is a metaphysical pestilence that can generate all kinds of nonsense when people are 'comforted' by being told that the spirits or souls of the departed indulge in all kinds of extraordinary activity. I would insist, however, that not all kinds of talk of the soul are nonsense. As Wittgenstein says, the best portrait of the soul is the body. That is precisely why the orthodox doctrine of life after death in Christianity is resurrection of the body.

This concreteness of Christian hope is what makes bereavement Christian. There is so much more to it than the comforting thought 'They've gone to a better place.' Such thoughts do not impinge on the awful sense of loss, let alone the guilt which is so often identified as a peculiar feature of bereavement. It is very easy to fall into the double trap which follows the secular attitude to death as something to be dismissed. We shuffle off death by an efficient funeral and ironically we adopt the fashion of calling a funeral a thanksgiving service. So we pretend that death does not really happen by pretending that the deceased is still there. But death does happen and bereavement is a pain that is mine. This is the corollary of Sartre's view that death is the triumph of the other person's point of view. But as death does happen so shall the dead live in Christ. My painful bereavement is the solitude that not even hope can remove; but I can hope and that hope is for the fulfilment of which Christ's resurrection is the promise.

References

P. Ariès, *The Hour of Our Death* (London: Allen Lane, 1981).

K. Barth, *Dogmatics in Outline* (London: SCM Press, 1958).

H. W. Bartsch (ed.), *Kerygma and Myth* (London: SPCK, 1953).

W. A. de Peter, *Immortality: Its History in the West* (Leuven: Acco, 1984).

H. Denzinger, *Enchiridion Symbolorum, Definitionum et Declarationum de Rebus Fidei et Morum*, 31st edn (Barcelona: Herder & Herder, 1957).

H. Denzinger and A. Schönmetzer, *Enchiridion Symbolorum, Definitionum et Declarationum de Rebus Fidei et Morum*, 33rd edn (Freiburg: Herder & Herder, 1965).

R. K. Fenn, *The Persistence of Purgatory* (Cambridge: Cambridge University Press, 1995).

A. A. Hodge, *Outlines of Theology* (London: Banner of Truth Trust, 1972).

F. J. Hoffman, *The Mortal No: Death and the Modern Imagination* (Princeton: Princeton University Press, 1972).

E. A. Litton, *Introduction to Theology* (London: James Clarke, 1960).

J. Locke (ed. I. T. Ramsey), *The Reasonableness of Christianity* (London: A. & C. Black, 1958).

R. Niebuhr, *The Nature and Destiny of Man*, vol. 1 (London: Nisbet, 1941).

K. Rahner, *The Theology of Death* (London: Burns & Oates, 1961).

K. Rahner, *Foundations of Christian Faith* (London: Darton, Longman and Todd, 1987).

P. Tillich, *Systematic Theology*, vols 1 and 2 (London: Nisbet, 1953).

T. Walter, *The Revival of Death* (London: Routledge, 1994).

6

Theologies of disposal

Douglas Davies

What Christian theological considerations underpin the final treatment of human corpses? For practically two millennia both the burial and the resurrection of Jesus furnished the root metaphor for Christian burial as, more recently, for burial at sea and cremation. It drew additional symbolic significance from images of death, burial and new life in baptismal and eucharistic liturgies. The full story of this symbolic assimilation still has to be told especially since, for example, the preference for burial over cremation in the Roman Empire during the early Christian period appears to have involved stylistic trends just as much as doctrinal influences (Nock, 1932). In other words we should not too readily assume that it was the rising tide of Christian burial orthodoxy which swept away pagan cremation throughout European cultures. From a slightly different perspective it is worth emphasizing the fact that while the practice of double burial, in which the bones were placed in urns after the decay of the body, was extremely popular in the Jerusalem of the time of Christ, and was practised in other forms in many parts of Christendom, it has seldom been given any serious theological interpretation.

Numerous contemporary issues, including the dramatic rise of cremation in western Europe, economic and ecological factors of ground and air pollution, aesthetic and psychological concerns, as well as changing theological interpretations of tradition, all encourage a reappraisal of the theology of many kinds of human disposal.

Which theology?

Because Christian traditions interpret life and death differently it is difficult to speak about theology in general. Though, for some purposes, there is a shared perspective derived from academic and ecumenical theology, certain topics inevitably demand denominational commitments.

One crucial distinction divides the dualistic model of the body as a container of the immortal soul from the model of embodiment viewing the body as the very organ of life itself. This complex issue can be far removed from popular levels of Christian belief. So, for example, while Thomistic theology formally views the soul as the form of the body in a radical unity of the person, this can easily be interpreted both liturgically and in popular thought as a belief in a separate body and soul. Practically speaking groups of Anglican clergy exhibit tremendous variation in responding to the question 'What makes us what we are?' Many speak of a body containing a soul departing at death while some stress only the unified single body, often with the associated assumption that this is somehow more true to a Hebrew conception of the self. Others retain the word 'soul' but only to refer to the religious or moral dimension of life. Yet others add the word 'spirit' to the discussion and talk about human beings as possessing a body, soul and spirit.

Sometimes human nature, death and eternity are shrouded in vague sentences reflecting degrees of human ignorance, the intrinsic mystery of death, and the supportive nature of pastoral practice which deals more in comfortable words than conceptual precision. Even formal theology acknowledges severe limits as when Rahner, half way through his study *On the Theology of Death*, says: 'We have spoken much of death, yet said very little. But who can say much of the mysteries of human existence' (1969, p. 79).

Disposal

Part of the paradox of death lies in the juxtaposition of mystery and disposal, words which sit so uneasily together. Yet this hostile proximity indicates the extent of the theological task lying to hand as disposal betokens impersonal and mechanical processes while few would classify corpses as useless objects, as disposable as domestic refuse.

Theological foundations

Here we approach a theology of disposal by the threefold path grounded in doctrines of creation, of incarnation and of society.

The doctrine of creation sees God making a real world containing valued individuals, a value reinforced in the doctrine of the incarnation where God's love brings divine nature to humanity in the person of Jesus of Nazareth. Men and women, boys and girls, are valued bearers of the divine image as God's material creatures and as designated for salvation through Jesus as the Christ. As social persons too they carry high value, indeed the foundation of Old and New Testaments, as of a whole tradition of social theology, lies in the fact that men and women were made to live in communities and not as social isolates.

The need to emphasize the significance of the dead as members of society lies in the theological conviction that society is also part of the divine creation. In doctrinal terms the Genesis myths stress the social nature of Adam and Eve as do the behaviour codes given to the Covenant people by God. It is not only plants and animals that constitute the created order; society also participates in the natural order of the world. As such society participates both in the divine creation and redemption, with its redemptive nature often described in terms of the church or the ideal Kingdom of God, which are to foster relationships through divine law and the ethic of love.

So, to describe dead human bodies as waste for disposal involves a threefold ignorance: of the creature before its Creator, of the redeemed person before its Saviour and of the deceased as a member of society. On this basis the theological rationale for human disposal is to honour God as Creator, Christ as Redeemer and the dead as a member of society. Not to provide a funeral is to denature human beings on all three counts. The provision of funerary memorials also reflects the social and historical nature of persons.

Burial theology

Christ's death and resurrection became central to belief and liturgical practice in baptism and eucharist while the death of martyrs reinforced the death–burial complex of Christian piety. Presumably they also lay at the heart of funerary rites but, as Geoffrey Rowell's important survey *The Liturgy of Christian Burial* demonstrates, we know relatively little about the actual content of early funerary rites (Rowell, 1977, p. 19). What is interesting is that general ideas of the soul were largely taken for granted in

Eastern and Western churches, in Aquinas's elaboration of Aristotle, in Luther's theory of the sleep of the soul between death and judgement, and in Calvin's theology and subsequent Reformation traditions. As against the extreme strength of this tradition it is important that contemporary theology addresses the alternative case of those who do not believe in souls.

Soul and body

Varied belief over concepts of soul and body stands as a serious divide not only between theologians of different traditions but also between professional theologians and lay members of their churches. Interestingly, the doctrines usually used to distinguish between denominations tend to concern church order in episcopal authority, ordination and the sacraments, and are closely linked to bureaucracy and ecumenism. By contrast, doctrines of body, soul and afterlife which really do have an important part to play in ordinary religious life are almost totally ignored. Catholic and Protestant traditions are related in interesting ways on this point. Starkly put, the Catholic Church officially teaches a doctrine of the soul while, if anything, the Anglican Church does not, even though many of its members, lay and clerical, may hold that view.

The new *Catechism of the Catholic Church* stresses the unity of human nature, reflecting the medieval perspective of Thomism that the 'soul is the "form" of the body', with each soul created by God and not 'produced' by parents. The soul is also 'immortal: it does not perish when it separates from the body at death' (*Catechism of the Catholic Church*, 1994, pp. 365, 366). Rahner's study *On the Theology of Death* (1969) offers a sophisticated interpretation of this general view as does Ladislaus Boros in *The Moment of Truth* (1962). But these discussions can appear tortuous in depicting the Thomist soul as the form of the body while arguing that this is not a dualist scheme in which body and soul can simply separate at death. Still, the soul is seen as immortal, passing into another kind of relationship with materiality after death because the soul cannot be itself apart from some sort of material substance.

General folk-belief in Britain, in Catholic and Protestant sub-cultures, reflects a much more direct dualism with a simple emphasis on the soul leaving the body after death. Prior compared Irish Presbyterian and Anglican culture in their rapid dispatch of the soul with the longer engagement with the soul in Irish Catholicism:

The disposal of the soul is a process which occurs quite abruptly in Irish Protestant culture. It occurs on the day of the funeral alone. After disposal there will be no prayers for the dead and no further ritualistic concern with the repose of the soul. Even in Irish Anglicanism this is the case. (Prior, 1989, p. 165)

Similarly Rory Williams studied attitudes to death amongst elderly people in Aberdeen showing how some accepted cremation, believing how it facilitated rather than hindered the reuniting of friends or spouses in a future world (Williams, 1990). Similarly, David Clark told of a Yorkshire fishing village where, 'as members of the family left the house (for the funeral procession) care was taken to leave the door open in the belief that this facilitated the departure of the dead person's soul' (Clark, 1982, p. 130).

In official terms the Anglican position is not as easy to ascertain as that of Rome. The Church of England's Liturgical Commission on *The Commemoration of the Faithful Departed* (1966) adopted the guideline that 'the rite should not assume that the soul of the deceased is, at the time of the burial of the body, in any particular place or state'. Though this seems to assume the existence of the soul, the Commission preferred not to commend the soul to God at the same time as the committal of the body but to introduce a new feature in the commendation of the whole man (*sic*) to the mercy of God. This shift from what is, practically, a dualistic belief in the soul and body to an emphasis upon embodiment as a single focus of human being can be better understood if we return to a consideration of a few elements in the history of doctrine of the soul.

Historical theology

From Rowell's study of early death liturgy we move to Reformation and to beliefs held in common by Reformed and Catholic theologians: beliefs reflecting the humane and rational attitudes of the Enlightenment which, in Protestantism, took the form of a biblically focused re-analysis of the past. Here we have the means of discovering beliefs so deeply installed in Christianity as to be taken for granted, as opposed to beliefs which were seen by the Reformers as dispensable accretions.

Calvin

Calvin's theology of death raised the issue of popular belief and disbelief in the resurrection. His commitment to biblical theology involved the desire to eliminate doctrines and practices perceived as excesses of Catholicism, religious enthusiasts and sectarians. Like Luther, Calvin happily draws on earlier Patristic tradition. But, and this is the important point, Calvin takes the soul to belong to a category of accepted and authentic tradition, even though it was only in 1513, at the Fifth Lateran Council, when Calvin was four years old, that the Catholic Church pronounced the immortality of the soul to be an official dogma of the Church.

By quite a different theological method from Aquinas, Calvin's *Institutes* speak of the human body as a 'cottage of clay', an earthen vessel which God chose to be 'the residence of an immortal spirit'. Spirit is synonymous with soul for Calvin (*ibid.*, I.XV.I). He categorically asserts: 'that man consists of soul and body ought not to be controverted' (*ibid.*, I.XV.II), and, 'when the soul is liberated from the prison of the flesh, God is its perpetual keeper'. Calvin argues for the existence of the soul not only by rehearsing biblical texts referring to soul and spirit but by seeing the existence and influence of the conscience as 'an indubitable proof of an immortal spirit'. The 'agility of the mind', despite the Fall of humanity and the contagion of sin, 'clearly demonstrates that there is concealed within man something distinct from the body'. More than this, Calvin believes that the 'image of God is in the soul' (*ibid.*, I.XV.III) and this leads him to name and favour Plato's doctrine of the soul over other pagan thinkers because Plato, 'considers the image of God as being in the soul'. So Calvin defines the soul as 'an incorporeal substance' (*ibid.*, I.XV.VI).

Calvin's commitment to the doctrine of bodily resurrection emerges in connection with human credibility. 'It is a thing difficult to be believed that bodies after having been consumed by corruption shall at length ... be raised again'. This is why 'many philosophers asserted the immortality of the soul', for 'the resurrection of the body was admitted by very few' (*ibid.*, III.XXV.III). He dwells at some length on the power of incredibility and unbelief in the resurrection of bodies that have suffered corruption. His ultimate advice to Christians is that their minds should be directed to the infinite power of God in achieving the resurrection of the dead and not dwell over-much on the impossibility suggested by human reason.

Hooker

Some of these points are reflected a generation later in the context of the English Reformation by Richard Hooker (1554–1600) as he develops his Anglican system of theology against the background of a strict Puritan scheme. His *Laws of Ecclesiastical Polity* produced at the close of the sixteenth century argues that Christian funerals are important for four reasons. They display the love grounded in our natural relationships, they allow honour to be shown in relation to persons' social status, they express the care the church should show in comforting the living and, finally, funerals express the hope that all should have in the resurrection of the dead (Hooker, Bk V.lxxv.2). Hooker thinks that the strict Puritan desire to hold silent funerals, devoid of formal rites, is misguided, not least because they did not allow an expression of the Christian hope in resurrection.

For Hooker, as for Calvin, the soul is taken for granted. Quoting Caesar's *Gallic Wars* he alludes to the fact that some ancient Britons believed in the transmigration of souls: 'It became a received opinion that the souls of men departing this life do flit out of one body to another. Which opinion, though false, yet entwined with a true, that the souls of men do never perish' (*ibid.*, Bk V.i.3). This truth concerning the immortal soul is one which Hooker, following Augustine, puts down to a discovery of human reason, and he contrasts it with belief in the resurrection which does not come from natural reason (*ibid.*, Bk I.xii.2). Augustine had, in his *City of God* in the fifth century, firmly committed himself to a belief both in the immortal soul and also to the resurrection of the body (St Augustine, XX:X,XX; XXII:V), which he considered in detail even arguing that as far as dead babies were concerned a 'sudden and strange power of God shall give them a stature of full growth' (*ibid.*, XXII:IV). While he was not so sure about abortions he remained open to the possibility that they too would be provided with bodies (*ibid.*, XXII:XIII).

Tillich

More recent theology on resurrection and the immortal soul reflects an awareness of complex cultural influences and philosophical debates on belief (McManners, 1981, p. 148). Some trends in Protestant theology reduce the significance of the soul to press subtle analyses of the meaning of resurrection. One important contribution is made by Paul Tillich's systematic discussion of 'eternal life' and 'immortality' as ideas which have become confused in popular religious thought. Tillich argues that both the idea of immortality and the biblical idea of the resurrection offer ways of expressing the Christian 'participation in Eternal Life' (Tillich, 1964, p. 436). He sees 'immortality', in the Platonic sense of the immortality of the soul, as not only coming into use in the early Christian Church but 'in large sections of Protestant thought' also replacing 'the symbol of the resurrection'.

He argues quite strongly that because the idea of immortality has come to be confused with belief in a soul it should be 'radically rejected by Christianity'. He would prefer to see the certainty of Eternal Life 'liberated from its dangerous connection with the concept of an immortal soul'. In both teaching and preaching 'it would be wise to use the term Eternal Life, and to speak of 'immortality only if superstitious connotations can be prevented'. Tillich is worried by the 'transformation of "immortality" from a symbol to a concept' (*ibid.*, pp. 437–9). He sees the Christian symbol of the resurrection of the body as retaining an emphasis both on the goodness of the material creation and also on the uniqueness of individual persons. These points should be influential in any theology of disposal and need careful consideration by liturgical reformers.

Temple

Such a stress on the doctrine of the resurrection of the body has for many Anglicans, and for the broad Reformed tradition, also involved an emphasis on the divine initiative as far as the future of individual persons is concerned. This was very clearly expressed by William Temple (1881–1944) who, as an Archbishop of Canterbury and an academic, counts among the influential theological voices in a church not given to extensive systematic theology. He is distinctively clear on the issue of eternal life: 'Man is not immortal by nature or of right; but he is capable of immortality and there is offered to him resurrection from the dead and life eternal if he will receive it from God and on God's terms' (Temple, 1935, p. 472).

Temple interpreted eternal life through the idea of resurrection and not through immortality. The dynamics of eternal life rest not in 'an inherent right of the human soul' (*ibid.*, 1935, p. 461), but as a divine gift. The only truly immortal being is God by virtue of the divine nature. Temple pursues a sharp distinction between the original Greek notion of immortal souls on the one hand and the gift of resurrection on the other, a gift which renders men and women immortal.

Moltmann

From the contemporary Lutheran tradition of Protestant German theology Jürgen Moltmann discussed 'the primacy of the soul' in his Gifford Lectures *God in Creation* (1985). Recalling Platonism's influence on Patristic thought and Aristotelianism on medieval theology he makes it obvious that notions of the soul have constituted the centre of Christian understandings of the self. This reflects very much, though without direct reference, Oscar Cullmann's long established critique of the immortality of the soul within Christian theology and faith (Cullmann 1951, 1958). Despite Cullmann's antagonism to immortal souls he still presses for some sort of 'intermediate state' in which the dead, 'live in a condition in which the tension between present and future still exists' (1951, p. 240).

Moltmann came to a different conclusion and went much more in the direction of embodiment as the conceptual basis for interpreting human life. In terms of pastoral theology he tellingly depicts the Platonic belief in the immortality of the soul as a desire to draw 'a protective circle around the soul to shield it from death'. This desire reflects, for him, a fundamentally unchristian attitude given that: 'the secret of life is easy to understand: anyone who wants to keep his life, and therefore holds on to it and keeps it back, will lose it ... becoming incapable of living' (Moltmann, 1985, p. 68).

All these historical perspectives have run alongside the practice of burial. Pastoral theologians have for the future the option of either supporting the soul–body dynamic and employing minor verbal modifications to burial rites to make them appropriate for cremation, or else adopting a radically distinctive theology of death grounded in embodiment with specific application both to burial and cremation. It is inevitable that in this kind of theological construction new motifs will have to be developed from within the Christian tradition, in relation to the motif of Christ's burial and resurrection but with an overriding concern with the quality of existence which can be deemed eternal.

Light, spirit and fire

My own earlier work concerning cremation tried to utilize a theology of light as a motif for a cremation liturgy alongside an argument pressing merit and denying the soul (Davies, 1990). Without repeating it here, I sought to establish a Christology focused on Christ the Light of the World within a liturgy grounded in a theology of grace, eliminating the belief that possession of an immortal soul guaranteed an eternal life.

Another possibility might take the motif of the spirit of God as expressed through fire. The problem with cremation is that in western Europe, though not in eastern Europe, fire is present only in word and not in public reality. Unlike burial where literal earth may be thrown onto the coffin, in cremation the fire is hidden and only referred to verbally in the service itself.

Still, in liturgical fashion, we may refer to the fire of the spirit. Just as the creative spirit of God brooded over the face of the waters at the birth of the world so the generative fire of the spirit brooded on the heads of the apostles at the birth of the Church. Similarly the creative spirit of God is responsible for our birth and baptism through water and, by faith, we might also see the same generative spirit attend our death. This is the symbolic expression that through death, the total death of the material body, hope has to be placed in divine creativity.

We cannot in any direct way identify the flames of cremation with the flame of the spirit because that would be to strain symbolism to breaking point. But it would be possible to refer to the flames as creatures of God – matching the water of baptism or even the eucharistic 'creatures of bread and wine'. To follow this line of thought would be to see these creatures serving God just like the many others cited in the hymn of the *Benedicite*: 'O ye Fire and Heat, bless ye the Lord: praise him and magnify him for ever.'

The funerary liturgy might decide to employ these or similar phrases to evoke the image of fire, not as purposelessly destructive, but as positively fulfilling God's purpose. This is an important point since fire in the Christian tradition tends to have negative connotations, from the burning place of Gehenna (Matthew 5.29), the lake of fire and brimstone (Revelation 20.10), the symbolism of hell, the flames that burned heretics and, in more recent times, the very directly chaotic furnaces of Holocaust crematoria.

Yet other biblical images of fire set very positive values over and against this negative picture. God is seen as a flaming and refining fire (Zechariah 13.9), while fire itself is central to the burnt offerings within the earlier temple cult. Perhaps it would even be possible to play with Paul's words in I Corinthians and, instead of saying 'though I give my body to be burned', say 'as we give his body to be burned, through Your love, let it profit him in life eternal'.

These varied features all offer promise for the formation of liturgical prayer that could accompany cremation services. The following is offered as one possible type of prayer in which the literal sense of fire is combined, metaphorically, with theological ideas of the nature and purpose of God:

O God, whose fire renders things of earth
To their frail dust,
So refine us by your mercy that we may attain
To your everlasting purposes.

Creative fire

One positive use of fire as an extended symbol of the penetrating and transforming nature of God within the spiritual life runs through Teilhard de Chardin's *Hymn of the Universe*, especially the section on 'Fire over the earth' set within 'The Mass of the World' (Teilhard de Chardin, 1974). In a meditation taking the form of what is best interpreted as prose poetry he associates God's creative power with fire. 'In the beginning there were not coldness and darkness: there was the *Fire*' (*ibid.*, p. 21). Linking the sunrise with the Mass he says: 'It is done. Once again the Fire has penetrated the earth ... once again the flame has lit up the whole world from within.' He goes on in a prayer to Christ, described as one 'whose eyes are of fire', to speak of him as the universal milieu in which all things have their being (*ibid.*, p. 33). Teilhard dedicates himself to that world 'become through your power and my faith the glorious living crucible in which everything melts away only to be born again' (*ibid.*, p. 35), just as he later reflects on his own death and asks that Christ may 'set me ablaze and transmute me into fire that we may be welded together and made one ... teach me to make a communion of death itself' (*ibid.*, p. 95), 'I shall have the joy, when death comes, of closing my eyes amidst the splendour of a universal transparency aglow with fire' (*ibid.*, p. 137).

All this serves not as some blueprint for approaching cremation but to show how a creative theological heart and mind can use the motif of fire to illuminate several streams of religious concern, whether it be creation, salvation, the Eucharist or death. It is this kind of theological meditation that liturgical reformers might employ to good effect. The cremation ritual of Hinduism offers an extremely interesting comparative case in which cremation possesses an extensive series of theological meanings. Jonathan Parry's brilliant study of *Death in Banaras* (1994) describes how the deceased is a sacrifice to deity in an act of cremation which rehearses a primal self-cremation of deity, with the fire as a vehicle for conducting the life-force elsewhere. It even acknowledges the violence done to the deceased through the act of cremation.

Constraints of burial

It may well be that burial restricted such liturgical creativity precisely because the tradition possessed an obvious grammar of discourse in the death and resurrection of Christ. Cremation introduces a new situation and creates new theological opportunities.

In terms of surveys of popular belief we have found that of rural Anglicans on parish electoral rolls, some 24 per cent assented to some sort of belief about a resurrection of a body (Davies *et al.*, 1990, pp. 243ff.; Davies *et al.*, 1991, p. 256). But even these individuals also tended to hold an idea of the soul going its own way. In practice the idea of the immortal soul is the dominant mode of practical Christian belief despite the fact that, except in Roman Catholic churches, the main liturgical language focuses on the body and its future rather than upon the soul.

While it is obvious that theology should not fashion itself according to statistical profiles of popular opinion it is good theological method to set theological issues in dialogue with contemporary philosophical issues and pastoral needs.

Death and popular thought

We have already alluded to the dramatically major feature of human relationships within contemporary thought about death, in the tragedy of loss and in the pain of grief. Relatively little stress is placed upon the divine frame into which the deceased may now be located. This has been argued by many, not least by Michael Perham in his sensitive study *The Communion of Saints* (1980), which not only shows the varied perspectives on death and afterlife present in the early Christian tradition but gives due weight to issues such as judgement and fear within the framework of liturgy and, indirectly, in pastoral theology.

In general life, psychological theories have replaced theology, stages of grief standing where the journey of the soul once lay, factors closely related to level of belief in life after death. One recent study (Davies *et al.*, 1991, p. 253) showed that 42 per cent of the general public believed in life after death, 32 per cent said they did not and 26 per cent were unsure. This compared with 69 per cent, 10 per cent and 21 per cent, respectively, of individuals on Anglican Church registers. This shows a large minority of disbelief or uncertainty and it was interesting to find that practically a third of those on church rolls were either unsure or did not know what they believed about life after death.

Another major study, based on interviews with some 1603 individuals in their homes in five different parts of England and Scotland, showed that of those claiming membership of the Church of England some 32 per cent thought death was the end compared with 30 per cent of Methodists, 22 per cent of the Presbyterian Church of Scotland but only 14 per cent of Roman Catholics. Amongst those assenting to a belief in an afterlife the great majority talked in terms of the soul passing on with relatively few agreeing to ideas of resurrection – 18 per cent of Roman Catholics, 4 per cent of Anglicans and no Methodists (Davies and Shaw, 1995, p. 93). This summary is discussed more fully in the second chapter by Davies below.

This reflection of mainstream denominations highlights the fact that practical religion may well confer other social and personal benefits upon participants which do not highlight death. For other churchgoers Perham's point ought not to be ignored that perhaps contemporary Christians have a sense that God will accompany them in death so that death does not possess a tremendous finality. Because of this death 'is not significant' for their way of living (Perham, 1980, p. 98). This is, perhaps, reflected in the way even a large minority of people claiming denominational allegiance opted for a general category of 'trusting in God since everything is in God's hands' when it came to attitudes to life after death. This was the position of 32 per cent of Roman Catholics, 32 per cent of Church of Scotland, 30 per cent of Methodists and 17 per cent of Anglicans (Davies and Shaw, 1995, p. 93).

Relationships

For most people relationships with others foster their sense of identity to a marked extent. This is a particularly important part of this chapter since it is the case that many ministers have to conduct services for people whose belief in the afterlife is as small as the loss of their partner is great. This challenges our pastoral theology and calls for a full appreciation of the life of the individual in community and also of the theological explanation of that human and social life as discussed at the outset of this chapter. Some of these points are now raised as matters for future discussion.

Creation and disposal

One practical issue pastors need to resolve is whether theologies of creation and society – apart from a Christological focus – can validate disposal through both burial and cremation. It is important given that they probably conduct funerals of many who are not specifically Christian.

An affirmative response might be grounded in a doctrine of universal salvation or might stress that all bear the image of God through creation and should, accordingly, be respectfully treated at death. Similarly, our divinely granted social nature is acknowledged by funerary rites and through memorialization. A sermon referring to a person's life is not, in any improper sense, to glorify the past but to state it as a fact. This transient person, as with us all, has occupied part of God's earth and attracted the attention and emotion of others. To ignore this particular lifetime is to ignore this one example of God's creativity. It is as fellow creatures of God that we mark the life before either 'passively' burying it in the earth or else actively engaging in destroying it through cremation.

Liturgical permission to destroy?

The issue of destroying a body is largely ignored in discussions of cremation. In burial human agents take no active part in what becomes of the body. Bodily decay and the earth itself destroy the body. There is biblical warrant for the earth to receive the dead. Cremation, by contrast, actively destroys bodies through humanly designed machines. It is hard to know just how aware people are of this. The Catholic Truth Society's explanation of how Catholics accepted cremation clearly referred to the act of 'violently destroying the corpse by fire' and of the body's 'violent destruction by fire' (McDonald, 1966, p. 2).

This raises the theological question of whether human beings have the right to burn bodies? Most Christians would, I assume, answer in the affirmative. But why do we feel we have this ability? Is it because of an underlying belief in the soul and not in an insignificant body? If that sort of neo-Platonist position is the motive force then the position is quite clear, but if one assumes that there is no soul as such and that the body is itself the total person then its destruction is a more demanding fact.

Under these circumstances what ought liturgy to say? The mere cumulative acceptability of cremation probably overlies any perceived problem with the practice but, in a reflective chapter like this, the question needs to be asked. Ought Christians, for example, to seek forgiveness for destroying the bodies of fellow creatures of God? And would this be of pastoral help for some who may think and feel that they harm their dead?

Does cremation involve a kind of symbolic vacuum, a process subjected to group amnesia, a forgetfulness which is polite and necessary precisely because there is no theological way of rendering the process ideologically significant? In other words, cremation is such a starkly mechanical process that we prefer to forget about it. This might account for the fact that, in practice, the actual incineration goes on behind the scenes, separate from the cremation service. Practically speaking, the cremation service is, if not a misnomer, at least only a partial description of events. Is this another example of Zygmunt Bauman's challenging thesis that social institutions exist to hide the fact of death from people lest they themselves lose the will to live? (Bauman, 1992).

Contemporary Swedish Lutheran funeral liturgy offers a fine example of what I mean, for their funeral services are identical whether aimed at burial or cremation. Even the liturgical rite of making an earthen cross on the coffin lid is identical in both cases. I suspect that British clergy would find it distinctly odd to use earth on a coffin destined for the flames, as though earth symbolized burial but not cremation. This category confusion is avoided in the Swedish case precisely because the funerary rite makes no distinction and offers no fundamental concession to cremation. This is reflected in the fact that the divide between the religious ceremony and the incineration is so complete that, unlike in Britain, they normally do not occur on the same day.

A *cremation disposal theology?*

These considerations return us to the issue of whether there could and, perhaps, should be a specific theology of disposal by cremation which is not largely derivative of burial? In my earlier small book *Cremation Today and Tomorrow*, I argued the case for such a distinctive cremation theology (Davies, 1990, pp. 30ff.). I need not rehearse that argument again, but simply stress how apt cremation is for stressing the finality of mortal life. Here Christianity stands as a realistic light amidst varied cultural avoidances of death, so our liturgy needs to express this in prayers like this:

Yours, Lord, is the gift of life.
In flesh and its empowering breath
You make us what we are.
As now we commit your servant's breathless body

to be cremated, we acknowledge that yours is the
right to give and take away,
Yours the right to return us to the dust from
which we came.

A similar note of realism is struck in the wedding service in the phrase 'till death us do part'. This is seldom emphasized or developed but might there not be a place to echo this phrase in funerals when the deceased is survived by a spouse? A prayer could address the issue in some way:

In your wisdom, O Lord,
You teach us that the covenant of marriage is
till death us do part.
Now, in grief we acknowledge this parting
and in its pain give thanks for the years together,
seeking strength for the way of life that lies ahead.

Such an integration of motifs between these occasional offices would make sense for many people who only attend church for major life rituals.

Sentimental memories and eternity

This type of prayer avoids the current sentimentalizing of death, especially in the belief that family relationships will be renewed in heaven. This view, potentially highly self-centred, lends itself to the criticism of being a simple wish-fulfilment of survival against destruction. A contemporary Christian eschatology ought to be more imaginative, not only to cope with the rather obvious point of serial polygamy in modern society but also to consider the astonishing challenge of eternity. Christian theologies of disposal necessitate a theology of eternal challenge for which theologies of hope provide a starting place.

Some popular views of life after death smack more of an eternally cosy family circle than of the call of a dramatically creative God. Because far too much stress is laid on death as stealing from survivors the cherished life of the loved one, practically no thought is given to eternity as anything other than making up for the loss by restoring family life. There is a parochial absurdity in this, hinting more of psychological counselling than of theology.

Any theology of disposal should mark the body as symbolic of ultimate significance, participating in what it represents and pointing to fulfilment and not futility. So too for cremated remains, a liturgical burial of them can set the deceased person within the ecclesiastical and social community while private placing in a treasured spot can simply reinforce a radically privatized existence. The churches have much ground to make up on this particular point, for most clergy are not involved with most cremated remains at all.

Conclusion

This chapter approached disposal through the three doctrines of creation, incarnation and society with the intention of raising rather than answering questions. What is obvious is that systematic theology, the philosophy of religion and sociology have integral parts to play in working towards a theology of disposal which can serve both liturgy and pastoral action.

References

St Augustine, *The City of God* (London: Duckworth, various editions).
Z. Bauman, *Mortality, Immortality and Other Life Strategies* (London: Polity Press, 1992).
L. Boros, *The Moment of Truth: Mysterium Mortis* (London: Burns & Oates, 1962).
J. Calvin, *Institutes of the Christian Religion* (Cheapside, London: Tegg and Son, 1838).
Catechism of the Catholic Church (London: Chapman, 1994).
Catholic Truth Society (see J. F. McDonald, 1966).
Church of England, *The Commemoration of the Faithful Departed* (London: Liturgical Commission, 1966).
D. Clark, *Between Pulpit and Pew* (Cambridge: Cambridge University Press, 1982).
O. Cullmann, *Christ and Time* (London: SCM Press, 1951).
O. Cullmann, *Immortality of the Soul or Resurrection of the Dead?* (London: Epworth, 1958).
D. J. Davies, *Cremation Today and Tomorrow* (Nottingham: Alcuin/GROW Books, 1990).
D. Davies and A. Shaw, *Reusing Old Graves: A Report on Popular British Attitudes* (Crayford, Kent: Shaw and Sons, 1995).
D. J. Davies, C. Pack, S. Seymour, C. Short, C. Watkins and M. Winter, *Rural Church Project Report*, vol. 1 'Staff and Buildings', vol. 2 'The Clergy Life', vol. 3 'Parish Life, Rural Religion', vol. 4 'Views of Rural Parishioners' (Cirencester: Royal Agricultural College and University of Nottingham: Department of Theology, 1990).
D. J. Davies, C. Watkins and M. Winter, *Church and Religion in Rural England* (Edinburgh: T. & T. Clark, 1991).

R. Hooker, *Laws of Ecclesiastical Polity* 5th edition, arranged by John Keble (Oxford: Clarendon Press, 1865).

J. F. McDonald, *Cremation* (London: Catholic Truth Society, 1966).

J. McManners, *Death and the Enlightenment* (Oxford: Clarendon Press, 1981).

J. Moltmann, *God in Creation* (London: SCM Press, 1985).

A. D. Nock, 'Cremation and Burial in the Roman Empire', *The Harvard Theological Review*, vol. XXV, pp. 321ff., 1932.

J. Parry, *Death in Banaras* (Cambridge: Cambridge University Press, 1994).

M. Perham, *The Communion of Saints* (London: Alcuin Club/SPCK, 1980).

L. Prior, *The Social Organisation of Death* (Basingstoke: Macmillan, 1989).

K. Rahner, *On the Theology of Death* (London: Burns & Oates, 1969).

G. Rowell, *The Liturgy of Christian Burial* (London: Alcuin Club/SPCK, 1977).

P. Teilhard de Chardin, *Hymn of the Universe* (London: Fontana, 1974).

W. Temple, *Nature, Man and God* (London: Macmillan, 1935).

P. Tillich, *Systematic Theology*, vol. 3 (London: Nisbet, 1964).

R. Williams, *A Protestant Legacy: Attitudes to Death and Illness among Older Aberdonians* (Oxford: Clarendon Press, 1990).

2

The experience of bereavement and the role of faith

7

The needs of bereaved people at the time of the funeral

Derek Nuttall

A caring organization received a telephone call recently from a woman very distressed after attending the funeral of a friend. Her natural distress at her loss had been made worse, she felt, by the unhelpful and insensitive way the funeral service had been conducted. Recognizing that personal grief is inevitable and subjective it was still the case that for her the way the funeral had been conducted had complicated her grieving. It is a reminder that a funeral is not outside grief, not a parallel event, but is closely woven in it. It is not a ritual standing by itself, without bearing or influence on those grieving the death. The fact that a funeral service may be experienced by those most deeply affected as if in a haze, carried along by what is happening rather than having a clear grip on it, is a reason, along with all the other reasons, for the content and conduct to be appropriate. A funeral is part of the grieving process, a necessary and crucial part, and conducted sensitively it can aid grieving, conducted badly it can hinder it.

This is not a new thought, but it is a relatively recent one. It comes, as so many things have, out of the research over the last 30 years into grief and bereavement, the greater openness in discussion about death, the experiences of those caring for dying and bereaved people and the sharing, in written and other forms of personal experience, by bereaved people themselves. Tracing human history back as far as we can, we see evidence in ceremonies and burial rites of the importance given to funerals in all civilizations (Bowlby, 1981; Hinton, 1967, especially Chapter 2). It seems there has always been deep instinctive awareness of the significance of burial rituals and the disposal of the dead. Whilst there is evidence of mourning rituals and some expression of the expectations of how bereaved people were to behave, it would seem, in the ancient world at least, that the emphasis was more on the dead than for the living. St Augustine, however, judged that Christian funerals benefited the survivors:

> ... earth has not been laid over many Christian bodies, yet no one of their souls has He kept out of Heaven ... Hence all these things, that is, anxiety about funeral, or place of burial, or funeral pomp, are rather a solace to the living than a help to the dead. (n.d., p. 12)

The knowledge gained in recent decades, and the continuing and increasing understanding of grief and its consequences, has helped us to a greater realization of the importance of the funeral for those who are bereaved as well as those who have died.

Why is a funeral important?

Why is a funeral important? Firstly, it is a ritual act and action. Death is awesome and grief powerful. They are major events in human experience, so major that ritual is needed better to express what is felt and known and believed. A ritual is a necessary thing when what we experience is too deep, too profound, too significant for ordinary expression and routine words. A death is such an event, its attendant grief such an experience.

Secondly, its importance lies in the fact that when someone we love, someone important to us, dies, we encounter change, both internal and external. Dr Colin Murray Parkes usefully helps us see something of the internal change in his concept of our assumptive world, our inner world, built around and upon things we have become accustomed to, that we take for granted, that we are dependent on, that we feel to be permanent (Parkes, 1975). We are thinking of all those essential supplies that go into and come out of a close relationship – love, companionship, opinion, nurture, stimulation, purpose and more. Death challenges and changes this assumptive world, the essential supplies cease, at least in the ways they have flowed before, and a new inner world has to be found and built and become trustworthy. The external changes are many, including all the practical tasks that previously have either been carried out by the deceased or were jointly executed.

There may have been some anticipation of the death, and some anticipatory grieving, or the death may have come without warning, or untimely, as of someone young. However it comes, bereavement means change. What these changes are and what they will mean are at first, in the early hours and days, barely grasped, if at all, but something fundamental has happened and things cannot be the same again. We know that the absorption of all this, the acceptance of what has happened, will take time, but the change has begun, the changes are set in motion. We are in, and entering more deeply into, a time of transition and significantly, without the person with whom we may have shared previous life changes. Like other major transitions in life, birth, growing up, marriage, divorce, retirement, a rite of passage is needed, to mark it and help us through it. A funeral is such a rite (Marris, 1974; Raphael, 1985, Kübler-Ross, 1973; Ainsworth-Smith and Speck, 1982).

A funeral, thirdly, is an opportunity for family, friends and the community to acknowledge the importance of what has happened, pay their respects, express their condolences and show and give their support. Those who are bereaved need to know that the one who has died mattered to others and will be missed by others. A funeral is the fusion of this being demonstrated and of the concern and sympathy felt for those who mourn most deeply. Some funerals only have a small number attending, but we have all heard the response, almost of surprise, from the individual or family at the centre of the loss, over numbers present larger than anticipated. It is more than the counting of heads. It has to do with the sense of respect and support.

A funeral importantly provides the opportunity for the saying of one of the many goodbyes, the speaking of gratitude for the life lived and what the deceased has contributed to people's lives, the expression of faith, the recognition of endings and the hope of new beginnings. It is a time for the shedding of public tears, though as individuals we differ in resisting this or permitting ourselves to do so. It is an occasion for comfort and pain, for hope and protest, for individual memory and corporate acknowledgement.

Finally, in an inevitably brief summary of why a funeral is important, it is so because it gives bereaved people the opportunity to be responsible for the final resting place of those they love. This would seem to be a fundamental human need, given the universal wish to have a formal farewell, the concern over where a body will be buried or ashes placed, and the distress often felt when a body has not been recovered and is not available for burial or cremation. Bereaved people who do not know where those who have died are buried or who cannot recover the body, often face a measure of unfinished business that can be lifelong. Recent years have seen many more pilgrimages to war graves abroad and often the outcome is relief and a sense of an unfinished task accomplished. Equally there are many examples of individuals who have now found it possible to visit the graves of family members or friends who have died, sometimes after many years, for the first time, and have found a release, a comfort and a completion. All this points to the deep need to be responsible for, or at the very least be aware of, the final resting place of those we love. It is also allied to the need bereaved people have for confirmation that the death has occurred, that the loved person has gone. In grieving it is often very important to have this confirmation by seeing the body, by attending a funeral, before acceptance can come and recovery begin. Some people may not wish to see the body and in some cultures it may not be permissible. For those who do and can it may prove to be an important step in a healthy grieving process (Hockey, 1992; Walter, 1990; Walter and Reader, 1993).

Bereavement and the funeral

The needs of bereaved people at the time of a funeral arise firstly therefore out of the significance of what has happened to them. Being bereaved and experiencing grief often produce profound reactions that for the majority of people are normal and natural and, given the blow they have taken, understandable. The emphasis in this chapter is on what may be called, without diminishing in any way the severity of the loss or the individuality of the grief, normal grieving. It is not an attempt to describe what may be the additional needs of those whose bereavement leads to abnormal responses, except to register the importance of being aware of them in the planning of the funeral. It is also important to stress the thought that should be given in funeral preparation to any bereaved people who may have learning or comprehension difficulties (Oswin, 1991).

What follows the arousing of these fundamental needs in bereavement are other needs concerning the funeral. These include the provision of clear, ample and simply put information. What may seem straightforward to those who conduct or arrange funerals regularly may be very unfamiliar, even totally unknown, to those who are bereaved and who have little or no understanding of what will happen at a burial or cremation or what procedures have to be followed. This is the first and only funeral that those who are bereaved are involved in for this person. It is far from easy for officiants to maintain a sense of uniqueness for every funeral, especially if there have already been several funerals in the week, but it is helpful if it can be achieved. In this regard Free Church ministers may have the advantage of generally fewer funerals than Anglican and Roman Catholic colleagues. The clarity of the information provided in the period before a funeral, whether it be the details of the arrangements from the funeral director's point of view or the service outline from the officiant's, is made doubly important by the fact that bereaved people may be finding it difficult to absorb and retain what is said. They are having to try and deal with matters at a time when they may still be in shock or their concentration is restricted. Much will depend on the circumstances of the death and the distress caused. It may be an elderly person where thought has already been given to the funeral, or a young person suddenly killed. It may be a self-inflicted death or a death following a period of deteriorating health. In some instances it may be very difficult for those responsible for the funeral to ask appropriate questions, make relevant requests or retain what is said to them. If there is someone who is less distressed and available to sit in on discussions this often helps. Equally if it is appropriate for some things to be written down and left with the individual or family this can also help.

The participation, both in the planning of the funeral content and in the service itself, will vary. Some prefer the officiant to do everything. Others provide material to be read or music to be played, and at times family members or friends may wish to read or be asked to give the tribute. The essential thing is for bereaved people to be consulted so that their involvement is as full as they wish.

This provision of information can be time-consuming. It may be difficult for clergy to spend adequate time with those who are bereaved but it does bring benefits in terms of discovering more about the person who has died and those who are left, and it increases the assurance mourners have over the procedure of the funeral. Time is certainly something bereaved people need. We recognize that working through grief and adjusting to what has happened takes time, often longer than we allow bereaved people in spite of our greater enlightenment on the process of grief. Time is also important in the days leading to the funeral, time to think about decisions, absorb details and suggestions and consider or reconsider parting actions, time to talk about the deceased to the person conducting the funeral. This may be setting an ideal beyond practicality but all who conduct funerals have to bear it in mind (Walter, 1996).

Underlying this issue of time is another basic need bereaved people have – for as personal a funeral service as possible. Reports are still received of funerals where the deceased is not mentioned by name and where all is generality rather than more personal reference to those principally bereaved. Every encouragement, in ministerial training and elsewhere, should be given to enable those conducting funerals to be aware of the comfort personalized funerals give, and of the lingering disappointment that can occur when they are impersonal.

It may be felt that personal references cause mourners more distress but the distress is already present and to hear a husband's or wife's or child's or parent's or friend's name spoken may well bring tears but it importantly conveys that the one who has died matters, that he or she was an individual with a personality. Those who are bereaved often say how some people find it difficult to mention the dead person's name in conversations when they may be longing for that personal recognition, and how they feel they have to speak the name first to break into the embarrassment and free the conversation from its restraints. A funeral service which includes the personal naming of the deceased brings comfort, helps make real, in the sense of confirmation stressed earlier, what has happened, acknowledges the individuality of the dead person and helps free people to talk more naturally about him or her.

Cultural factors

One major cultural change in Britain in the last fifty years has been the growth in the numbers of cremations compared to burials. Seventy per cent of all funerals are now at crematoria. What difference, if any, the means of disposal makes to the process of grief, the experience of bereavement and the needs of bereaved people, at this time, still needs to be more fully researched and understood. The principal thing would seem to be that the choice is knowingly made by those responsible for the funeral and we may wish to deduce that this having been done there would be little, if any, difference in the grief reactions and the personal needs. This is a deduction awaiting more study. One thing it has done is reduce the provision of graves and gravestones, which are traditional places for the paying of respects, remembering anniversaries and other dates, laying flowers and spending times of quiet; a focus for grief. For bereaved people who do not have a grave to visit, this focus may have changed to a name in a Book of Remembrance, a rose tree, a plaque on a cemetery or crematorium wall, or an inscribed seat in a park. It seems that for many bereaved people this need for a focus for grief remains, and is met sometimes in the ways listed or in some other way. A question that could be asked is whether this change in marking cremated remains, or perhaps not marking them, is an indication of a change in the needs of bereaved people or a pattern emerging as by default because less encouragement is given to have an obvious memorial. Is it a sign of change in bereavement responses, a fulfilment of Orwell's *1984* picture of once dead then forgotten, a diminishment of personal faith, or less adherence to a sense of continuity between generations in a highly mobile world? Are we doing a disservice to bereaved people by not encouraging more consideration of memorials of some kind? These are questions rather than answers but this area of bereavement need requires study (Jupp, 1990; Cleiren, 1991; Walter, 1990).

Another major change has been the development of our multifaith, multicultural society. This affects the care of the body after death, the speed at which a funeral may need to be arranged, the funeral practices themselves and the provision of support for those who are bereaved.

Funeral directors and those in nursing and medicine who have to prepare bodies after death are having to learn practices appropriate to the culture and faith of the deceased. Officiants at Christian funerals may benefit from a closer study of the rites of other faiths and vice versa. This is true also in the fields of bereavement care and mourning rituals. Rigidity of ritualistic response following bereavement is unlikely to be helpful but some framework of ritual is supportive. We have largely moved away from what many can still recall as rituals after a death, typified by drawing shut curtains in the street where the funeral begins, the doffing of hats as the cortege passes, the allowing of all the funeral procession cars to follow in close convoy rather than being broken up by other vehicles. Frequent comments on the absence of these community rituals seem to indicate something more than simple nostalgia. The Church has a responsibility to create appropriate rituals for the deceased and those who are bereaved and a consideration of funeral differences in different faiths would be helpful to everyone (Neuberger, 1987; Green, 1993).

The growing availability of Humanist services has marked a further change in funeral practices. The deceased may have indicated that there should be no formal religious content or it could be the choice of the mourners. It would be an interesting area of study to consider what differences if any are to be found in the grief responses of those who have shared in a Humanist funeral compared with a formally religious ceremony. Is the honesty of the atheist itself a strength and comfort or does the finality remove a necessary hope of some kind of continuing spiritual life from bereaved people?

Again we enter the discussion over who the funeral is for and the recognition of the needs of those who grieve. The choice of a Humanist funeral could involve several factors, including: the honesty of those without religious belief; a wish to have much greater, if not total, control over the ceremony; a decline in the belief in eternal life; and a negative view of the funeral rituals provided by the faith communities.

A further cultural change deserves mention: the discussions about euthanasia, the greater use of Living Wills, and the possibility of making more formal plans for your own funeral in advance of dying. These will have an impact on grieving and may influence, in both positive and negative ways, the needs of bereaved people. Clearly they will influence the arrangements made for funerals if the details have been worked out in advance and those who are now bereaved feel they can have no say in what happens. Being guided by the wishes of the deceased can be helpful for those deciding what to do but it may also leave them with a sense of having not participated fully enough, nor been able to express in the funeral what their needs may be. Could this lead to some of the grief being left unexpressed? A funeral is for the one who has died, but it is also for those left to grieve.

Children and funerals

No distinction has been attempted so far between the needs of bereaved adults and bereaved children when considering the funeral. Some of the needs discussed are not necessarily dependent upon age but it is important not to overlook children's needs, at any stage, and certainly not when thinking of funerals. What is clear and should never be neglected is that children grieve. A significant attachment to another person, parent, sibling, grandparent, or any other, that is broken by the death of that person, will lead to a sense of loss and to its consequence, grief. Its shape and expression may vary with the age of the child but loss is experienced and as it is important in an adult's bereavement for grief to be expressed, so it is in a child's bereavement. Part of that expression involves the funeral.

Whether or not children go to a funeral usually depends on a number of factors. Age is clearly one and there may be reluctance to allow a young child to attend. One concern expressed by parents is the upset he or she might cause mourners by being restless and noisy. One aid to the decision will be how possible it is for the child to understand and discuss what has happened and what will happen at the funeral, and take a share in the decision about attending for himself or herself. This raises again the issue of information and explanation and if children do attend it is important that someone is able to explain in advance what will happen. This will reduce fantasies, prepare them for what will happen, particularly at the moment of committal when the coffin disappears from view, and help them feel included.

A further factor in the decision will be the culture of the family and its openness or otherwise to talking about loss and about pain and death. It may be a family where children have been excluded from painful events both through physical absence and by lack of open discussion. It is still the case that some children are sent to school on the day of the funeral of someone significant in their lives. Such exclusion is often explained as a wish not to cause the child pain and upset. In contrast the family may be one where there is open sharing of feelings and it would be natural for children to attend a funeral.

When considering the needs of bereaved children at the time of the funeral it is important not to exclude them from something they are already part of anyway. Children grieve and their grief needs and deserves acknowledgement. To do things that make them feel that their loss and sadness are inferior to other people's grief will be unhelpful and may hinder their own grieving. If children do not go to the funeral it is very important that they should not be sent away for the rest of the time that day so that they miss the post-funeral gathering, and it is best if it can be arranged that they spend the time while others are attending the funeral with someone they know well.

If children are old enough, whether or not they go to the funeral, they could be asked if they have any suggestions for the service. This again reinforces the importance of their experience. All these comments about bereaved children carry essentially the same message – that more thought needs to be given than is the case at times to their needs, and that nothing should be done to make them feel left out, their grief unrecognized, their loss unacknowledged (Wells, 1988; Kremetz, 1986; Black, various dates; Furman, 1974).

In what ways then can a funeral aid the grieving process? By its being an opportunity for the expression of grief, by the recognition it signals of the depth of loss felt, by acknowledging that the deceased person mattered and matters, by creating an occasion for public respect, sympathy and support, by providing a setting for thanksgiving for life, prayers for the dead and grieving and hope in eternal things; by laying a loved person to rest, closing a chapter of grief and making a future possible. If we did not have funerals for our dead it would be much more difficult for us to work through our grief and to move on.

Faith and grieving

Having a religious belief will not necessarily reduce the pain of loss nor remove the need to work through the stages of grief. Such belief, however, can be an aid to grieving.

It will include belief in an afterlife for the one who has died, however simply or sophisticatedly construed. A passing of the spirit or soul not into nothingness but to a state of glory, peace, joy and freedom. We would prefer our loved ones to be with us but if they cannot be, to believe they have eternal life is a comfort and a source of hope. In Christian belief there is resurrection, a new life, an unfettered life, and within it the hope that we will meet again with those we love and go on loving. There will be a reuniting.

Christian belief speaks of a loving, sharing and suffering God. In bereavement we need to know we are not alone, that our agony is understood and in some way shared. At the heart of Christianity is faith in a fatherly God who through Christ has shown he loves us, shares in what we experience and through the cross suffers with us.

Those who are involved in and are part of the fellowship of a faith community have access in their grief to a caring group who, it is hoped, will provide not only emotional and spiritual support but practical and social help as well. Bereaved people often find it difficult to re-enter social life and a ready-made group, such as a church fellowship, can greatly aid this step in the process.

References

St Augustine, trans. M. Allies, *How to Help the Dead* (London: Burns & Oates, n.d.).

I. Ainsworth-Smith and P. Speck, *Letting Go* (London: SPCK, 1982).

D. Black, various articles in *Bereavement Care* (Richmond-upon-Thames: Cruse-Bereavement Care, various dates).

J. Bowlby, 'Mourning in other cultures', *Attachment and Loss*, vol. 3 (Harmondsworth: Penguin, 1981).

M. P. H. D. Cleiren, *Adaptation after Bereavement* (Leiden: Leiden University Press, 1991).

E. A. Furman, *A Child's Parent Dies* (New Haven and London: Yale University Press, 1974).

J. Green, *Death with Dignity* (London: Nursing Times Publications, vol. 1, 1991, vol. 2, 1993).

J. Hinton, 'Death no more', in *Dying* (Harmondsworth: Pelican, 1967).

J. Hockey, *Making the Most of a Funeral* (Richmond-upon-Thames: Cruse-Bereavement Care, 1992).

P. C. Jupp, *From Dust to Ashes: The Replacement of Burial by Cremation in England 1840–1967* (London: The Congregational Memorial Hall Trust, 1990).

J. Kremetz, *How It Feels When a Parent Dies* (London: Gollancz, 1986).

E. Kübler-Ross, *On Death and Dying* (London: Tavistock, 1973).

P. Marris, *Loss and Change* (London: Routledge & Kegan Paul, 1974).

J. Neuberger, *Caring for Dying People of Different Faiths* (London: Austen Cornish, 1987).

M. Oswin, *Am I Allowed to Cry?* (London: Souvenir Press, 1991).

C. M. Parkes, *Bereavement: Studies of Grief in Adult Life* (Harmondsworth: Penguin, 1975).

B. Raphael, *Anatomy of Bereavement* (London: Hutchinson, 1985).

T. Walter, *Funerals and How to Improve Them* (London: Hodder & Stoughton, 1990).

T. Walter, 'A new model of grief: bereavement and biography', *Mortality* 1:1, 1996.

T. Walter and I. Reader (eds), *Pilgrimage in Popular Culture* (Basingstoke: Macmillan, 1993).

R. Wells, *Helping Children Cope with Grief* (London: Sheldon, 1988).

8

Bereavement and belief: an Anglican perspective

Peter Speck

Introduction

> The interval between the decay of the old and the formation and the establishment of the new, constitutes a period of transition, which must always necessarily be one of uncertainty, confusion ...
> (Calhoun, 1850).

It can often be difficult to know what to say or do when a crisis occurs since our usual means of coping may seem inadequate. Therefore, all societies have developed forms of ritual which are built into their culture and provide acceptable ways for someone to behave in a disturbing situation (Speck, 1978). These 'rites of passage' are not necessarily religious but frequently mark the passage from one social or religious status to another.

It is important to note that the rituals associated with the care of the dying and the bereaved, and the disposal of the dead, do not replace the grief process. If a ritual is to aid the natural grief process, then it should meet needs at three levels:

(a) the psychological level – by giving a framework for the full expression of feeling (grief) and to reduce anxiety;
(b) the theological or philosophical level – by which one seeks to make some sense and existential meaning out of what is experienced;

(c) the sociological level – through sharing the experience with others and being re-accepted into society with a new status.

Ideally ministry to the dying person and their family will have commenced long before the closing stages of life are reached so that clergy do not come as complete strangers. Sadly, this is not always possible.

Nevertheless one has to respond sensitively to the needs of the time and try to help people devise an appropriate way of saying 'goodbye' to the person who has died, against the background of the natural grief response which will often take more than two years' adjustment.

Shock and disbelief

Initially people may find it difficult to acknowledge the reality of a death and may deny that death has occurred. This may last for a few hours or a few days. It is important to be clear and direct in stating to the bereaved frequently what has happened. Grief and shock are very physical and people may resist reality because of the pain it brings. We must, therefore, sensitively stick to the reality. Viewing the body can be important in helping people through this first part of the grief process and this includes giving children the opportunity to talk and to view. The nature of the death frequently influences the degree of shock and denial. Worden provides several examples of ways in which we can enable the bereaved to face the reality of the death through our use of language, writing, symbols and memories (Worden, 1991, p. 53).

Growing awareness

Reality gradually impinges and a variety of feelings flow back and forth making the person feel out of control. This can be frightening if the person does not feel supported while this happens. We should not force people to express emotions not yet experienced, rather give permission and opportunity for expression of feelings of emptiness, sadness and desolation.

People need to be able to express their grief in their own way and we need to respond flexibly, allowing for cultural differences. Recent texts provide information on some of these cultural patterns (Irish *et al.*, 1993; Green and Green, 1992; Neuberger, 1987). However, care is needed not to assume that all who profess a particular faith or culture are equally strict adherents. It is important that the carer pays attention to his/her own assumptions as to how people should feel or behave. People need practical details but they also need someone who can simply 'be' with them, with the skill to listen, and perhaps tells 'you the bitter truth and stays with you to the inexorable end' (Illich, 1995, p. 1653).

There may thus also be a corresponding grief reaction in the carers (Speck, 1994).

Resolution

People usually come to terms with the loss without the need for any professional intervention, provided they have adequate support. This can take at least 18 months to two years.

People may well have experienced a variety of forms of loss before they actually come to personal death, and therefore do have some experiences to draw upon. I believe that the psychological understanding of the processes of letting go provides us with an understanding of the human reaction to such situations. It is important to understand that process so that any theological interpretation and understanding that we may offer will not cut across what the person is experiencing at a psychological level. Grief is frequently experienced as chaos, and what we frequently have to offer is some structured order, some rite of passage, which might provide the boundaries of safety within which the individual can experience the chaos. Malinowski (1974) refers to a 'fruitful chaos' within a rite of passage whereby the confusion and disorientation experienced by people can lead to the emergence later of a new life in the ceremonies of incorporation. Grainger makes a similar point in relation to the important function of the wake (Grainger, 1988, pp. 53–5, 155–67).

Our rituals at the time of a death should seek to bring healing to the bereaved. We help to redefine the relationship between the person who has died, with others and with God, so that the bereaved may ultimately be free to relate to others in the future. This process is discussed by Grainger and Worden when they speak of emotional relocation which permits the survivors to find a new place in their life for the deceased person (Grainger, 1988, pp. 48ff.). Loss, therefore, forces us to re-evaluate our interpretation of life and its purpose.

The funeral and associated events

The funeral is an extremely important event since the manner in which we dispose of our dead can be a reflection of our attitude towards death, and towards the deceased.

What is the purpose of the funeral?

In the mid 1960s the Church of England Liturgical Commission tackled the question 'What ought we to be doing at a burial service?' (Church of England Liturgical Commission, 1965, pp. 105–6) with a five-fold answer regarding the funeral's purpose:

(a) to secure the reverent disposal of the corpse;
(b) to commend the deceased to the care of our heavenly Father;
(c) to proclaim the glory of our risen life in Christ here and hereafter;
(d) to remind us of the awful certainty of our own coming death and judgement;
(e) to make plain the eternal unity of Christian people, living and departed, in the risen and ascended Christ.

It would perhaps be natural to add a sixth point, namely the consolation of mourners; but the Commission believed that this would be attained by means of the five objects already detailed. In giving liturgical expression to this answer, the Commission set itself the following practical aims:

(a) that one burial service should suffice for all baptized persons (including suicides) but an exception has had to be made in the case of burying children;
(b) that the rite should not assume that the soul of the deceased is, at the time of burial of the body, in any particular place or state;
(c) that as much as possible of the existing material should be used even though some parts must be simplified or used in a different way;
(d) that the congregation should be given a more active part than at present;
(e) that as little as possible of the service should be required to take place out of doors;
(f) that the orders of services provided should, the committal of the body being omitted, be suitable for use as memorial services.

The same thinking carried forward to the Alternative Service Book of 1980. The five-fold answer, however, does not address the need for awareness of the process of grieving which affects the family as they prepare and attend the funeral.

Van Gennep used slightly different language to describe the aim of a good rite of passage (Van Gennep, 1977). He saw these rites as a means whereby

VAN GENNEP

individuals might be eased, without undue social disruption, through the difficulties of transition from one social group to another. Van Gennep proposed three distinguishable and consecutive stages in this process:

(a) separation or pre-liminal (before the threshold);
(b) transition or liminal (at the threshold);
(c) incorporation or post-liminal (past the threshold).

The person, or group, on whom the rite focuses is first symbolically separated from his or her old status, then undergoes adjustment to the new status during the period of transition. Finally there is incorporation into society with a new social status (Ainsworth-Smith and Speck, 1978).

The funeral service and the events surrounding it can be very significant for both the deceased and the mourners since, if the ritual is to facilitate grief, the family and the community must be involved in all three aspects of the rite of passage.

Separation – transition – incorporation

Separation for the deceased and the bereaved

Whilst the commendatory prayers at the time of death have the prime intention of commending the dying to God's mercy and love, they can also act as a means of giving permission for the dying to die. It not infrequently happens that following anointing, prayer and commendation, the person dying will visibly relax and begin to 'slip away'. It is as if they feel that permission has been granted to let go.

The bereaved must also allow the dying to die and, having died, to let them be dead. Hence the need to declare the deceased to be dead in any prayers or ritual at this time, since it can aid separation. This is especially true if there is no physical body to see and touch as may happen if the person is lost at sea or the body is donated to medical science.

Viewing the body

If the family were not present at the time of death they may wish to see the body. This can help many relatives who are denying the reality of the death. Whilst not everybody will wish to see the deceased, the opportunity to do so should be given to them, and the local minister/hospital chaplain[1] may be invited to accompany the family and offer suitable prayers (Church of England, 1991).

Children may also need an opportunity either to be present or not, since we cannot 'shield' a child from what has happened. However, their choice will need to be informed by some explanation of what they might see and hear. If we are not able to face the fact of death children will also find it difficult. To tell the child that 'mummy is in hospital', when in fact mummy is dead, can lead to a multitude of problems later. It does not help to shut a child out of the grief that a whole family shares (Kremetz, 1986; Judd, 1989; Abrams, 1995; Wallbank, 1991).

Around the time of the funeral the bereaved become temporarily separated in order to become the focus of care from both the family and the community. If that support is not there it can precipitate great loneliness. Similarly, condolence cards and letters are appreciated. Whilst they may not be read properly until much later, they do signify the support and prayers of others.

Pre-funeral visits by the clergy

Clearly there needs to be a good relationship and liaison between clergy and funeral directors. With those families who have no church connection the funeral director can fulfil an important caring role and may often pave the way for a visit by a member of the clergy whom they have not met. In many places clergy and funeral directors work closely together and, as far as possible, funerals are taken by the clergy who are likely to have continuing pastoral contact with the bereaved. The pre-funeral visit to a family where one is known and welcomed is quite different from that where clergy have no previous pastoral contact. It is not usually a time for one-to-one bereavement counselling. There is often much coming and going, with relatives and friends in and out of the room, and the next-of-kin perhaps shocked and numb. To the family the main purpose for the visit is seen to be the necessity of arranging the funeral.

There will be discussion about the service, mode of disposal and other practicalities. It may also be a time of prayer with the bereaved, either using available prayer books or praying spontaneously. There needs to be a spirit of openness which echoes and offers up to the love of God what has been shared in the visit – the positive and the negative, the rage and doubt, submission and bewilderment (Lambert, 1994, pp. 149ff.). However, a prayer should not be a means of wrapping it all up, silencing the family or protecting the minister!

A home visit can enable one to build up a picture of the various and different reactions of family members, to assess where they are in their grief and to gain information about the deceased. Various members of the family may be at different points in their grief which, coupled with previous rivalries, can lead to friction. While they need the minister to conduct the funeral they may also resent his presence and intrusion.

Transition for the deceased

The transition for the deceased is related to the anxiety expressed by many bereaved people as to where the dead person has gone. The concept of a journey is prevalent with many people and there can be great anxiety about 'hell and heaven'. Linked with this can be the anxiety that the dead in some way may be able to do harm. 'Never speak ill of the dead' has overtones of fear of reprisals as well as genuine respect.

What we should be seeking to express in the liturgy at this time of transition is our faith and hope in God's love and grace, and not in what we have achieved in life. Eulogies, elaborate arrangements and sentiment can sometimes cloud this for us, whereas a genuine act of thanksgiving for the deceased and the family may reaffirm our dependence and trust in God. What is crucial is that the funeral relates to the real person with whom the mourners related whether positively or negatively. This has implications for the sermon (see Perham, Chapter 13 below).

An important part of liturgy, therefore, is to reaffirm the continuity in Christ of the living and the dead and the appropriateness of commending the departed to the love of God. In the liturgical revision of the burial service (subsequently renamed the Funeral Service following the Cremation Act, since not every body would be buried), the Requiem and associated prayers for the dead became an area of sharp division in the Church of England (see again Perham's chapter below). One of the purposes of ritual is to reduce anxiety and the anxiety about what has happened to the deceased has influenced aspects of the religious ritual throughout the history of the Church and led the Church, in its early days, to baptize the dead. Whatever our personal doctrinal position regarding prayers for the dead (Report of the Archbishops' Commission, 1971), many of the relatives one meets are looking for reassurance and an easing of the anxiety about what has happened to the person who has died.

Before offering any prayer at the time of death, therefore, the minister needs to spend a little time picking up the feelings that are around in the family regarding both the deceased and God. This reflects what was said earlier, that if a ritual is to be seen as relevant it must be in tune with needs at the psychological, theological and sociological levels. This sensitive 'picking up of the atmosphere' will enable the clergyman to formulate a prayer or prayers which express the reality of what is being experienced. Hence the importance of visiting the family beforehand. The ambivalence may be heightened if there has been a breakup of the family through divorce, dispute or poor communication within the family.

It is for many the Eucharist and the Requiem which symbolize this the most clearly. The Holy Communion and the Requiem represent a unique meeting point between God and man, between the living and the departed. For those who believe in the sacramental presence of Christ in the consecrated bread and wine, they can also feel very close to the faithful departed (who are in Christ) when they go forward to receive communion. It is for this reason that many find that, apart from their normal regular attendance at Communion, a special annual occasion, such as All Souls' Day on 2 November, can be especially significant and reassuring regarding incorporation for the deceased (Mitton and Parker, 1991).

Transition for the bereaved

For the bereaved the transition phase of the rite of passage is the time when the past is left behind and the future has not yet begun. It is the period between Good Friday and Easter Day. One's point of reference has gone and time seems to stand still as an endeavour is made to discover and accept a new identity and status, e.g. the spouse is beginning the transition from wife/husband to that of widow/widower. It is as if one's entire world has been destroyed and one is left with a deep sense of insecurity (see Gardiner, Chapter 10 below). Sometimes, after a stillbirth, the parents may feel that the world is now such an unsafe place that they cannot contemplate another pregnancy. As one father said to me: 'How can you bring children into a world where people are bombed, raped, hijacked or murdered?' His ability to protect those he loved had been badly damaged by the experience of stillbirth. The funeral ritual and associated events are vital here because the funeral has the capability of encapsulating the full process of separation, transition and incorporation and thus enabling the bereaved to move forward in their grief. It does not do the grief work for them, but it can act as a catalyst.

The funeral service

During the course of the Christian funeral rites our eyes are to be turned away from the physical remains towards the things 'that are unseen'. Away from who we are and what we have done in life to spiritual resources, what God in his love has done for us through his Son, Jesus Christ.

If the funeral ritual is to be effective, as a rite of passage, in facilitating the grief of the bereaved then those present must be actively involved. This begins with the pre-funeral planning whereby the mourners begin to 'own' the event as theirs. This may continue by their contributing material, joining in with the responses, the saying of the psalms together, one of the group reading a lesson, offering a tribute, singing a hymn, as well as the non-verbal ways of touching and holding each other and passing tissues. Most people need careful direction so that they can be caught up in the ritual without becoming anxious about whether they should be standing, sitting or kneeling.

The minister is invested with authority and looked to for leadership in seeing that the 'ritual is effective' and that 'Bert has a good send off'. It can be a daunting task to be faced with a varied group of distressed people, about whom one may know very little, and to try and unite them into a meaningful act of worship within the space of a few minutes. No other helping profession in our society possesses a ready way to exhibit ritually its representation of a distinct tradition of helping (Clebsch and Jaekle, 1995).

The sermon

Historically there has been a reluctance to say too much about the deceased at the funeral and the earlier Church of England Prayer Book made no provision for a sermon. In the new Alternative Service Book the sermon is optional. While the funeral is not a time for an exposition of the psychology of grief, there is still a need to acknowledge the sense of loss and, where they are known to the minister, to reflect some of the emotions represented in those present. It is usually possible to include a note of thanksgiving with details acquired during the pre-funeral visit. Even when there is ambivalence in the various relationships it should be possible to find aspects of the person for which to give thanks, and to make some offering of the 'loose ends' of a person's life. This can be especially challenging if the deceased was well known locally as a 'bad character'. It might be necessary to acknowledge this fact, but also to point people to God being the final judge of a person's life and that that judgement occurs in the context of God's mercy and love. Similarly a sensitive but realistic message is required if the circumstances of the death are especially painful, as in suicide or murder (see Nuttall, Chapter 7 above).

What if there is no body?

If the deceased is 'lost at sea', blown up or donated to medical science there will be no body at the time of death to bury or cremate. In all such cases it is advisable that there should be some ritual to mark personally and socially what has happened. Failure to do something at this time may leave the bereaved very unsure and anxious about how and where to express what they are feeling. People often need 'permission' to grieve, otherwise grief may be postponed and this can be the prelude for abnormal grieving patterns subsequently. A memorial service or a requiem is often the right way to proclaim publicly the fact of the death and to enable separation to take place.

Incorporation

This third part of the rite of passage aids the re-entry into the community of those who have been branded or stigmatized by death.[2] In that the funeral encapsulates the entire rite of passage, in miniature, then such re-entry can be symbolized by the return to the house of family and friends following the funeral. It is time for offering support to the next of kin, for reminiscence, renewing old acquaintances and perhaps for settling old scores. Traditionally there is a meal and drinks. A great deal of emotion is expressed as laughter or tears, and on occasion it can lead to a riotous party. In some parts of the country it is also practice for the family to attend their local church on the Sunday following the funeral and for the deceased and family to be referred to, and prayed for, during the course of the service. This helps to encourage the ongoing concern for the bereaved by the local Christian congregation who may be involved in post-funeral visiting as part of a lay pastoral scheme.

Full incorporation of the bereaved back into the community is parallel to the final phase of grief which we described earlier as 'resolution'. We are, therefore, thinking in terms of a period of time nearer to 18 months than the two or three months that people usually allow. Attempts to hurry the grief process are often an expression of our anxiety and embarrassment in the face of grief. A difficulty that faces many people in our own society is the lack of a structure within which to do their grief work, and which would mark off the end of grief. A memorial service, a visit by the minister, or an act of remembrance around All Souls' Day can help the bereaved feel they have permission to end the main part of their grieving.

Conclusion

In this chapter we have looked at ways in which ritual, and the funeral in particular, does not replace 'grief work' but can, if used effectively, enable the grief process to happen. In that people in a crisis usually benefit from having a structure within which they may safely express very powerful feelings, the desire to reduce ritual to a minimum is not something necessarily to be welcomed. If we dispense with ritual we may leave people with a further sense of loss and abandonment. There needs to be a sensitive and flexible approach to the needs of each particular family which should then lead to a more relevant and effective ritual which can acknowledge and aid the grieving process, and be reflective of the faith of the participants, without imposing a rigid belief framework. Since an inappropriate and ill-prepared ritual may serve to block the grief process, this places a large measure of responsibility on those who arrange the ritual, as well as on those who participate in it.

Notes

1. Hospital chaplains should check the mortuary chapel/viewing room arrangements at their hospital, and the policies dictating how they are used. They should also ensure that these areas are adaptable for use by non-Christians. Department of Health guidelines also exist which require hospitals to review their policies and practices regarding the care of dying and bereaved people DA(84)17.
2. An individual who is seen as being socially 'abnormal' may be reacted to by others in a variety of ways ranging from rejection to over-hearty acceptance or plain embarrassment. Close contact with death can lead to social contamination (stigmatization) and therefore the need for some form of cleansing prior to reintegration into society. One example of this process is seen in the healing of the ten lepers who were sent to the priest to be pronounced clean in order to rejoin their family and community (Luke 17.14). For further discussion of 'stigma' see E. Goffman, *Stigma* (Harmondsworth: Penguin, 1968).

References

R. Abrams, *When Parents Die* (London: Thursons, 1995).

I. Ainsworth-Smith and P. Speck, *Letting Go – Pastoral Care of the Dying and the Bereaved* (London: SPCK, 1978).

J. Calhoun, *A Disquisition on Government* (1850), quoted in the *Oxford Dictionary of Quotations* (Oxford: OUP).

Church of England Liturgical Commission, Alternative Services, 2nd Series (London: CIO, 1965).

Church of England, *Ministry at the Time of Death* (London: CIO, 1991).

W. A. Clebsch and C. R. Jaekle, *Pastoral Care in Historical Perspective*, 2nd edn (New York: Aronson, 1995).

R. Grainger, *The Unburied* (Worthing: Churchman, 1988).

J. Green and M. Green, *Dealing with Death – Practices and Procedures* (London: Chapman Hall, 1992).

I. Illich, 'Death undefeated – from medicine to medicalisation to systematisation', *British Medical Journal*, vol. 311, 1995.

D. Irish *et al.* (eds), *Ethnic Variations in Dying, Death and Grief – Diversity in Universality* (Bristol: Taylor & Francis, 1993).

D. Judd, *Give Sorrow Words – Working with a Dying Child* (London: Free Association, 1989).

J. Kremetz, *How it Feels When a Parent Dies* (London: Gollancz, 1986).

C. Lambert, 'Bereaved families and funeral arrangements: options for change', *Resurgam*, vol. 37, 1994.

B. Malinowski, *Magic, Science and Religion* (London: Souvenir Press, 1974).

M. Mitton and R. Parker, *Requiem Healing* (London: Darton, Longman and Todd, 1991).

J. Neuberger, *Caring for Dying People of Different Faiths* (London: Austen Cornish, 1987).

Report of the Archbishops' Commission, *Prayer and the Departed* (London: SPCK, 1971).

P. Speck, *Loss and Grief in Medicine* (London: Ballière Tindall, 1978).

P. Speck, 'Working with dying people: on being good enough', in V. Roberts and A. Obholtzer, *The Unconscious at Work: Individual and Organisational Stress in the Human Services* (London: Routledge, 1994).

A. Van Gennep, *The Rites of Passage* [1909] (London: Routledge, 1977).

S. Wallbank, *Facing Grief – Bereavement and the Young Adult* (Cambridge: Lutterworth, 1991).

W. Worden, *Grief Counselling and Grief Therapy*, 2nd edn (London: Tavistock, 1991).

9

Loss and gain

David Forrester

No one knows precisely how he or she will react when someone dear to them dies. This is so whether the death of such a person comes at the end of a painful and terminal illness and might reasonably be expected for all concerned to come as a relief, or whether death occurs suddenly and unexpectedly and is therefore traumatic for those left behind. In various ways we may already be acquainted with serious loss, whether it be the loss of a faculty such as one's hearing or eyesight, the amputation of a limb, a separation or divorce from a partner, the loss of a child in a miscarriage, and even such losses as that of status or usefulness when one retires, and sometimes the loss of purpose when one's children leave home for good. Nevertheless, the death of a loved one is at first usually devastating. Furthermore the extent to which we grieve often differs greatly from person to person, depending on a variety of circumstances and factors. An author who feels passionately about the subject has recently remarked that, 'Bereavement works through us, rather than the other way round. Our responses are as different as our experiences: some need privacy, others need to shout their grief from the roof tops. Some find tears crucial, others find repression the answer; others still that there is nothing to repress.'[1] In extreme cases, such as that of Dora Carrington, the lover of Lytton Strachey, for example, such was her grief that it ended in despair and ultimately suicide:

I dreamt of you again last night. And when I woke up it was as if you had died afresh. Everyday I find it harder to bear. For what point is there in life now ? ... I look at our favourites, I try and read them, but without you they give me no pleasure. I only remember the evenings when you read them to me aloud and then I cry. I feel as if we had collected all our wheat into a barn to make bread and beer for the rest of our lives and now our barn has been burnt down and we stand on a cold winter morning looking at the charred ruins ... It is impossible to think that I shall never sit with you again and hear your laugh. *That every day for the rest of my life you will be away.* (Carrington, *Diaries*, 12/17 February 1932)[2]

Even so, given the fact that Carrington is an extreme case, there are reactions which we all more or less experience in our loss and most authorities also speak of 'stages' of bereavement. Incidentally, the term 'bereavement' comes from the word 'reave' which means to ravage, rob and leave desolate and it is the so-called stages of bereavement that it is initially most useful to explore. This is so in order that we may to some extent prepare ourselves for the time we can hardly bear to think about; the time when we shall irretrievably be separated from someone whose life may be at present intimately bound up with our own. Even so, it cannot be emphasized sufficiently that these so-called 'stages' are only useful guidelines and, as Virginia Ironside has observed, they are not set in stone. Some people may never feel anger or guilt, whilst others may wonder whether the day will ever come when they do not feel these emotions; some people adjust to the death of a loved one only with extreme difficulty; others feel released. The use of the term 'stages' when applied to the subject of bereavement is simply a useful device to assist people to understand some of the reactions they may face when someone close to them dies. Nor are the emotions described below always to be found in the order mentioned.

Most authorities on the subject of death and bereavement are agreed that in the main a person grieving the loss of a loved one passes through a period of mourning which may last up to as much as two years.[3] Moreover this period may be roughly divided into three stages, each possessing its own characteristics: firstly that of shock and disbelief, followed by increasing awareness of what has actually happened, and finally acceptance of the death of the loved one.

According to the researches of E. Lindemann (1944), the initial stage of grieving, that of shock and disbelief, is characterized firstly by the bereaved person experiencing a numbness, a lack of appetite and strength, a proneness to sighing, choking feelings and breathlessness, and a reluctance to speak directly of the one who has died. Outwardly, however, the bereaved may appear to cope well and indeed demonstrate practical skills, such as arranging the funeral and registering the death, but what is probably happening is that the shock has insulated the bereaved from his or her deeper emotions. Indeed, according to Elisabeth Kübler-Ross in her book *On Death and Dying* (1973), the first identifiable response to the subject of death is denial.

These signs of distress are succeeded by a preoccupation with the images of the deceased. This is similar to day-dreaming and in some instances may even involve hallucinating. Such experiences are commonplace during bereavement and should not be the cause of alarm or scorn, indeed they sometimes provide an opportunity for the bereaved to release their suppressed pain. The close unseen presence of the loved one who has died might also be keenly felt and for the bereaved be an added source of comfort, making them feel less deserted. Under no circumstances, however, should mourning be denied to the bereaved. According to John Hinton it is a firm antidote to denial:

> The practice of mourning provides more than this socially approved catharsis of grief. It insists that the death has occurred, repeatedly demonstrating this fact in various ways ... over a few days so that the bereaved, whatever their state of mind, accept the painful knowledge, assimilate it and can begin to plan accordingly. Viewing the body and taking part in the funeral emphasizes beyond all doubt that the person is really dead. The condolences, the discussion of the deceased in the past tense, the newspaper announcements, the public recognition of the death, all affirm the loss. (Hinton, 1967, p. 187)

Following denial, feelings of guilt may arise, with the bereaved either regretting not having done more for the deceased during his or her lifetime, or blaming themselves for having been insufficiently loving when they had the opportunity. Guilt on a large scale sometimes leads the bereaved to engage in what is termed compensatory behaviour and to regard the dead person as though he or she had led the life of a saint. In reality, as other people who were acquainted with the dead person might testify, such an image may be quite contrary to reality. Moreover it is guilt such as this that largely accounts for the anger and hostility the grieving person now often projects either on to others such as family members, doctors and nurses, attendant clergy and social workers, God, or even the loved one who has died. This is particularly so if the loss is of a partner upon whom the bereaved was highly dependent. Even so, as Martin Israel remarks: 'Unexpressed anger is dangerous since it may recede into the depths of the psyche and precipitate a depression. Unacknowledged anger is likewise to be avoided since it may flare up into destructive hatred' (Israel, 1995, p. 106).

Indeed, it cannot be emphasized enough that the bereaved must be allowed to vent any of the emotions so far mentioned. If grief is denied expression then suffering of some kind, either physical or psychological, will almost inevitably follow. As Geoffrey Gorer has asserted: 'It would seem correct to state that a society which denies mourning and gives no ritual support to mourners is thereby producing maladaptive and neurotic responses in a number of its citizens' (Gorer, 1965, quoted in Enright, 1983, p. 103).

From shock and disbelief with all its different characteristics, a person grieving the loss of a loved one then usually proceeds to the second stage of mourning. This stage is characterized by the mourner acquiring an increasing awareness of the fact that the loved one has actually died, together with all the implications involved. It is not surprising therefore that the bereaved should now often yield to pangs of grief, indulge in pining, experience deep sadness and give way to apathy. This latter is vividly described by C. S. Lewis after the death of his wife when he speaks of 'the laziness of grief' and his loathing of any activity requiring effort (Lewis, 1961). It is also most natural at this stage for the bereaved to weep and nothing should be done to stop this, since tears usually bring relief.

After this, most people gradually move on to the third and final stage of mourning in which acceptance (but not forgetfulness of the death of the loved one), is the chief feature. As J. Tatelbaum (1981) remarks, the bereaved now moves to what he terms 'recovery'; a time when the deceased is no longer the primary focus of the bereaved's thought. This is not to suggest that there will not be occasions of regression, often when least expected, and from time to time there will be a return of bouts of anger, tears and even guilt, but this stage is essentially one in which hope becomes a key emotion.

One of the most important reasons why it is usually so painful for a bereaved person to reach the third and final stage of mourning, that of acceptance of the death of the loved one, is the mysterious nature of death itself. In addition to shouldering the often devastating pain at being irretrievably separated from someone they held dear, there is the difficulty for a mourner of understanding death itself, not as a physiological phenomenon but in its ontological character. Not only does the bereaved have to accept that the loved one has ceased to exist in former ways, but there is the problem of trying to grasp the significance of death for human existence. As the Fathers at the Second Vatican Council asserted:

> It is in the face of death that the riddle of human existence grows most acute. Not only is man tormented by pain and by the advancing deterioration of his body, but even more so by a dread of perpetual extinction. He rightly follows the intuition of his heart when he abhors and repudiates the utter ruin and total disappearance of his own person. He rebels against death because he bears in himself an eternal seed which cannot be reduced to sheer matter. All the endeavours of technology, though useful in the extreme, cannot calm his anxiety; for prolongation of biological life is unable to satisfy that desire for higher life which is inescapably lodged in his breast. (Abbott, 1966, pp. 917–18)

Indeed, until someone we love dies, we may have always fled from such considerations and preferred to employ euphemisms when speaking of death. Hitherto, we may have refused to face the fact that humans are creatures who are 'beings unto death', that death is untransferable, and that we have no way of knowing when death will occur in our lives. The knowledge that 'Man is always old enough to die' fills us with fear and like the biblical man who built his house on sand (Matthew 7.26–27) we tend to base our lives on illusions instead of the Christian faith. This is the difference between what John Macquarrie terms authentic and inauthentic existence:

> Authenticity is properly a character of something which is not given in its nature, but stands before different possibilities of being. It is, therefore, a character of man ... Man exists authentically when his original possibilities, belonging to his being as man, are fulfilled. His existence is inauthentic when his possibilities are projected on something alien to himself ... We are told (in the Bible) that man was formed in the image of God. His original possibility is to be a child of God. But by worshipping and serving the creation rather than the Creator, man has lost that possibility and fallen away from his original being ... The Christian religion claims to restore man to his original being and his lost possibility of being the child of God and enjoying communion with God ... The Christian life may fairly be called the authentic existence of Man. (Macquarrie, 1973, p. 129)

If a bereaved person has hitherto led an 'inauthentic' life, it is often during that period of mourning in which the bereaved comes to terms with the death of a loved one that he or she may be most open to responding to the Gospel message. Indeed, the bereaved may now undergo a conversion experience. Many years ago, Viktor Frankl, the founder of logotherapy, discovered that in their struggle to survive traumatic experiences human beings most often succeed if they have a purpose for living (Frankl, 1978), but a Christian maintains that only faith brings lasting fulfilment:

> Although the mystery of death utterly beggars the imagination, the Church has been taught by divine revelation and firmly teaches that man has been created by God for a blissful purpose beyond the reach of earthly misery. In addition, that bodily death from which man would have been immune had he not sinned will be vanquished, according to the Christian faith, when man who was ruined by his own doing is restored to wholeness by an almighty and merciful Saviour. For God has called man and still calls him so that with his entire being he might be joined to Him in an endless sharing of a divine life beyond all corruption. Christ won this victory when He rose to life, for by His death He freed man from death. Hence to every thoughtful man a solidly established faith provides the answer to his anxiety about what the future holds for him. At the same time faith gives him the power to be united in Christ with his loved ones who have already been snatched away by death; faith arouses the hope that they have found true life with God. (Abbott, 1966, p. 918)

It is this faith indeed that assists a Christian to negotiate the pain of bereavement, for it enables us to heed the words of St Paul that we must not grieve 'as others do who have no hope' (1 Thessalonians 4.13).

Finally, it is essential that those of any faith and any community should be aware of how they may be of assistance to bereaved persons in their midst. In the earliest stage of mourning the most effective support that friends and relatives in particular can provide for a bereaved person is that of taking on the role of a listener. In saying this, it should be remembered that Bonhoeffer once remarked: 'The beginning of love for the brethren is learning to listen to him' (Long, 1990, p. 33). Genuine listening includes not being in the least surprised by any unusual and, occasionally, even irrational utterances on the part of the bereaved. Listening also requires sensitivity of a high degree and discerning when it is more appropriate to act as a companion or to allow the bereaved their privacy. True listening often eventually enables the one mourning to begin to look to the future, a task which in the initial stages of grief may not only be difficult but be resisted by the bereaved. If counsel is sought by the bereaved, it needs to be stressed, however, that the period of mourning is not one in which any vital decisions should be taken, such as what should be done with the deceased's belongings or whether the grieving person should sell their home and move.

According to the writer Henri Nouwen, true listening is one of 'the highest forms of hospitality' (Nouwen, 1976, p. 89) and of the kind that does not attempt 'to change people but to offer them space where change can take place ... Hospitality is not a subtle invitation to adopt the lifestyle of the host, but the gift of a chance for the guest to find his own' (*ibid.*, p. 69). To this description of listening, Nouwen links the healing that may result from it. 'Healing means first of all, the creation of an empty but friendly space where those who suffer can tell their story to someone who can listen with real attention' (*ibid.*, p. 88). To these words should be added those of Robert Carkhuff, the American psychologist, who having researched and analysed many counselling interviews, considers that the six qualities required of an effective listener are respect, genuineness, empathy, concreteness, confrontation and immediacy (Carkhuff, 1969).[4] And Alistair Campbell, the author of *Rediscovering Pastoral Care*, is of the view that integrity in those who care (in this case the listener) is of the utmost importance. He remarks that 'all genuine care for those assaulted by doubt and guilt proceeds from this integrity and without it no ecclesiastical role or counselling technique will be of help to others' (Campbell, 1981, p. 12). For him integrity consists of 'steadfastness' which is the product of wisdom and life's experiences.

On the strictly practical level there are measures that can be taken almost at once to assist the bereaved. Immediately after a death, for example, assistance may be required by the bereaved, especially if they are elderly, infirm or without family, in such matters as arranging the funeral, acquiring a death certificate and registering the death, notifying insurance companies, contacting the Department of Social Security and publishing the death in a local paper. All these necessitate negotiations with clergy, undertakers and civil servants and require qualities of sensitivity and tact on the part of those offering their help.

Because of the shocked state of the bereaved, however, often it is only close family members, the local clergy or the local GP whom the mourners feel able to turn to or trust immediately after a death. Hopefully many of these will already be well aware from previous contacts of the situation and circumstances of mourners, unless a death comes totally unexpectedly. In the Roman Catholic tradition this usually means that a priest will have previously visited the dying person, have anointed him or her as part of the Sacrament of the Sick, and have met and prayed with relatives and friends at the bedside. On these occasions his concern will have been to comfort everyone present, including deliberately holding the hands of the dying person, to eliminate the fear of death in everyone, and to foster an atmosphere as much as possible of normality.[5]

Again, it is part of the Roman Catholic tradition for a priest to be called immediately after anyone has died; his presence being a powerful symbol for many of the support they are entitled to receive from the church community. At such times it is customary for prayers for the dead to be offered, the deceased's body to be blessed and the bereaved persons present to be comforted. Whereas the custom of holding a 'wake' in the home and around the open coffin of the deceased may nowadays be dying out, the practice of receiving the body of the dead person into church for a vigil service, with appropriate prayers and biblical readings, the night before the funeral is greatly to be encouraged. This permits not only the family and friends but anyone in the wider parish community to come and, as an expression of solidarity, both pay their respects and pray for the deceased and the bereaved.

Just as significant is the fact that Catholics of every kind are usually keen to have Masses offered for the repose of the soul of the deceased and for the comfort of the bereaved. It is not unusual these days for coffins in church to be covered not only in flowers but also in Mass cards, sent by people anxious to express their condolences. Such Masses, if celebrated with emphasis on the resurrection of the dead, invariably provide the bereaved with immense hope, a sense of healing and renewed joy (see the chapters by Speck and Steel in this book). At the same time, however, every parish should also at least be aware of the different organizations offering counselling services to the bereaved, such as Cruse-Bereavement Care and the National Association of Bereavement Services.

Since bereavement may last as long as two years, it is essential that the bereaved be regularly visited in their homes, their needs be monitored and, above all, that their views be heard. As time goes on and the stage arrives at which the bereaved are more able to accept with relative equanimity the death of the loved one, they could be encouraged to participate in parish and community activities and to adopt new interests. Most of all they should be made to feel a real part of their community and not just as recipients of charity. Even the housebound bereaved are often open to hosting parish prayer groups, being visited by young members of the community, especially if they have been commissioned to bring them Holy Communion, and to demonstrating that they have a contribution to make to life around them.

It is at this point that the clergy and members of any parish community can play a vital role in integrating the bereaved into what might be termed the local Body of Christ. Much of course depends on how alive a community may be, but one which is so will use the occasion of bereavement to bring the Gospel or Good News to those downcast by grief. The Gospel's emphasis on the resurrection and what this means for all believers is able to bring a unique form of hope to the bereaved, with its message that earthly life is simply a preparation for an eternal life, in which they will one day be reunited with those they presently mourn. 'Because we look not to the things that are seen but to the things that are unseen; for the things that are seen are transient, but the things that are unseen are eternal' (2 Corinthians 4.18).

Notes

1. V. Ironside, 'Nearly every book I read on bereavement enraged me', *Independent*, 19 April 1996. See also V. Ironside, *You'll Get Over It: The Rage of Bereavement* (London: Hamish Hamilton, 1996).
2. Quoted in D. J. Enright (ed.), *The Oxford Book of Death* (Oxford University Press, 1983).
3. See P. Speck, *Loss and Grief in Medicine* (London: Ballière Tindall, 1978), p. 13, where the author draws up a table showing the similarities in their views on this of G. Engel, E. Kübler-Ross, and J. Bowlby and C. M. Parkes.
4. See also A. Long (1990).
5. One of the most useful books on practical matters is P. Mares, *Caring for Someone Who is Dying* (London: Age Concern, 1994). See also I. Ainsworth-Smith and P. Speck, *Letting Go: Caring for the Dying and Bereaved* (London: SPCK, 1982).

References

W. M. Abbott (ed.), 'The pastoral constitution on the church in the modern world', *The Documents of Vatican II* (New York: America Press, 1966).

A. V. Campbell, *Rediscovering Pastoral Care* (London: Darton, Longman & Todd, 1981).

R.R. Carkhuff, *Helping and Human Relations: A Primer for Lay and Professional Helpers*, vol. 1 (London: Holt, Rinehart & Winston, 1969).

V. Frankl, *The Unheard Cry for Meaning* (London: Hodder & Stoughton, 1978).

G. Gorer, *Death, Grief and Mourning in Contemporary Britain* (1965), quoted in D. J. Enright, *The Oxford Book of Death* (Oxford: Oxford University Press, 1983).

J. Hinton, *Dying* (Harmondsworth: Penguin, 1967).

M. Israel, 'Mourning: the song is over but the memory lingers on', in D. Cohn-Sherbok and C. Lewis (eds), *Beyond Death: Theological and Philosophical Reflections on Life After Death* (Basingstoke: Macmillan, 1995).

E. Kübler-Ross, *On Death and Dying* (London: Tavistock, 1973).

C. S. Lewis, *A Grief Observed* (London: Faber & Faber, 1961).

E. Lindemann, 'Symptomatology and management of acute grief', *American Journal of Psychiatry*, 101, pp. 141–8 (1944).

A. Long, *Listening* (London: Daybreak, 1990).

J. Macquarrie, *An Existentialist Theology* (Harmondsworth: Penguin, 1973).

H. Nouwen, *Reaching Out* (London: Collins, 1976).

J. Tatelbaum, *The Courage to Grieve: Creative Living, Recovery and Growth Through Grief* (London: Heinemann, 1981).

10

Confronting the abyss: the relationship between bereavement and faith

Anthony Gardiner

This chapter is part of a personal journey that is not yet complete, and may never be. The terrain over which I have travelled has often been both hard and bitter. Its landmarks, such as they are, can be very confusing, while paths are difficult to find and often seem to lead round in circles. This is the journey of grief, and while it has been painstakingly mapped many times before, I hope to explore a particular facet of it which has been of vital importance to me – the challenge to faith posed by the experience of bereavement. Let me try to lay bare the starkness of that challenge.

The Christian faith is life-affirming. It accords to our human existence meaning, purpose, worth. This sense that human life is supremely precious is expressed in scripture in a variety of ways. We are made 'in the image of God', while the price that was paid for us is awesome indeed – it was 'paid in precious blood ... the blood of Christ'. So the value of our human life is affirmed. But the experience of intimate bereavement would seem to be the ultimate challenge to any such affirmation. For it raises, with inescapable sharpness, the spectre of meaninglessness. If something of such potential, such vitality, something apparently so precious – for me, my wife of eighteen months, a young woman on the verge of motherhood – can be broken and destroyed in a moment, then how do you speak of meaning, of worth?

The pain of grief can seem unbearable. The cry of King David, learning of the death of his son, echoes still, haunting in its hopelessness, a lament for eternal loss: 'The King shuddered. He went up to the room over the gate and burst into tears, and weeping said, "My son Absalom! My son! My son

Absalom! Would I had died in your place! Absalom, my son, my son!"' (2 Samuel 18.33).

Even after three thousand years, listening to those words, I can still feel like an intruder, blundering in where I have no right to be, his anguish is so overwhelming. There is something almost frightening in the violence of his grief. Yet bereavement commonly brings, mingled with the numbness, the aimlessness, the exhaustion; times of such searing pain when we are confronted, inescapably, by the enormity of our loss.

That sense of loss is devastating. It has been likened many times to an amputation, the tearing away of part of oneself, leaving you maimed, crippled, stumbling – and empty (the very meaning of the word 'widow' in the original Sanskrit) drained of life and purpose. And the loss is absolute. There is no appeal against it. C. S. Lewis, struggling to cope with his wife's death, wrote:

> I look up at the night sky. Is anything more certain than that in all those vast times and spaces, if I were allowed to search them, I should nowhere find her face, her voice, her touch? She died. She is dead. Is the word so difficult to learn? (Lewis, 1966, p. 16)

This is the deepest fear, that the dissolution death brings is total, that death is an abyss of nothingness into which everything falls. 'The abyss', 'the pit' – the choice of such images is not accidental. Expressing a stark and terrible vision of death as the ultimate loss and deprivation, it is deeply rooted in the Old Testament. The psalmist can speak of death as a fearsome thing. Those who pass that way are 'forgotten' by God, 'deprived of (his) protecting hand'. The poet continues:

> Do you perform miracles for the dead? Do they rise up and praise you? Is your constant love spoken of in the grave, or your faithfulness in the place of destruction? Are your miracles seen in the place of darkness, or your goodness in the land of the forgotten? (Psalm 88.10–11)

To every question the context demands the answer, no. The dead are gone, beyond even the reach of God. So terrible does death seem that *She'ol* can only be described as 'the place of destruction', 'the place of darkness', 'the land of the forgotten' – stark negatives, as if to emphasize the 'non-entity', the 'non-being' of the dead.

Death robs us of those we love. But it has a still more awesome power: it can also destroy our world. What do I mean? Quite simply this: that though not everyone may or can articulate it, the experience of ultimate bereavement, the destruction by death of a close, deep and crucial relationship, can seem to strike a deadly blow against the very idea that human existence has meaning. I think of my own experience. When lives are so intimately interwoven as this, when we have invested so much of ourselves, our love, our hopes, our dreams, in a relationship, then the shattering of that relationship knocks away one of the foundation pillars on which our world stands, and we are left all at sea, adrift on the waters of chaos. These echoes of ancient cosmology – the pillars on which the world stands firm amidst the chaotic and turbulent waters – again are not accidental. They were chosen to emphasize the magnitude of the catastrophe that befalls us in intimate bereavement. It is the fundamental experience of human insecurity, and from it there springs that sense of existential dread which forms so potent an ingredient of our human psyche: the fear that, in the end, nothing is solid, all will let us down; that at the last we shall be left totally alone with 'darkness ... (our) one companion left' (Psalm 88.18).

It might, of course, be argued that such a position is nonsense. My experience of bereavement does not change the nature of the world one iota, or even my perception of it. The world is a dangerous place. Our hold on life is tenuous in the extreme. The one certainty is that we will die. How, when and where are the only mysteries. C. S. Lewis, reflecting on the death of his wife, seemed stunned by the depth of his pain, as if it were unexpected, and commented in bewilderment: 'I knew already that these things, and worse, happened daily. I would have said that I had taken them into account ... I've got nothing that I hadn't bargained for' (Lewis, 1966, p. 31).

It could, however, be argued that our century has witnessed events which no-one could have 'bargained for', and which have radically reshaped our perception of reality, and quite properly so. One might think of the battles of the First World War, which led the poet Wilfrid Gibson to write of 'the heart-break in the heart of things'. Or consider humanity's first venture into the nightmare of atomic war in August 1945. In our generation the apocalyptic vision has been revived in a new and terrible way, and perhaps our greatest fear, still, is that one day that vision will become reality: that this fragile earth will be incinerated in a moment of madness. Confronted by such an appalling possibility, how can one still speak as if our human life has meaning?

And then there is that other 'Holocaust', which awakened the world to an appalled awareness of the depths of human bestiality. Names and words like Dachau, Buchenwald, Auschwitz-Birkenau, gas-chamber, crematorium,

Xyclon-B, have become part of a new vocabulary of horror and despair. For in the face of such agony one can surely no longer cling to the old delusions peddled by religion. The Holocaust, surely, marks the end of all religious interpretation of reality. In such a universe as this, where no divine voice answered the cries of the victims, and no divine hand was stretched out to help, how do you speak of God? Where can you look for any signs of his presence or his activity? Moltmann quotes Elie Wiesel, a survivor of Auschwitz:

> The SS hanged two Jewish men and a youth in front of the whole camp. The men died quickly; but the death throes of the youth lasted for half an hour. 'Where is God? Where is he?' someone asked behind me. As the youth still hung in torment in the noose after a long time, I heard the man call again, 'Where is God now?' and I heard a voice in myself answer: 'Where is he? He is here. He is hanging there on the gallows.' (Moltmann, 1974, pp. 273–4)

But is that any more than a last, desperate sleight-of-hand, a futile attempt to smuggle God back into a universe which has no place for him? And what a God – broken, emasculated, useless. Does not the fact that we are forced to countenance such a paradox in order to speak of God at all mark the bankruptcy of religious faith?

It may seem absurd to claim that the experience of close personal bereavement raises the spectre of meaninglessness as inescapably as, say, the Holocaust. And yet it does have that same profoundly disturbing quality. We find ourselves standing at the edge of a precipice. At our feet, the seemingly so solid and dependable ground drops away ... into what? We can side-step the grief of others, and we do, even literally. How many bereaved people have had the experience of friends, neighbours, acquaintances, crossing over to the other side of the street to avoid an encounter they could not cope with? How many bereaved people have been denied the opportunity to talk about their loss even by members of their own family? Death reminds us too much of our own mortality: it threatens to break through the brisk and brittle facade of our own self-assurance. As long as we can hold it at bay, as long as we can maintain our denials, we will. But our own grief is inescapable. Attempts to evade our own pain bring, not peace, but deep-rooted psychological and emotional disturbance. It becomes a yet more intolerable anguish which we must bury deeper and deeper still. A friend lost his only daughter in a road accident sixteen years ago. He has never spoken of that daughter, never even uttered her name, from that day to this. Seeking to avoid the pain of grief, he has condemned himself to a lifetime of torment. One senses the rawness of the wound even after so many years. Faced with our own grief, evasive action is not possible. We cannot skirt around the abyss that opens before us.

The challenge posed by the experience of bereavement comes with special sharpness and poignancy when we are faced with the death of the young, particularly the death of a child. We find it hard to accept a young life cut short, its promise unfulfilled. It strikes a bitter blow against our longing to believe that life is, at its heart, trustworthy.

As a pastor, I have shared with parents the trauma of miscarriage, stillbirth, neonatal death, a fatal accident to a child, the death of the young in many forms. I have faced, myself, an experience not vastly dissimilar. Each of these experiences was quite devastating to those caught up in it, a moment when life dissolved into chaos and easy answers were no longer possible. Sharing the grief of parents, I have also shared something of their journey back from grief, back from the abyss to something like solid ground.

'Amy was born 18 weeks early, too early to survive and medically classified as a miscarriage.' So begins a letter from Amy's mother. I call her 'Amy's mother' because that is how she thinks of herself. Amy was a real child to Vivien. She *was* Vivien's daughter. The letter goes on: 'By the time I was 22 weeks pregnant she and I had been working together as a team for her survival so long that she was very much a little person to me.' Because she was premature, Amy's birth could not be registered. Yet she was real. So many hopes and dreams had already gathered around her: so much, psychologically, had already been invested in her. She could not go away without leaving behind her terrible pain. You cannot dismiss miscarriage as a gynaecological accident. This was a real bereavement, as the baby lost was a real child, already the object of love. Time and again in her letter Vivien returns to this vital point:

> People said I coped very well. I think I coped in public and grieved in private. Having a name for her helped, though I can only refer to her by name to Roland, members of the Baby Lost Support Group and yourself. The few times I have said her name to others they have looked at me in amazement and obviously thought it odd. The Baby Lost Support Group was a great help, being able to talk to others who had suffered, and talk openly about a person that most people refused to accept existed. I think that the inability of the majority of people

around me to accept that Amy was a person and very real was the most difficult thing to cope with.

Under the guidance of the chaplain of St Mary's Hospital in Portsmouth, the Baby Lost Support Group has begun holding an annual memorial service in the hospital chapel, an opportunity for families who have lost children to come together: this includes families where the loss has come by miscarriage or stillbirth. It is described as 'a time for sharing our memories and our sadness, and for offering each other sympathy and support'. For Vivien, being present at that service just a few months after Amy died played a vital part in her recovery. Again, the uniqueness, the value, the worth of her child was being recognized. She writes:

The Memorial Service held by the Baby Lost Support Group four months after Amy was born marked a turning point. It was a form of relief to have her treated as a person, to hear her name read out by the chaplain, to have a Christian service to mark her existence and death. From that point on I began to be positive again, to be determined to have another child and to keep Amy as a part of my life that had been and had gone.

This need to assert the reality and magnitude of their loss, against any attempts to deny or minimize it, is felt by many parents caught up in similar circumstances. Rosemary and Neil, Rebecca's mother and father, were told that Rebecca was not developing properly in the womb, that she had physical problems which would make an independent existence impossible. Suddenly they were faced with a stark choice, to terminate Rosemary's pregnancy or to allow it to continue knowing that, at best, the child to be born would live no more than a few hours. They found it impossible to think of the child Rosemary was carrying being 'written-off' as a termination: already she was precious to them. They felt that she must not simply be discarded, but welcomed, acknowledged, as a real child. In the end Rebecca was stillborn, weeks premature; but still there was a need to affirm her uniqueness, her worth. They held her, cuddled her, wept over her, for they felt the need to maintain, against the world if need be, that Rebecca was a real child and deeply precious to them (see Saunders' chapter below).

It would seem, then, that the pain is lessened, or at least made more bearable, not by denying the value of what we have lost, but by affirming it; and how could it be otherwise? In bereavement, to take the path of denial, evasion, pretence, will almost certainly be deeply damaging. It is only as we are able to acknowledge and accept how deeply we have been hurt, and how much we have lost, that we shall be able to come to terms with the experience, and even, perhaps, grow through it. Even the death of the young? Yes. There will still be questions, sharp and disturbing, that will not yield to us. But the vital fact remains that facing the reality and magnitude of our loss, being willing to confront the abyss without evasion, does not necessarily lead to collapse and despair. Rather, down this road alone lies the possibility of healing.

But here lies the dilemma: if our healing can come only through facing our pain and loss and anguish, through confronting squarely life's darkness when it assails us, can faith survive such a confrontation?

There is, quite clearly, nothing to be gained by evading the truth. And the plain truth is this: that the face life turns towards us is not always a smiling face; sometimes it is vicious and ugly. As we contemplate the grim toll of human suffering – and who can quantify the pain of the Holocaust, or the pain caused by the death of a child? – it is sometimes easier to believe that we can discern behind it all not the face of a loving Father, but the grotesque, distorted features of some half-crazed, sadistic demon. So, in his agony, Job can speak thus of God:

> I was at ease, but he set upon me and mauled me, seized me by the neck and worried me. He set me up as his target; his arrows rained upon me from every side; pitiless, he cut deep into my vitals, he spilt my gall on the ground. He made breach after breach in my defences; he fell upon me like a fighting man. (Job 16.12–14)

Like a lion tearing at its prey, like a man of war bereft of pity – this is God? Is it possible? The fact is that life does sometimes take on just such a nightmarish quality, leaving, surely, no room for complacent, easy answers, or what Kingsley Amis called an 'eager, cruising credulity'. But our search is not for complacency or credulity. It is a search for faith. Can faith find a place in such a world as this, and among those who have been deeply wounded? Can we see beyond life's demonic face to the face of the Father?

I begin with something that I have always, instinctively, intuitively believed from the time I first committed myself to Christ. It can be summed up in what Moltmann calls 'Luther's lapidary statement: *Crux probat omnia*' – the cross is the test of everything – which deserves to be called Christian, the benchmark against which all else must be measured. What happens when you take that with absolute seriousness? Does it not demand a revolution in our image of God?

Our problems begin because we try to impose upon the Christian faith a ready-made concept of God, born out of man's inherent religiosity, itself the product of our radical insecurity. John V. Taylor writes of this in *Weep Not For Me*:

> We human beings are physically puny in a world of brute force. From our childhood we long for greater power and more perfect control. We admire the strongest, the victor, the one who outsmarts the others. So, with our gift for fantasy, we project those images of domination out into the skies and call it God.
>
> God is imaged as the super-potentate among the emperors, the master-mind over all clever controllers. God (unlike us) can do exactly was God wants at any moment. God (like our secret wishes) fixes everything. Get him on your side and you can't lose. And what human psychology brought to pass, the philosophers were quick to rationalise. (Taylor, 1986, p. 7)

That is one image of God. But let me offer you another very different image: 'And when they came to the place which is called "The Skull", there they crucified him' (Luke 23.33).

'The place which is called "The Skull" ' is in Hebrew, 'Golgotha', in Latin, 'Calvary'. All three have the same meaning: the place where Jesus was led was a place full of violent killing, human agony and humiliation. The nails are placed, the hammer lifted, there is the clang of metal upon metal. The cross-beam is raised – man and beam together – and Jesus hangs upon the gibbet, alone between earth and heaven. And, as the hours pass, there is wrung from his lips that terrible cry of desolation: 'My God, my God, why have you abandoned me?' (Mark 15.34).

There he hangs, forsaken by men – save for the little band of women who huddle, broken-hearted, at the foot of the cross – and now God-forsaken too. The heavens grow dark as if in grief, as if to draw a veil over his suffering, as if the whole of creation, in its bereavement, donned widow's weeds. Muslims believe that Jesus the prophet was miraculously taken from the cross and another victim substituted in his place; for Muslims it can not be that one so close to God should suffer such desolation. The Christian faith will never countenance such a travesty. There is no divine sleight-of-hand to let God off the hook. He hangs there to the bitter end. God does not bare his strong right arm, except to receive the nail through his palm, pinning him, like a butterfly, to the cross. And he hangs there, alongside all life's victims, impotent and forsaken, as helpless as his tragic compatriots who, nineteen hundred years later, were herded into cattle-trucks for their last journey ... to Auschwitz, or Dachau, or Buchenwald. Could it be that Elie Wiesel's words are more than a cry in the dark: 'I heard the man call again, "Where is God now?" and I heard a voice in myself answer: "Where is he? He is here. He is hanging there on the gallows."' (Moltmann, 1974, pp. 273–4).

Could it be, not that this is blasphemy, but that any other answer would be blasphemy? I have no doubt. *Crux probat omnia.* At the cross, the old pictures of God, fantasies created by man in his religiosity and insecurity, come crashing to the ground. But then, did we not already suspect – more than suspect – that they were false? The harsh and bitter facts of our own human existence suggest that they are fundamentally flawed. Whether it is the Somme or Dachau or Hiroshima, the death of one young woman, the death of one small child, or Golgotha, there is little room here for the Arch-manipulator, or, indeed, for any other triumphalist image of God. In their need, in their pain, in their distress, in their loneliness, men look to God for help: they look to God to save them, and find instead that he is alongside them, as helpless as they. In *Letters and Papers from Prison*, Bonhoeffer said this:

> God allows himself to be edged out of the world and onto the cross. God is weak and powerless in the world; and that is exactly the way, the only way, in which he can be with us and help us ... It is not by his omnipotence that Christ helps us, but by his weakness and suffering. This is the decisive difference between Christianity and all religions. Man's religiosity makes him look in his distress to the power of God in the world; he uses God as a 'Deus ex machina'. The Bible, however, directs him to the powerlessness and suffering of God; only a suffering God can help. (Bonhoeffer, 1959, p. 122)

The cry of suffering humankind is: 'Does anyone care?' From the midst of our grief and pain and loss, we look for someone who will be with us, someone who will simply 'be there', even in the depths of the abyss, expressing love. In Christ, the 'man of sorrows, acquainted with grief', who is called Immanuel, 'God with us', I receive the assurance that God is indeed beside us, sharing our suffering; and I learn that the abyss is not an abyss of meaninglessness, but an abyss of love. I am reminded forcibly of the words of George Fox, recorded in his *Journal*: 'I saw ... that there was an ocean of darkness and death, but an infinite ocean of light and love, which flowed over the ocean of darkness. And in that also I saw the infinite love of God ... ' (West, 1962, p. 49). Here is the love that is revealed in all its depth and glory on the cross, the love that plumbed the abyss of death and was not destroyed. From this love nothing can separate us. In this love we may journey even through the valley of deep darkness unafraid – unafraid, at least, of final annihilation, of meaninglessness. For the God of love holds us in life, in death, and beyond death – in time and in eternity.

References

D. Bonhoeffer, *Letters and Papers from Prison* (London: Collins, 1959).
C. S. Lewis, *A Grief Observed* (London: Faber & Faber, 1966).
J. Moltmann, *The Crucified God* (London: SCM Press, 1974), quoting from Elie Wiesel, 'Night'.
J. V. Taylor, *Weep Not For Me* (Geneva: World Council of Churches, 1986).
J. West, *The Quaker Reader* (New York: Viking, 1962).

11

Contemporary belief in life after death

Douglas Davies

The complexity of human life guarantees that matters of belief are not simple. Those concerning life after death are no exception. In the population at large some individuals hold clear beliefs, others change their minds with ease or hold their views but tentatively. As far as religious institutions are concerned some demand acceptance of sharply formulated doctrines while others foster a variety of beliefs amongst members. Indeed, religious positions often bear their own code of spirituality: some adherents view firm dogma as a sign of deep commitment while others see it as an immature stage in the journey of faith.

This chapter reflects this spectrum of belief by considering quantitative information derived from social surveys of various British populations. Obtaining information through interview techniques is not easy but the benefits can be great as long as both caution and open minds are, appropriately, adopted (Kaldestad, 1992, pp. 70ff.). This is important since some people seem, instinctively, either to distrust statistical material or to accept and quote it uncritically.

The complexity of beliefs is partly associated with basic differences between people reflected in their gender, age, occupation and religious affiliation. I would emphasize the fact that while individuals' general beliefs may change over time, as life-experience exerts its transforming power, this change may be especially true for views of life after death. It is also important to remember that the way questions are posed is of vital importance. This complicates the comparison of different studies even when they are related to the same topic.

Because attitudes may change over time between generations, it is worth considering aspects of altered belief over recent decades, insofar as evidence exists for it. Geoffrey Gorer, for example, compared studies of 1950 and 1963 showing that men were more unbelieving than women over a period which showed remarkable similarity of responses (Gorer, 1965, p. 166):

Belief in afterlife

Gender	Year	Yes (%)	No (%)	Uncertain (%)	Total (%)
Male	1950	39	28	33	100
	1963	41	26	33	100
Female	1950	56	14	30	100
	1963	55	16	29	100

Further data from Steve Bruce's 1995 sketch of changes in belief in life after death (Bruce 1995, p. 51) give a picture in which the level of belief drops in each period from 54 per cent in 1957, to 45 per cent in 1981, to 43 per cent in 1987, and down to 27 per cent in 1991.

Most recently, some 1603 individuals were interviewed at length in their homes on matters concerning funeral ritual (Davies and Shaw, 1995). They were shown cards indicating a list of possible attitudes towards life after death and asked whether they agreed or disagreed or did 'not know what to think' about each of the following statements. These statements had already proved their worth as questions in an earlier research project (Davies, Watkins and Winter 1991, pp. 253ff.).

1. Nothing happens, we come to the end of life   29%
2. Our soul passes on to another world   34%
3. Our bodies await a resurrection   8%
4. We come back as something or someone else   12%
5. Trust in God, all is in God's hands   22%

In addition a substantial minority of 9 per cent (145 individuals) did not know what to think, while another 1 per cent (23 individuals) gave a response unconnected with the above options. What was particularly interesting, however, was that the great majority (79 per cent) of the 1603 individuals interviewed chose only one of these options as best reflecting their own position. This suggests that this scheme of options reflects popular outlooks fairly well. It also means that the majority had some sense of life as possessing a wide framework not entirely bounded by death.

Death as the end

In general we see that a significant minority of 29 per cent, slightly less than a third of all those interviewed, saw death as simply the end of life with no existence lying beyond it. This picture can, however, also be complex. For example, a very small number (eight people) believed both that death was the end of life and that they might come back as something or someone else. Perhaps they saw death as a literal end and the prologue before some quite different identity was assumed. For these eight, then, it might be unwise to speak in terms of an afterlife as this word implies continuity of identity.

By using data from the 1995 study (Davies and Shaw, 1995), but published here for the first time, we can glimpse the complexity of afterlife beliefs. Two particular groups are a case in point, one describing itself as atheist (129 individuals) and the other as agnostic (39 individuals). The numbers are small and due caution is necessary in evaluating their responses. Still, they are worth recording for two reasons. First, it takes very large samples of the general population to yield even such small groups of those calling themselves atheist or agnostic. Second, their responses appear to contradict some of the assumptions we might otherwise have made.

Responses	Atheists	Agnostics
Nothing happens, we come to the end of life	55%	43%
Our soul passes on to another world	18%	15%
Our bodies await a resurrection	2%	0%
We come back as something or someone else	7%	5%
Trust in God, all is in God's hands	0%	0%
Don't know	10%	28%
No response	8%	9%

These results are very difficult to interpret if we operate on the strict assumptions that people defining themselves as atheist would, inevitably and naturally, neither believe in an afterlife nor agree with any statements involving the name of God. The survey reveals a more complex picture: 18 per cent of atheists and 15 per cent of agnostics accepted a viable option of an afterlife, 'the soul passing on' after death. Furthermore, a smaller number of each group, 7 per cent of atheists and 5 per cent of agnostics, also accepted the idea of 'coming back' as something or someone else. These surprising results indicate that reference to souls or to some form of continuing life-force is, too easily, assumed to involve some reference to God, and suggest that such an alliance of concepts is not necessarily wise. Again, while we might have correctly assumed that no atheist or agnostic was prepared to say 'all is in God's hands', the two atheists who agreed with ideas of a resurrection provide a difficult task to interpret.

This finding on atheist belief assumes greater significance in the light of a recent study of 16,000 teenagers in England and Wales (Kay and Francis, 1995, pp. 5–26). Using the basic statement 'I believe in God' to differentiate between theists, atheists and agnostics, Kay and Francis found that in relation to the further statement, 'I believe in life after death', the theist group registered a 60 per cent agreement but the atheists registered a 26 per cent level of agreement. The authors commented 'surprisingly, about a quarter of atheists do believe in life after death' (*ibid.*, p. 14).

This is of particular interest in the light of a survey involving 2068 individuals conducted by MORI for the British Humanist Association in April 1996. Asked for their response to the statement, 'I do not believe there is an afterlife', 21 per cent agreed. Yet the survey reveals a notable gender difference. While 25 per cent of the men reckoned not to believe in an afterlife, this was so of only 18 per cent of the women. We shall return to gender differences below, but these results show that beliefs are complex and do not necessarily follow the neat assumptions often held in explicit philosophical positions.

The soul

The most favoured belief in an afterlife was some notion of the soul. In our 1995 study the single most frequent option chosen by those who gave life after death a serious place in their thought focused on the idea that the soul passes to some other world after death (34 per cent of the respondents). Furthermore, of those who selected two of the afterlife options in the list provided, most placed the soul-idea alongside some other option. Fifty-four individuals linked the soul with 'trust in God', 26 linked it with 'coming back as something or someone else' and 21 linked the soul with a belief in 'our bodies await a resurrection'. These responses together show not only the widespread nature of the idea of the soul, but also its adaptability in

conjunction with other views of future identity. This was especially apparent
for those 42 individuals who combined the three beliefs of 'soul passing on',
'body awaiting resurrection' and 'trust in God' as their view of the future.
Altogether, we see how the soul plays a major part in thinking about death
for those who believe in an afterlife. With this in mind it is now worth
examining the influence of religious affiliation upon belief in the soul along
with the other options provided in our 1995 survey of religious affiliation
and afterlife beliefs.

Religious affiliation and afterlife beliefs

Belief in life after death has, in some way or another, constituted a major
dimension of formal religious belief in the major religions of the world
whether in the Eastern or Western traditions (Holm and Bowker, 1994).
The Christian tradition has, in particular, taken its theological stand upon
the belief in the resurrection of Jesus along with the promise of a future
resurrection for believers. Belief in an immortal soul came to be accepted by
many Christian traditions as the major means by which individual identity
was perpetuated after death even though it might have been believed that,
at some later date, a resurrection of the body would occur (Sullivan, 1987).
Later on, some Christian theologians in the Anglican and Protestant traditions have very firmly opposed belief in an immortal soul as an intrusion into
Christian thought and as a contradiction of the doctrine of the resurrection
grounded in a new divine creation, while Roman Catholic theology has
increasingly developed a theology of the soul in relation to the body as
argued elsewhere in this volume (see the chapters by Sheppy and myself
above).

Formal theology is not, however, always reflected in the popular religion
of active church members, let alone of the wider public who may attend
church only periodically. To examine empirical aspects of popular belief on
life after death, we return to our 1995 study (Davies and Shaw, 1995,
particularly pp. 93ff.). We should bear in mind that the following percen-
tages represent options taken by people and that some individuals, albeit
relatively few, chose more than one option. The majority of those reckoning
allegiance to the major churches of Britain reckoned to believe in an
afterlife of some sort.

A substantial minority did not. Those who said they thought life came to
an end at death included 14 per cent of Catholics, 30 per cent of Methodists
and 32 per cent of Anglicans.

These figures may seem surprising. Given the emphasis upon eternal life in those denominations, it should seem odd that just under a third of Methodists and of Anglicans appear not to believe in an afterlife. But this result should be compared with an earlier study undertaken between 1988 and 1990 (Davies, Watkins and Winter, 1991, p. 253). This focused not only on members of the general public who might claim to be Church of England but also on active Anglicans in rural areas of Britain. Those results showed that while 32 per cent of the general public did not believe in life after death only 10 per cent of those on Anglican Church rolls did not so believe. This distinction is important, given the way the English religious and social world uses the identity of Church of England as a nominal sign of religious adherence, whereas being on a church roll requires explicit assent each year and implies a degree of activity on the part of the member.

These, along with other responses mentioned below, indicate that adherence to religious institutions may play a great variety of parts in people's lives quite separate from issues of eternity. Much more research needs to be conducted in these areas and it may well be worth exploring the networks and patterns of faith in different groups because, for example, it would seem as though belief in life after death is more centrally located within the total scheme of Roman Catholic thought than it is in that of either Anglican or Methodist belief. With such patterns in mind it is worth comparing Anglican and Roman Catholic responses to the set of afterlife beliefs listed above.

Anglicans and Catholics

The Anglican pattern took the form of a basic belief in the soul passing on at death (33 per cent of Anglican choices) with another 17 per cent opting for a general trusting in God. Only 4 per cent of Anglican choices fell upon the idea of the body awaiting a resurrection. This is an important observation and well worthy of comment given the importance of the idea of the resurrection of Christ and of ordinary believers in the Creed and in the basic theology of the Church of England. Whilst it cannot simply be assumed that the idea of the resurrection and of a resurrection body are clearly intelligible to all, it might be expected that the very word 'resurrection' would evoke a response in people's own grammar of faith when responding to survey questions on life after death. Yet this seems not to be the case. Belief in a soul and in a broad trust in God seems to cover the basic Anglican grasp of life after death. There is a clear third option which, though a minority response, stands as an oddity as far as Anglican theology is concerned. This is the issue of a dead person coming back as something or someone else. This item is clearly important and will be discussed below in a section of its own along with Catholic responses on the same topic.

The Roman Catholic pattern was also grounded in belief in the soul but at the higher response rate of 48 per cent. This may reflect aspects of the Catholic funeral liturgy in which language of the departing soul is more explicit than in Anglicanism. Along with this went a high proportion (32 per cent) of those opting for a broad trust in God. Some 18 per cent emphasized resurrection of the body. We may thus observe in the Catholic case a greater degree of unity of ideas between personal belief and formal church teaching than in that of the Church of England. This is likely to be because more of those identifying themselves as Catholic in England are engaged in church life than is the case with many who identify themselves as Anglican and may be but loosely linked to formal church life. It should nevertheless be noted that recent Catholic research has demonstrated that traditional Catholic beliefs in the afterlife are weakening (Hornsby-Smith, 1991, pp. 98–104).

Returning as another

So far, this chapter has not used the word 'reincarnation'. This reflects the fact that in the research currently being discussed we have always focused on the term 'coming back as something or someone else' and found it to be one which has been understood by most of those interviewed. We have assumed that the term reincarnation would pose greater difficulties for some in the general public. We have also reasoned that the term reincarnation tends to be associated with Indian and other Eastern forms of thought, especially that of *karma*. These have no direct significance in non-Indian contexts except perhaps for those who espouse new forms of non-ecclesiastical spirituality. In her research on contemporary British Pagans, Amy Simes has shown that practically all identifying themselves as Pagans accepted a belief in reincarnation (Simes, 1995, p. 376). Steve Bruce has also drawn attention to the acceptance of reincarnation ideas by those in New Age circles (Bruce, 1996, p. 212).

The Davies and Shaw study of 1995 showed that of the 1603 asked, some 195 (12 per cent) said that returning again as something else expressed something of their own view. Of those claiming a religious adherence some 14 per cent of Church of England people opted for it, 11 per cent of Roman Catholics and 6 per cent of Methodists. Amongst the Scots in the sample some 206 belonged to the Presbyterian Church of Scotland. Six per cent of these opted for coming back as something or someone else. Bruce has also cited a study in Belgium showing that 20 per cent of Catholics who attend Mass believe in reincarnation (Bruce, 1996, p. 212).

We may add to this evidence the findings of the earlier study conducted between 1988 and 1990. This involved face to face interviews with some 341 members of the general public and 186 individuals whose names were on the electoral rolls of Anglican parishes in England (Davies, Watkins and Winter, 1991). Of the general public some 56 per cent firmly rejected the idea of coming back in another form, about a fifth were unsure but 12 per cent accepted the idea. This is a direct match in response for the Davies and Shaw study of 1995. As far as those on Church of England registers were concerned, i.e. individuals who can be viewed as more than nominal adherents of the state church, only 4 per cent accepted the notion, some 18 per cent were unsure while 69 per cent were firmly against it (*ibid.*, pp. 256–8).

If we may compare these two surveys – always bearing in mind that the earlier one represents more rural populations while the later was drawn largely from urban areas – an interesting feature emerges. At first glance one might suggest that the more religiously involved persons were less given to ideas of returning to earth than were more nominal adherents. By contrast, the later study hints at general urban Anglican adherents being a little more given to beliefs in reincarnation than the urban public at large.

More research needs to be completed on this issue of transmigration of souls in Western societies, especially to explore the precise dynamics of that belief within an individual's overall network of faith. It may be that ideas of returning as someone or something else are grounded in a variety of experiences including attitudes to nature and family traditions. It may well reflect a sense of being part of a this-worldly system of life and not some other-worldly domain, especially as ideas of nature and ecology enhance the notion of this-worldliness, making it less materialistic than has tended to be the case in traditional sociological analyses. In this sense, such ideas of a return may reflect a kind of religiosity focused on nature which differs both from traditional Christianity and also from Indian notions of the transmigration of souls within the framework of moral causation. All we can say at present is that there appears to be a significant minority of people who seem to accept a view of an afterlife quite contrary to the traditional religious teaching of their historical culture. In fact more opted for this view than for the explicit and traditional dogma of the resurrection.

Gender, belief and experiencing the dead

Another variable which always needs to be considered in relation to religious factors is the sex of respondents. After all, many societies possess a practical division of labour over religion irrespective of their formal theology. Data gathered in the Rural Church Survey (Davies, Watkins and Winter, 1991) show a clear difference between men and women as far as belief in life after death is concerned.

Belief in life after death

Response	Men		Women	
	Number	%	Number	%
Yes	79	38	166	60
No	77	37	46	17
Don't know	51	25	65	23
Total	207	100	277	100

In terms of levels of uncertainty, both men and women were very similar indeed. A sharp difference between them comes in actual belief and actual disbelief in life after death, as the table shows.

This pattern of male and female beliefs in life after death is closely repeated in the 1995 study shown in the following table and published here for the first time.

Belief	Number	Male	Female	Total
Soul passes on	546	37%	63%	100%
Life ends	461	61%	39%	100%
All in God's hands	348	38%	62%	100%
Come back as something	195	37%	63%	100%
Resurrection	126	45%	55%	100%

This shows that of all the 546 people who acknowledged that the soul passed on the great majority (63 per cent) were women. This general proportion of women to men was reflected in all of the other options except that of resurrection where, of the 126 who opted for this position 55 per cent were women and 45 per cent were men. Yet, though the fact of this gender difference can now be regarded as firmly established, we are still far from being able to explain why these differences exist. Tony Walter has suggested a set of social-psychological reasons for the broad spectrum of women's beliefs (Walter, 1994) and Grace Davie has added her own emphasis on the experience women derive from their experience of giving birth as a source of awareness of the mystery of life (Davie, 1994, pp. 118–20). Though there is much truth in their arguments, I think any explanation is likely to be multi-faceted and would add to these another feature, one closely associated with bereavement and which, I think, has much to do with either reinforcing or stimulating belief in an afterlife. It is the phenomenon of sensing the presence of the dead which also demonstrates a female weighting.

Presence of the dead

Though this sense of presence has previously been noted in qualitative terms by, for example, David Hay (1990, p. 47), the Davies and Shaw research has pursued this phenomenon, of individuals who gain some sense of the presence of the dead at some time after a death, more quantitatively (Davies and Shaw, 1995, pp. 96–8; see also Davies, 1993). Though the majority of respondents, 63 per cent of the total, had never had such an experience, this still left a significant minority of approximately 35 per cent who could recall some such moment. The following table, also published here for the first time, is derived from the data of that research and focuses on the significant gender differences.

Gender and sensing the presence of the dead

Sensing a presence	Number	Male	Female	Total
Often	136	17%	83%	100%
Occasionally	218	34%	66%	100%
Rarely	95	35%	65%	100%
Once only	117	33%	67%	100%
Never	1011	55%	45%	100%

This table shows, for example, that of those who said they often experienced the presence of a dead person the great majority were women while only 17 per cent were men. The three categories of occasionally, rarely and once only can easily be combined, revealing a very similar pattern of women having these experiences nearly twice as often as the men.

The important fact in interpreting this material is that those with these experiences say that the presence they feel is that of someone who is a close relative, very often a parent or a spouse. Given that men tend to die before women, more wives lose their husbands than husbands lose their wives. This demographic factor may be significant as a reason why women obtain more of these experiences than men. Women are likely to spend a disproportionate amount of time in the home and this very domestic context is the one in which most people reckon they experience the dead. Demography plus environment may thus serve as additional factors for the female experience of sensing the dead. Emotionally speaking, these experiences are usually reckoned to be positive and moreover, I think, they also reinforce ideas of an afterlife in those who experience them. Thus the disproportionate belief in life after death may be, in some small part at least, due to actual experiences which enhance the belief.

Conclusion

Belief in life after death has been so widespread that no brief account of it can claim to be adequate. Here we have sought simply to document its presence today. We have emphasized the importance of gender differences and the way this item of belief may be related, often in unsuspected ways, to other beliefs, attitudes and religious affiliation.

These are significant matters not only for sociologists of religion but also for those ministers who are engaged in that task of pastoral correlation between the great traditions of theology and the daily attitudes of people at large.

The research described above has implications, both immediate and long-term, for the way in which we conduct funerals. Firstly, it clearly indicates that there are widening varieties of belief among the people sitting in the front pew of the crematorium today. Compared with the widow, the widower is less likely to believe in a Gospel of an afterlife (see Wilcock, in Chapter 12). Compared with the elderly, the middle-aged and younger are less likely to believe in such a Gospel at all. Even the churchgoer may entertain firm ideas about reincarnation or the finality of death.

This information has immediate repercussions for our message, its plausibility and its relevance; and for their hearing, comfort and healing. The content of our sermons, readings, prayers and gestures at funerals is, of course, a less easy matter for clergy who are bound to use set forms of liturgy. The primary way in which we can articulate and express the Christian message so that it speaks to the mourners' condition is by careful and sensitive contact with the mourners beforehand. This will prepare both the congregations and ministers for the funeral.

Prior pastoral contact is more vital than ever before. The result of such preparation will be a funeral perceived by mourners as far more relevant and personal. Funerals must address not only the situation of the bereaved, they must address the situation of the deceased. The more difficulties people have with their beliefs, the more they are concerned for their certainties. I have written elsewhere of clergy presiding at a funeral or at a subsequent disposal of ashes. The Christian tradition at funerals is the 'prospective fulfilment of identity', the traditional belief in a 'resurrection to eternal life in Christ Jesus our Lord' (Davies, 1995). Today's more agnostic people are more certain of the past than the future life. They prefer their funeral ceremonies to concentrate at least as much on the life once lived than a next life only predicted. Hence the increasing habit of the scattering of cremated ashes in a place meaningful to the deceased, like a favourite hillside, woodland or football field.

It may be, of course, that the future of religion in Britain is more fundamentalist than sceptical. Either way, if we may take religious belief as one expression of adaptation to environment, then the environment of death is one of the major fields in which change can be expected as social values alter. If bereaved people are the primary beneficiaries of a funeral, those who conduct funerals must be prepared to minister to a variety of faith positions, whether these merge with or become separated from the official teachings of traditional churches.

References

S. Bruce, *Religion in Modern Britain* (Oxford: Oxford University Press, 1995).
S. Bruce, *Religion in the Modern World: From Cathedrals to Cults* (Oxford: Oxford University Press, 1996).
G. Davie, *Religion in Britain since 1945: Believing without Belonging* (Oxford: Blackwell, 1994).
D. Davies, 'The dead at the eucharist', *Modern Churchman*, new series, vol. XXXIV, no. 3, 1993.
D. Davies, 'The theology of cremation', in P. C. Jupp (ed.), *Clergy and Cremation Today* (London: The Churches' Group on Funeral Services at Cemeteries and Crematoria/The National Funerals College, 1995).

D. Davies and A. Shaw, *Reusing Old Graves: A Report on Popular British Attitudes* (Crayford: Shaw & Sons, 1995).

D. Davies, C. Watkins and M. Winter, *Church and Religion in Rural England* (Edinburgh: T. & T. Clark, 1991).

G. Gorer, *Death, Grief and Mourning in Contemporary Britain* (London: Cresset Press, 1965).

D. Hay, *Religious Experience Today: Studying the Facts* (London: Mowbray, 1990).

M. Hornsby-Smith, *Roman Catholic Beliefs in England: Customary Catholicism and Transformations of Religious Authority* (Cambridge: Cambridge University Press, 1991).

J. Holm and J. Bowker, *Human Nature and Destiny* (London: Pinter, 1994).

E. Kaldestad, 'Questionnaires for belief and morality', *Journal of Empirical Theology*, vol. 5, no. 1, pp. 70–85, 1992.

W. Kay and Leslie J. Francis, 'The young British atheist', *Journal of Empirical Theology*, vol. 8, no. 2, 1995.

MORI Survey for British Humanist Association (London: May 1996).

A. Simes, 'Contemporary Paganism in the East Midlands' (unpublished PhD thesis, University of Nottingham, 1995).

L. E. Sullivan, *Death, Afterlife, and the Soul* (New York: Macmillan, 1987).

T. Walter, *The Revival of Death* (London: Routledge, 1994).

T. Walter, *The Eclipse of Eternity: A Sociology of the Afterlife* (Basingstoke: Macmillan, 1995).

12

Contemporary issues

Tony Rogers, Penelope Wilcock,
Margaret Saunders and Hazel Addy

Introduction

Tony Rogers

A vicar in a rural parish in Norfolk once told me of the 25-year old surviving twin who came in search of the grave of his stillborn brother. No such grave existed, because that stillborn baby would have been placed in the coffin of a totally unrelated adult and no record kept of his whereabouts. That's not a tale from the distant past, but within the lifetime of most readers of this book. It's only in the space of a very few years that the Churches have addressed this issue in their funeral services, and even in the wake of these provisions, it is not unknown for parents who have been through such an experience to be brushed off with a claim that the Church has nothing to offer, and that such families must make their own arrangements.

It's never easy to be selective on contemporary issues. No-one could claim that a brief treatment on non-standard funerals, funerals of children who have died before or close to the time of birth and of AIDS victims, will cover the ground adequately. But it will help bring to the forefront situations which, though not everyday occurrences, are both opportunities for pastoral care or door-closing brush-offs.

We marvelled at the availability and sensitivity of the clergy and people of the Dunblane churches after the tragic shooting of young children and their teacher in 1996. Liverpool's ability to respond so quickly – and so appropriately – to the Hillsborough disaster won the admiration of all. While no-one can predict tragedies of this scale, the experience of each one that is past will in some way raise our expectations for the future, and the churches will look to these as models and patterns for worship and care. These and other more unusual settings for funerals will doubtless be the subject of some future work, but for the moment we offer the following three contributions, all written from the standpoint of clergy close to the pastoral situations of which they speak.

Non-standard funerals
Penelope Wilcock

The funeral is a vital ingredient in the process of separation from the dead. It often is the first point of moving on from the numbness of shock and disbelief into the experience of exploring the re-shaped landscape of life without this companion. Not, of course, that the funeral is a turning point concluding the work of grief; on the contrary, it often allows this work to begin; but it is almost invariably a landmark of significance.

The period of time between the death and the funeral is often experienced as a kind of limbo time, waiting for the funeral to happen, with its formalization of goodbyes. When this period of waiting is extended (maybe awaiting a post-mortem result, or to give time for overseas friends to organize their attendance) it can feel almost unbearable to those who are left behind.

And when it comes, the funeral is a milestone of parting. It is a chance to encapsulate in a brief space of formal ritual the love, pain and grief of those who are left, and the character, life and faith of the one who has gone. Often anticipating it with dread as a harrowing experience, many people are surprised by the uplifting and comforting experience the funeral can be; a time to cherish memories, to celebrate love and to acknowledge this parting with reverence and dignity.

The funerals of those with a definite faith – Christian, Muslim, Jewish or Hindu, for example – will normally be conducted by their religious leaders. There is a small but growing proportion of secular funerals. Meanwhile it has been estimated that 70 per cent of the funerals in England are conducted by Anglican clergy. So, in the case of Christian people, and people who are of no faith or of indeterminate religious views, it is likely that the funeral will be conducted by a Christian minister.

This presents no problems when the deceased and the mourners are also Christian, but when they are not, there is a need for the officiant to consider with care an appropriate approach.

Essentially, a funeral is a rite of passage, a ceremony expressing fundamental human need to grieve and to say goodbye. Even if at the time mourners feel numb and can find no sense of mourning, certainly when for whatever reason there is no funeral, bereaved people are left with unfinished business, and are hindered from moving on. So even people who have no religious faith need a ceremony, a ritual goodbye; such a rite of passage has older and deeper roots than Christianity.

Some Christian ministers see the funeral as an opportunity to preach the Gospel; a chance to present Christian doctrine and the words of Scripture to those who never hear them. Certainly all Christian ministers are used to understanding a funeral as primarily an offering of worship – ' ... grant us grace in the presence of death to worship you ... '.

But many mourners perceive the funeral differently. They may wish to have no Bible readings and no prayers, because they do not interpret life and death in the language of the Church. Or (more frequently) they may feel the need to pray, but in simple and direct expression of their situation, not in reflection of the doctrine and ideology of the Church. And, not infrequently, the mourners look to the officiant to bridge the gap between different ideologies: maybe to find words that will express the spiritual instincts of those mourners who believe, without betraying the atheistic viewpoint of the one who has died.

Most mourners do not feel confident or emotionally composed enough to plan and conduct the funeral service themselves. They need our training in leadership of public ceremony; but even in this largely post-Christian age, there is no other public figure who can fulfil the same role. They also turn to the clergy to fulfil a priestly role, as persons representing mystery and solemnity. Mourners look to clergy to create with words and gestures the reverential space of this solemn goodbye, to lead them competently and with compassion through the scary territory of holy ground, to lay their beloved dead to rest with dignity and tenderness.

Problems commonly arise over the mismatch of the needs of the mourners and the expectations of the minister. If the minister offers nothing but a prayer-book service for the funeral of an agnostic or sceptic, then it does not function as an appropriate memorial. If the minister does not know the mourners, the fact that the service reflects the minister's faith but not the faith of the mourners or the deceased subtracts from the occasion and fails to facilitate the work of grief and parting. Those occasions when the officiant has made no house-call, or appears not to know the name of the dead person, certainly will not commend the words of the prayers and the Scriptures to the mourners, however sincerely the officiant may believe them.

In these days of word processors, it is easy for officiants to keep a large bank of prayers and readings that will enable them, without unrealistic effort, to create a ceremony which is person-centred rather than church-centred. The mourners have paid a fee to engage the service of a public figure professionally trained in conducting funerals: it seems right that these professionals should take care in considering the ideology and the emotional need of those who have hired them.

As for the preaching of the Gospel, there are more ways than one of doing that. The mourners know that the minister is a Christian. And, knowing that, the minister's attitude and behaviour will be his or her loudest sermon, not the words. It is even possible to preach entirely without words, but it is not the Gospel of Christ without humility, gentleness and love.

And when it comes to words, the Gospel can be preached in many languages, even the language of atheism. The blessing concluding the funeral of an atheist might say: 'May the light of truth and integrity shine upon all your roads ahead.' Why should either atheist or Christian have any quarrel with such a blessing? And does not the courtesy of hearing and understanding others' outlook on life, humbly helping them to make their farewells as they, not we, need to do, in itself preach the Gospel?

Some clergy are uneasy with this, feeling that they are denying their religion, asking God to look away for a moment while we pretend God is not there. But perhaps God is abler than we think at communicating with people in their own words. It might help us to understand God not so much as a commodity to be marketed as a Someone to be encountered. We may act with less anxiety too, if we begin to see salvation and faith in terms of the wonder, surprise and uncertainty of growing relationship, rather than the doctrinal position of secured acquiescence. Jesus spoke of a vision of worship offered in spirit and in truth; conformity and submission was never his style – he preferred honesty. Perhaps the professional help of a minister who hears, who understands, who uses his or her skill with words to express the momentousness of the occasion, will do more than reading the prayer book ever can to speak to the people of Christ.

For too long the Church has tried to preach a humble Christ with an attitude of arrogance, demanding that people come to us, speak our words, submit to our constructs. At various stages in our history, we have tried most means to obtain their acquiescence, including threatening souls with hell-fire, and burning the bodies of heretics. In years gone by, those outside the pale of the Church – the bodies of suicides and of stillborn children – were buried outside consecrated ground. Now is our chance to learn our own Gospel, to practise our own doctrines of humbleness and love, to do what Christ did and to be the icon of grace, God who comes where we are, who is with us, who speaks our language, who in his own body makes a path for us to a touching place with the holy.

Peri-natal death
Margaret Saunders

Last autumn we held a remembrance service for bereaved parents in our city centre church. After the service a woman in her sixties came up to thank me. It was the first time, she said, since her baby died forty years ago that she could publicly acknowledge the life of her stillborn child and mourn her loss.

One mother I visited recently told me of her mother's experience when her first child was stillborn over thirty years ago. She never saw her baby, nor even knew whether it was a boy or girl, she did not know what happened to it – or where it might have been buried. This was so she would not be upset! She was not able to talk about any of this until her daughter, in her turn, shared her experience of giving birth to a stillborn baby. It was then that she realized how much she needed to begin to mourn for her own child.

Over the last ten to fifteen years parents, through support groups like the Stillbirth and Neonatal Deaths Society (SANDS), the Miscarriage Association, and Support After Termination for Abnormality (SATFA), have started to share their experiences with one another and to give guidance to the professionals who care for them. Particular attention has been given to the parents whose baby has been miscarried or stillborn. They are helped to spend time with their child and to create the memories that enable grieving to take place. When a child dies at the time of birth his or her mother has little sense of her child's separate identity, and they need time with their baby to help them accept their child as a separate person and so to start to grieve. Midwives now encourage parents to see and hold their baby, to take photographs and to show the baby to all the family.

In my work as chaplain to a hospital with a busy maternity department I am often called in to hold a simple service to name and bless the baby; sometimes parents welcome my suggestion that they ask other members of the family to be there and affirm the significance of their child's life. Some of the many meanings of their loss are identified by Kohner and Henley:

> The loss of a baby is the loss of a person ... the loss of a future. Even a baby lost in the earliest stages of pregnancy may have this significance for parents. Parents may also have invested so much of themselves in their baby that when the baby dies a part of them dies too. Parents who lose their first baby lose their new identity as parents; those who already have children lose an expected new member of their family. (Kohner and Henley, 1991, p. 9)

Parents whose child has lived for some time, either on the Special Care Baby Unit or at home, have had the opportunity to get to know their baby as a person and have memories of their relationship which help them to grieve, and this can be reflected in the funeral service. I remember one very premature baby, Lorna Louise, who lived for three weeks in our Special Care Baby Unit – as her parents said, she lived as long as the daffodils – she was born on Mothering Sunday and died on Easter Day. Although she was very tiny she was alert, wriggly and responsive, and we all hoped against hope that she would survive. I had shared her parents' hopes and fears through those three weeks, and had baptized Lorna one night soon after her birth. I was with them when she died. Her funeral was held at the parish church where her parents had been married, the service taken by their own minister. I gave the address and, because of my involvement in the brief span of her life, could describe Lorna and the love which her parents had been able to give her. Friends and family were there, as witnesses to Lorna's life and to the status of her mother and father as new parents. Their faith provided the context in which they could entrust her into God's care. As we went to her burial on the Chiltern Hills the breeze blew myriads of pink petals across the grave.

Lorna was a baby who had both lived and died; we planned a funeral in thanksgiving for her life, and her parents' faith provided a positive framework for the difficult and painful task of letting go. When I go to see parents whose baby has been miscarried or stillborn I am very aware that they too need a chance to recollect and remember their child and all that he or she has meant to them. Memories make the grieving possible, so I give them the opportunity to talk about their child; the labour and delivery and their feelings at the time of birth. They need to speak too of their anger, guilt and bitterness at what has happened. 'Why me?' and 'Why has God let this happen to me?' are pressing and important questions for which they have no obvious or easy answers. Even when there is a medical reason, and often no medical cause of death can be found, other deeper questions emerge. Kohner and Henley quote June, who learned that her son Philip died after an infection contracted in pregnancy:

> Even if you have logical answers they don't address the real why. Why me? Why now? Why this innocent babe? We were endlessly reassured that it wasn't our fault, but although after long grief-stricken months I have come to accept what happened, to take renewed interest in myself and my career, even to understand how much good came out of the tragedy, I think the search for the answer to that why – the search for the very meaning of life – is a lifetime's work. (Kohner and Henley, 1991, p. 86)

In my working with the parents I try also to help them articulate their hopes for their child, the good memories of pregnancy and their experience of seeing and holding their baby. I may ask to see the photographs. Some young parents are numb with shock, but it is helpful whenever possible to help them speak for themselves and not to be taken over by well-meaning grandparents. It will often take at least two visits to help parents prepare for their baby's funeral. Slowly, they can be encouraged to decide on the shape the funeral should take. They may need help in making the choice between cremation and burial. Burial may be important if parents need a place to return to remember their child. Crematoria are rarely able to ensure that there will be ashes after the cremation of babies lost earlier in pregnancy and parents may need sensitive and informed guidance about this. Susan Hill wrote very movingly of the death of her baby Imogen in her book *Family* (1989). She spoke of the way in which planning the funeral helped her to come to a sense of resolution. They were advised: 'You should make it your service, for your child. It should bear your mark upon it' (Hill, 1989, p. 243).

During the period before the funeral some parents will want to visit their baby each day. They may have chosen clothes for their baby or found a shawl or soft toy to go in the coffin. The funeral will then crucially become the point at which the separation becomes real. One mother said to me: 'I still think she's sleeping – it won't be real until the funeral.' The memories of the funeral are an important bridge; the mother is helped through this painful physical relinquishment of her child by being able to express her continuing love and grief. When I talk through the funeral with the parents it is a natural point to talk about their beliefs about what happens to their baby when the physical connection has been severed. Often they talk about a relative – a grandma or great-grandma in heaven – who will look after the baby. Particularly when they feel angry with God or the Church, it is important to find ways for parents to express their love, hopes and belief for their child and for me to try to find words which can help them to do this.

When a baby has been born dead before 24 weeks gestation there is no legal requirement for a funeral. Many parents are helped by the suggestion that they arrange a burial or cremation for their baby, and they can do this through a local funeral director, who often will keep costs at a minimum. Not all parents wish to do this and hospitals have to ensure that all babies have an appropriate and dignified disposal. Some hospitals make special arrangements for incineration within the hospital but very many hospitals arrange services at the local crematorium or cemetery which parents are invited to attend. Not all parents wish to be there but are glad to know when and where the service is taking place.

Often parents choose their own words, bring flowers, a shawl for their baby. One couple even bought a coffin and carried their baby to the crematorium in their own car. This opportunity to care for and express their feelings for their child is crucial. Leon comments: 'If a mother is able to cherish some aspect of the child she produced her wounded self esteem may begin to heal' (Leon, 1990, p. 45).

Not all parents are able to be as articulate: some need to be cared for and to have words chosen for them. If parents are given the opportunity to be as involved as they wish to be in the funeral, the funeral can provide a containment for their grief and their endeavours to care for their child whom they have loved and from whom they are parted too soon. Clergy and chaplains have a pastoral, liturgical and interpretative role at these critical times.

References

S. Hill, *Family* (London: Penguin, 1989).
N. Kohner and A. Henley, *When a Baby Dies* (London: Pandora Press, 1991).
I. Leon, *When a Baby Dies: Psychotherapy for Pregnancy and Newborn Loss* (New Haven: Yale University Press, 1990).

A pastoral case study
Hazel Addy

I only really got to know John when he was admitted to hospital after a holiday abroad. Previously, he had been a face that had grown familiar at funerals. He lived with an HIV diagnosis and then an AIDS diagnosis for four years. When he died I was devastated and exhausted.

I have changed names and some details, to protect his family.

John had known he was gay since he was thirteen. He told me early on how his parents had responded when he told them. It was then that he started cottaging. When he was about fifteen, he started to bring girlfriends home. No doubt his mother breathed a sigh of relief. Then John started talking about Rita, whom he didn't bring home. In fact, Rita was Nick, with whom it had been love at first sight; they moved in together. Nick was older than John. He had come out of the closet years before. But now, he had to go back in, because John didn't want his parents to know the real nature of this relationship. John loved his mother, and didn't want to hurt her. They were understandably close for John's father had run out on the family when the children were little and had only returned in the last few years.

With the AIDS diagnosis, the facts emerged. John told me initially his parents had accepted his being gay and the AIDS diagnosis. That was not my perception. John's father would tower over me outside John's hospital room, earnestly explaining that homosexuality was a perversion, unnatural and condemned by Scripture. If John hadn't been homosexual, he wouldn't have this disease now. His father was sure what nature intended: our genitalia were made like hands for gloves, our natures were made so that men and women were attracted to one another. We might have had a long conversation about this, but he was the father of a man of 26 who would be dead in a few weeks' time, and I was the only pastor that any of them had.

As I got to know John better, I longed for his parents to be proud of their son. Their heterosexist assumptions had forced John into lying and deceit. In turn, they were lying to neighbours, and even to family, who asked why John was in hospital. So John's parents became isolated with their secret, and from possible support.

Things turned worse for them when John announced he would pretend no longer. John came out to his family. To his friends, he was not ashamed of what he was or of anything that he had done. He had a partner whom he loved. He had friends who affirmed him.

John's HIV diagnosis had proved a turning point in his life. He had believed in political protest and self-help. He had seen how this enabled people to live longer, healthier lives with AIDS. Once he was diagnosed, he educated himself and then set about educating others. He was concerned that people thought if they weren't gay and didn't do drugs they were safe. He became a counsellor and held offices in local support organizations. As an integrated person, John had turned towards other people's needs for care and for justice and they became his holy work.

Sadly, John's parents knew nothing of these commitments until after he died. They didn't know their son. They couldn't celebrate his successes with him. They never talked with him about his friends who died. His new freedom did nothing to change their perspective.

Many people living with HIV or AIDS are more aware than many doctors of the nature of their illness and its treatment. With his own doctor John could speak frankly. This allowed him to turn his attention to dying, but his parents wanted to believe that he had 'just a tummy bug' caught on holiday. In many ways, John was in charge of his own dying but he never wanted to die in hospital. Several weeks before his death, he had begged his parents to take him home. The clinical nurse said that would be possible if there was 24-hour care. No offers were forthcoming, either from his partner or his parents. Two days before he died, there was an argument in the hospital corridor. His parents now insisted that John go home to die at Nick's, and that was what happened.

The funeral was next. Nick rang me to say that he had arranged for us and the parents to meet. John had proposed specific ideas for his funeral, of which I was the guardian. I outlined his choice of music, readings and testimonies from friends. His parents said that, while they meant no disrespect for John's wishes, they couldn't have any mention of AIDS or of his being gay. Other members of the family would be attending and they were unaware.

I had to think of those closest to him: his parents; Nick who had lost his partner; and their many gay friends. These had become John's family when his blood family had turned their back. From Nick his parents heard about the son they never knew. They heard of his commitment to the AIDS/HIV support organizations. In his funeral, I explained, we needed to acknowledge some of these things in order to celebrate John's life. Friends would also want to share their memories.

His parents began to realize how little they knew John. His model of open living challenged them from beyond the grave to risk a degree of openness.

They must have begun their mourning months ago at his bedside. I felt they had now begun to mourn the death of a son they had not previously known, a son about whom such positive stories could be told.

At the funeral, John's adopted family rallied round his blood family with expressions of sympathy and friendship which they accepted. There was hardly a dry eye in the crematorium as the coffin was carried in, draped in pink balloons. This funeral service had not followed any book. It probably wasn't a proclamation of the Resurrection in the traditional sense. However, the many testimonies to John's life proclaimed that there is life after HIV, and that there will be a world beyond AIDS. This was not the sterile production-line service that people who are not particularly religious expect from the church. The last thing they wanted was to hear religious clichés about Jesus dying for our sins, or easy reassurance about there being life after death. They were deeply spiritual people, searching for a path through their distress as they said goodbye to John.

John's mother said she couldn't believe what wonderful friends her son had. John's father said he'd now thump anyone who dared say anything against him. A transformation had taken place. Had they shaken off some of the stigma? Would there be more honesty, more truthfulness?

This case study illustrates several issues for funerals where AIDS and homosexuality are factors. Firstly, our death-denying culture is challenged by people who, having faced the death of many friends from AIDS, leave detailed instructions for their own funeral. It was one of the many loose ends of his life that John wanted to tie up, and having done so, he felt more at peace. For his friends, the funeral liturgy was a legacy.

Secondly, the relationships with and between those who are most closely bereaved may be difficult. Funerals traditionally focus on the deceased person as a heterosexual family member. If they were gay or lesbian, then a partner or close friend, who may have been more important to the deceased than blood family, may be excluded. Parents and partners, blood relatives and adoptive communities all have relationships which cry out for recognition. The minister must be ready to face a range of emotional responses, anger or shame, vengeance or forgiveness. There may be inner voices pleading both for judgement and forgiveness. These may all have changed direction during the period preceding death.

Thirdly, involvement in funerals like John's challenges us to meet the best expectations of both the dead and the bereaved, and demands our best pastoral skills. Careful listening is more important than talking. Most important, however, is openness to the possibility that, at a funeral, people with no theological or liturgical training may actually be better placed than we are to know how to say goodbye to their friend.

Fourthly, what theology and beliefs are incarnate in John's story? Most of John's family and community would not describe themselves as practising Christians. However, particularly within John's gay community, there is a deep spirituality. Theology written from a gay perspective invites recognition of the gay community as a community of resurrection faith, having more in common with the communities out of which the Scriptures grew than mainstream religious society. John overcame homophobic oppression to live a life marked by a belief that nothing could separate him from his own integrity or from the love of God: that there is life beyond oppression, beyond HIV, AIDS or death. John's belief was expressed in a commitment to justice, which we would recognize as being Gospel. The pink balloon, with its associations of torture, prejudice, death and celebration, functions as the Cross might for Christians, had we not lost sight of the horror of it all.

Lastly, how far is the church – its ministry, theology and ritual – a better agent of reconciliation in this second decade of AIDS? All funeral ceremonies must address the problems raised by the specific death as well as the challenges raised by human mortality in general. The better we can work creatively with all the conflicting demands of an AIDS funeral, the more we can make funerals a positive factor in helping people come to terms with all their losses.

Liturgy and its context

13

Anglican funeral rites today and tomorrow

Michael Perham

To write in the late 1990s about Anglican funeral liturgy is a difficult task. It is difficult because the Church of England has embarked upon, but not brought to fruition, a revision of its contemporary funeral liturgy found in the Alternative Service Book of 1980. It is also difficult because the indications are that, in a normally fairly law-abiding church, those who lead worship depart from the legal provisions when conducting funerals more than on any other liturgical occasion. There is much pastorally-driven doing of 'one's own thing' by clergy at funerals. It is easy to understand why. The provision in both the Book of Common Prayer and the Alternative Service Book (ASB) is light years away from where most mourners are. And Anglican mourners are a particularly diverse bunch because of the Church of England's historical role, by virtue of being an established church, as the provider of funerals for men and women of little faith, nominal faith and even none.

The rite in the Book of Common Prayer is a simple and austere rite. Just as it stands, it is probably rarely used, and when people ask for 'the old service' they tend to be asking for something in the style of the 1928 rite, later legalized as Series 1 in 1966. The austerity of the Prayer Book rite owes much to the theological controversy of the age out of which it came. The burial office was only a part, and not the most significant part, of the rites for the disposal of the dead in the medieval church, for at the heart of these rites was the Requiem Mass, removed for doctrinal reasons, together with all prayers that prayed for the dead. The Prayer Book rite, not very different from its 1552 predecessor in Thomas Cranmer's second Prayer Book, is not much more than a procession with Sentences, the recitation of Psalms 39 and 90, the reading of much of 1 Corinthians 15, and the Committal and a few prayers at the graveside (Rowell, 1977, pp. 84–93).

The 'old service' received fresh treatment in the proposed Prayer Book of 1928, when a very different theological and social climate existed, influenced deeply by the First World War only a few years before, with its huge waste of human life and all the consequent sense of loss and grief (Wilkinson, 1978). The 1928 service introduced alternative psalms and readings and new prayers, some more positive in tone and more than one of them expressing the belief that Christians could legitimately pray for the dead, or at least for 'the faithful departed'. Long before its authorization in 1967, it established itself as the normal rite and its use has continued beyond the introduction of the Alternative Service Book. The abiding popularity of this service is no doubt partly because of the poverty of the 1980 rite, but also because the fine and resonant language of the Prayer Book, even when not entirely understood, has sufficient gravity to 'carry' the deep emotions people bring to funerals. Part of the honouring of the dead is in commending them to God in words that carry authority and give the occasion dignity.

The funeral rite in the Alternative Service Book accepted, without much question, the basic liturgical shape it inherited. Sentences of Scripture lead to psalmody. Psalmody leads to prayer. Prayer includes Commendation (of the person) and Committal (of the body) (Jasper and Bradshaw, 1986, pp. 396–409). One innovation is the use of verses of the Te Deum. Another is a prayer near the beginning after the Sentences, and that idea was well intentioned, for the old rite lacked an opening prayer that set the tone right at the start, but the choice of prayer was wrong. Transposed from its position in 1928 near the end of the rite to this position at the beginning it reads:

> Heavenly Father,
> in your Son Jesus Christ
> you have given us a true faith and a sure hope.
> Strengthen this faith and hope in us all our days,
> that we may live as those who believe in
>   the communion of saints,
>   the forgiveness of sins,
>   and the resurrection to eternal life;
> through your Son Jesus Christ our Lord.
> (ASB, 1980, p. 308)

This is an inappropriate text at the beginning of the service. The task of the minister may be to lead the people to this expression of faith at the end of the service, but at the beginning prayers must arise from where people are, fragile, worried whether they will cope with the next half hour, let alone life for years ahead.

The language of the 1980 rite is, of course, more immediately accessible, but what it gains in intelligibility it loses in dignity and resonance. It also marks a just perceptible theological shift, a slightly more confident celebration of the death of the Christian in relation to the resurrection of the Lord, and reflects a 1970s attempt to find a way through the doctrinal difficulties surrounding prayer for the dead. It has long been a problem for Anglican liturgical revisers in England that the Church cannot come to one mind on praying for those who have died. Although mainstream Anglican theology would be suspicious of any sense that the dead rely on our prayers, most Anglicans are happy to pray for the departed, or at least for the Christian departed. There is, however, a significant minority that believes this contrary to Scripture.

Difficulty with prayer for the departed is a peculiarly Anglican problem. In the Roman Catholic Church it is taken for granted. In the Free Churches, though there may be little provision for it in liturgical texts, it is a not a matter that arouses fierce debate. In the Church of England it has done so and texts brought to the synod for approval are scrutinized for any shift in doctrinal emphasis. Any discussion begins, of course, from Scripture. The difficulty is that Scripture is not much interested in the subject. The early Christians lived with the expectation of the imminent end of all things. The issue of the state of the departed before the final consummation was an academic one, and there was too much to do in preaching the gospel and saving the world to stop to address it. But the emphasis on the imminent end contained an essentially social approach to life after death: the judgement would be communal and universal. There was little thought of an individual moment of judgement. Each individual would be judged for his or her own deeds, but only within the context of the consummation of all things.

Here is the root of the contemporary problem. Within a theological framework that has a much weaker view of the *eschaton* and where in any case it seems delayed indefinitely, does the individual come to the judgement seat of God at the moment of his or her own death or is there a provisionality about everything until the end? Interestingly both Catholic and Reformed theology have tended to go with the former yet, to be truthful, Scripture, inasmuch as it has a single and systematic view, tends to the latter. Classic Protestant theology within Anglicanism believes that prayer for the dead is improper because at the moment of death eternal destiny, for better or worse, has been decided. Classic Catholic theology permits prayer for the dead, indeed urges it, because the departed one, judged at death worthy of salvation but in need of purgation to be fit for heaven, may properly be supported by the prayers of those on earth. But both are working from a model that sees death as the key moment and both play down that corporate consummation to which the New Testament writers looked forward.

These writers were also more interested in the unity of all things in Christ than drawing distinctions between categories of people. There was a sense of communion and fellowship, and death was almost an irrelevance to that. Although some prayer for the dead does sometimes betray signs both of anxiety about the eternal destiny of the departed and also of a desire to influence God or to change his mind, at its best it is much more about this sense of communion and fellowship unbroken by death. What is more natural than to share with God one's love and care for one's departed family and friends? And who is to say that remembering and thanking can suddenly be turned into an improper sort of prayer? In the end praying for the dead is more about affection than influence. Protestant Christians have misunderstood others when they think we are trying to change God's mind or even to know more than we can. Bishop John Taylor expresses it tellingly in *The Primal Vision*:

> Surely the 'tender bridge' that joins the living and the dead in Christ is prayer. Mutual intercession is the life-blood of the fellowship and what is there in a Christian's death that can possibly check its flow? To ask for the prayers of others in this life, and to know that they rely on mine, does not show any lack of faith in the all-sufficiency of God. Then, in the same faith, let me ask for their prayers still, and offer mine for them, even when death has divided us. They pray for me, I believe, with clearer understanding, but I for them in ignorance, though still with love. And love, not knowledge, is the substance of prayer. (Taylor, 1963, p. 160)

It follows that, whatever the precise words that are used, the mood of prayer for the departed (and on the whole Anglican prayer has been faithful to this) is one of unity ('the whole Church, living and departed', 'one communion and fellowship in the mystical body' of Christ), with a proper agnosticism about the exact conditions or needs of the dead, a sense of the need for divine mercy and forgiveness, a lively faith in the resurrection, a recognition of the 'radical incompleteness' of things until the end of time, and the expression of mutual affection.[1]

The Doctrine Commission produced in 1971, under Bishop Ian Ramsey's chairmanship, an essay with a series of appended texts that tried to find an approach to which all could subscribe in good conscience (Report of the Archbishops' Commission, 1971). Its key text is found in the 1980 rite: 'May God in his infinite love and mercy bring the whole Church, living and departed in the Lord Jesus, to a joyful resurrection and the fulfilment of his eternal kingdom' (ASB, 1980, p. 315).

But the almost inevitable result of this compromise document was to produce texts that were harmlessly bland and carried little conviction. Traditional words about the departed – 'grant them rest', 'have mercy on their souls', 'Give them refreshment, light and peace' – were eschewed. Nothing was said of the dead that was not also said of the living. Whilst the prayers still said more than some wanted to say, they said a good deal less than the majority wanted to articulate in prayers at a funeral. Thus theological dissatisfaction has been one of the factors in the abandonment of legal forms of service by the clergy in developing funeral liturgies.

There remains a more basic difficulty with the official rites, a difficulty that alongside the theological poverty of the texts, has contributed to the abandonment of legal forms. This difficulty lies not in the rites themselves, which stand full square within the historic tradition. It resides in the radical change in the kind of community, if 'community' be the word, that gathers for a funeral. There are occasions, of course, when the funeral is that of a committed Christian, with a church-going family, an articulate Christian faith among the congregation, and all set within the parish church and perhaps within the eucharist. But such occasions are rare indeed, and most funerals have an altogether different set of conditions[2] (see Wilcock in Chapter 12 above).

Whereas in the past, the parish church was the setting for the funeral, today the setting is more likely to be the crematorium or cemetery chapel. Whereas the parish church has associations with a variety of liturgical occasions (not only funerals, but baptisms and weddings, Christmas, Easter and Harvest, to name only the most obvious), the crematorium or cemetery chapel has no associations except with death and funerals.

In the past, the minister at the funeral would, more often than not, have been the parish priest, known to his people, familiar with the deceased and familiar to many of the mourners. Now the chances are that the minister, even if he or she be the parish priest, will not have known the deceased and will be unfamiliar to most of the mourners, except perhaps through one pastoral visit a day or two before the funeral.

In the past, the liturgy itself would have been familiar. Church-going was at least an occasional part of the lives of a great many people and when they went to church what they found was what they expected. There was a bank of liturgical text (much of it hymnody, but certainly including the Lord's Prayer and probably texts like 'Glory be to the Father ... ') that was part of a shared familiarity. Now the vast majority of people share in Christian worship only at weddings and funerals, and even these rarely, and when they do, the service forms they find are unfamiliar and unpredictable. The bank of common texts is very small indeed and the art of community singing almost dead (Martin, 1980). Even the Lord's Prayer, 'in the traditional version' as the minister may put it, can prove a challenge without the text in front of the congregation. Beyond that there is now the desire for the customized or personalized service. Though some want nothing more (or less) than the official rite (probably 'the old service'), which they see as decent, proper and appropriate, others are more interested in a service that reflects the personality of the deceased than one that allows the Church's liturgy to carry all their emotions.

In the past the faith proclaimed in the service would have been known. People may well have had some odd ideas about Christian belief on death and resurrection and the life of heaven. Heaven may have been seen rather too often as a garden, and justification more in terms of works than faith, but there was a basic shared view that there was life beyond death, that Christ had been raised, that the cross was the key to salvation, that the Christian came to judgement trusting the mercy of God. The minister could reasonably assume that set of beliefs or at least a familiarity with it. Now it is not only Christian worship that may be unfamiliar, but the Christian faith itself, and at some funerals only a small minority have any idea what the Church teaches (Davies and Shaw, 1995, pp. 92–6; see also Davies' Chapter 11 above).

In the past the mourners, more often than not, saw the funeral service as but one stage in a series of (mainly shared) experiences that took them through the grieving process. Sudden death is not a new phenomenon, but in the past more people died surrounded by family, visited in illness by friends. Fewer people arrived at a funeral protected from any involvement with the dying and the mourning until that moment. Today the funeral has to carry so much more of their shock or grief. Sometimes there is the guilt felt by family members who lived too far away. Sometimes the death is not real for them until they enter the building and see the coffin. The funeral has to ritualize for them so much more of the taking leave than in the past. Mourners were also a greater support to one another in the past. They knew one another and talked to one another and knew how to comfort one another. Today very often they are strangers to one another, even within families. All they have in common is that in different departments of his or her life they knew the deceased.

What all this adds up to is that today much much more is demanded of the minister and of the liturgy. There is no longer a community that gathers to mourn. There are individuals who need to be drawn into community for a short time to mourn together. There is no longer a shared expectation, faith or culture. The minister needs a liturgy that can provide these and provide them very fast. To do this the minister needs, first of all, a liturgy that binds people together, gives them some sense of direction and a common cause. Without intruding his or her own personality overmuch, the minister needs to be an anchor, a president and a spokesman. A rite is required that allows this to happen.[3]

The liturgy is not likely to begin with the recitation of sentences of Scripture, unintroduced and undiluted, or with a prayer that assumes a developed sense of Christian faith. It will probably need a greeting and an introduction. The minister may be tempted to resort to the spontaneous, but too often that will not carry sufficient weight. A solemn moment calls for texts that carry conviction. The beginning might be along these lines:

We meet in the name of Christ,
who died and was raised
by the glory of the Father.
Grace and mercy be with you all.
We have come here today to honour the memory of *N*.
We give thanks for his/her life and our share in it;
we commend him/her, lovingly and confidently,
to the infinite mercy of God
and into the fellowship of the saints.
We pray for strength and courage in the face of this loss.
Therefore I welcome you into this house of prayer,
that here today you may know the peace of Christ
in communion with all God's faithful servants.

God of all consolation,
whose Son Jesus Christ was moved to tears

at the grave of Lazarus his friend:
look with compassion on your children in our loss;
strengthen in us the gift of faith,
and give to our troubled hearts the light of hope.
We make this prayer in the name of Jesus Christ our Lord.[4]

Such a text (and this one is a preliminary draft Church of England text as at May 1997) begins from Christian conviction but does not demand that people immediately embrace it, recognizes their fragility and invites them to give thanks, to remember and to pray. It makes them welcome and invites them to find peace. Whatever text is adopted, these things need to be spelt out; older rites could afford to take them more for granted.

What other features need to be prominent in a funeral rite for today? There could be a long list. High on it should surely be these five needs:

(a) to proclaim the Christian faith confidently and sensitively;
(b) to give space to remember;
(c) to articulate the sense of sin, guilt and failure;
(d) to recognize that actions speak louder than words;
(e) to identify a moment of farewell or committal.

A Christian funeral cannot be less than that. Individual ministers can use their pastoral good sense to know when a particular text is inappropriate or where something a little different needs to be said, but the liturgy must proclaim the Church's faith in the death and resurrection of Christ, in the communion of saints and in the forgiveness of sins. Indeed it will nearly always be better to let the liturgy do that than to urge it too forcefully in a homily. The formality of liturgical texts allows them to urge the Christian faith on their hearers in a way that is less intrusive, and yet often more effective, than the minister's own words. Strong words and images and confident presidency of the rite are both needed if the funeral is to be a genuine gospel experience. As much as anything an authorized funeral rite preserves objectivity where otherwise personal choices of the deceased, the mourners or the minister might produce more of a memorial meeting than a Christian liturgy.

The need for space to remember is more fundamental than the need to be told a life history. A funeral service has to have the proper blend of the universal and objective with the personal and subjective, but there is an art to be communicated to those who lead funerals that will enable them to say just enough to create an atmosphere in which each can remember in the silence. It does not all have to be told, and the funeral address or prayers that read like a biography will hardly ever create that atmosphere as tellingly as a very few carefully chosen words that set the memory free, followed by silence to let that process develop. Nevertheless those who devise the liturgy need to understand the role of the minister as 'spokesman'. It is a subtle and demanding role, for it involves articulating the words of the gospel, being the spokesman for God and for the Church to the community, and standing just sufficiently apart from it to do that. Yet, at the very same time, to be the spokesman of the community, articulating its thoughts and fears and prayers to God; and that demands a proper identification with the community. The texts and the rituals of the liturgy need to help the minister in that role.

Never is that role more difficult than in helping people to articulate complicated feelings about sin, guilt and failure, linked with the judgement and mercy of God (Walter, 1990, pp. 243–52). A funeral service that has no hint of that darker side is both dishonest and unhelpful.[5] Yet a funeral where the minister tells the mourners either that the deceased was a sinner or that they stand under judgement will often offend, and an opportunity to press home the gospel will be lost. However, people do need to be able to recognize that the departed stands under God's judgement, that there are things to be forgiven. They also need, often, to unburden their own sense of guilt, their angry words, their resentments or, quite simply, their absence when they were needed.

This all found expression in the language of the Book of Common Prayer:

> In the midst of life we are in death: of whom may we seek for succour,
> but of thee, O Lord, who for our sins art justly displeased?
> Yet, O Lord God most holy, O Lord most mighty, O holy and most
> merciful Saviour, deliver us not into the bitter pains of eternal
> death.

The Alternative Service Book retained that text (optionally) and any new funeral rite is likely to do the same. But how are these emphases to be expressed also in a more contemporary idiom? Prayers of Penitence at the funeral might read like this:

> As children of a loving heavenly Father,
> let us seek the forgiveness of God,
> for he is full of gentleness and compassion.

Call to remembrance, O Lord, your compassion,
and your loving kindness,
for they have been from of old.
Lord, have mercy.
Lord, have mercy.

Remember not my sins nor my transgressions;
but according to your mercy think on me.
Christ, have mercy.
Christ, have mercy.

O keep my life, and deliver me,
put me not to shame, for I have put my trust in you.
Lord, have mercy.
Lord, have mercy.

May God our Father forgive us our sins,
and bring us to the eternal joy of his kingdom
where dust and ashes have no dominion. Amen.

And later, in Prayers of Intercession, words like these need a place:

Bring him/her and all who rest in Christ into your kingdom where
there is forgiveness of sins and fullness of joy ... Heal the memories of
hurt and failure. Give us the wisdom and grace to use aright the time
that is left to us on earth, to turn to Christ and follow in his steps in the
way that leads to everlasting life.[6]

All this concerns text. Yet one of the clearest insights of recent thinking
has been the recovery of the need for symbolic action. People need to get up
out of the pews and do something. Where the Church gives them nothing to
do, they will find their own action and, inevitably, it will sometimes be
sentimental and with little symbolic meaning. The flowers thrown into the
grave at the Committal are an example of a growing secular ritual. It is
interesting to compare it with the older, theologically richer symbol, of
throwing dust into the grave. Words, even liturgical words, will always be
inadequate at a funeral. What are we to do?

The Church of England looks likely to follow other churches down the
path of allowing suitable symbols of the life and faith of the departed person
to be placed near the coffin during the service. Such a symbol would be the
person's Bible or a cross, but would the provision also extend to the golf
club, the darts trophy or the teddy bear? It is a difficult area into which to

enter. It is easier to find a place for these very personal symbols if the liturgy itself is strong, Christian and objective, but here pastoral decisions will always be quite hard to make.

But doing is more than simply bringing symbols. The crucial need is to find a way of honouring the body in the coffin. Too often it is all but ignored in the funeral. Of course it is true that, in the end, for the Christian what matters is not the body, but the 'soul' (but see the chapters by Sheppy and Thomas above). Nevertheless it is the body of which we need to take leave and it ought to be a focus at some points in the rite. For Christians the obvious and traditional thing to do is to sprinkle the body with water and thus to make the identification with Christ in his death and resurrection. With words like these:

> With this water we call to mind *N*'s baptism.
> As Christ went through the deep waters of death for us,
> so may he bring *N* and all the redeemed
> to the fullness of the resurrection life[6]

the coffin can be sprinkled, either as it passes the font on entering the church or at the Commendation. It may be done by the minister. Rather better it may be done by members of the family. It gives them something to do, and something rich in Christian meaning. But there is still, in Church of England terms, a suspicion of sprinkling as 'not the kind of thing we do' and some rather patient teaching, beginning with Romans 6, is needed in most communities.

Gathering around the coffin is part of the saying farewell that ought to be a clear feature of the funeral rite. When is that moment to be? There are funerals when it never seems to happen. Every prayer is much of a muchness and there is no moment of farewell. Or, at the family's request, no coffin is lowered or no curtain drawn at the crematorium, or the last sight of the coffin is waving it off at the church door (see Walter's chapter below). Other funerals have too many key moments and, in particular, a double committal, of the body to the fire one day, and of the ashes to the ground some time later (Lampard, 1993). Psychologically, as well as liturgically, there ought to be one moment that expresses quite intensely the taking leave, and it probably involves walking away leaving coffin or ashes behind, not simply waving them off on a journey. For the Christian it is the return to the ground, the much quoted 'earth to earth, ashes to ashes, dust to dust', that is theologically the richest farewell. The rite ought to make that the norm. Committal at a church door or even at the crematorium may be pastoral necessities, but we should work for a rite that at some stage returns the departed to the dust of the ground and gives the mourners an identifiable place to which to come should that later prove helpful to them.

Sometimes this is impossible, or simply not wanted. Indeed, with cremation – where the body is reduced to practically nothing – the churches need a theology of cremation, or else it will always seem a poor substitute for the return to the earth. The significance of Davies' chapter ('Theologies of disposal', above) is because the Church of England encouraged the practice without first developing a theology about it.

The dilemma for the Church of England is that all these considerations call for a much more measured approach to funeral liturgy than can be contained within the fifteen to twenty minutes permitted in the crematorium or cemetery chapel, and a dual approach is now needed to change attitudes. There are many reasons why people opt for a short service in a crematorium – the funeral director advises it, it is cheaper, family mourners are not sure they can cope with anything longer, they would feel hypocritical going into a church they have rarely attended. Sometimes the reason is that previous church funerals have proved no more worthwhile than what they have encountered in the crematorium. Even in the parish church, the crematorium approach has become the norm. This has to be reversed. Parishes and their clergy must be trained to give church funerals a quality all of their own that will make people say: 'That's what I want for me or for my family.' Nevertheless, if the Church of England is to go on ministering to its wider constituency, it must, at the same time, learn to use the twenty-minute funeral slot in a way that serves and satisfies.

In so doing it has to wrestle with its second dilemma, how shall it celebrate the funeral rite for those where faith is hard to detect, whether that be the faith of the deceased or the faith of the mourners. There are those who argue for two orders of service, one for 'Christians', one for others, but that involves a judgement that no pastor would seriously want to make (Wilcock, 1996, and Chapter 12 above). I suspect that the Church must offer a Christian funeral for all and let people appropriate it at the level of which they are capable; the judgement must be left to God. The only possible way forward to provide more than one rite would be a different rite for the unbaptized. It is an objective criterion and one that will apply more often as we move into a society where baptism will be a more deliberate choice than for many generations. The Prayer Book rite, it may be noted, is not to be used with the unbaptized, so this would represent no new departure, though the Prayer Book does not go on to provide an alternative in the way the

Church today would need to do.[7] A church that makes more in funeral liturgy of the relationship between baptism and the death and resurrection both of Christ and of the Christian will find it increasingly difficult to use that rite of those who have not come to baptism.

The need to minister to people at so many stages along the path of Christian discipleship will make it almost impossible for the Church of England to go for a eucharistic norm for funerals even in church. It may adopt a basically eucharistic shape – preparation, liturgy of the word, prayers – but it will not usually be a shape that leads into the eucharistic prayer and the sharing of communion simply because of the kind of culture in which we live. Nevertheless, if it is to offer funeral liturgy that celebrates tellingly the Christian doctrines of the death and resurrection of the Lord and of the communion of saints, the Church will need to give the eucharistic option more prominence, print it as a full service, rather than a table of contents, such as the Alternative Service Book does, and take the opportunity, whenever it is appropriate, to use this form. If it is true that in funeral liturgy actions speak louder than words, the action of the eucharist proclaims deep truths and brings true comfort in a way that no other form can do. Where there is still some theological suspicion of the eucharist as the funeral rite (medieval requiem masses still raising hackles), fresh thinking is needed to lay that ghost to rest.

In an ideal world the Church can offer a series of staged rites to enable people to take leave of their dead and entrust them to the Lord. There can be prayers at home, prayers when the coffin is brought into the church the night before the funeral, a vigil, a eucharist, a main rite, a committal and prayers at points further along, including anniversary rites, each liturgy both reflecting the stage of grieving and also helping to move that process on (see Steel's chapter below). Most funeral ministry is not celebrated in that ideal setting but in one short service. Nevertheless it remains an awesome duty of the Christian Church to help people commend their dead to the mercy of God, a duty charged with potential both for proclaiming the gospel and for revealing the love of Christ. There is a need for well trained and liturgically imaginative ministers, but the rite with which they have to work needs to command their confidence and that of the whole Church.

Notes

1. The question of prayers for the dead is fully discussed in M. F. Perham, *The Communion of Saints* (London: Alcuin Club/SPCK, 1980), pp. 90–114.

2. A survey at York Crematorium in 1993 revealed that in a crematorium which has approximately 2300 cremations a year, 65 per cent had the entire service at the crematorium, 32 per cent had held a pre-committal service elsewhere, 3 per cent had no service. Seventy-nine per cent of services were conducted by Anglican clergy, 8 per cent by Free Church clergy and 5 per cent by Roman Catholic clergy.

3. For another discussion of this area, see M. F. Perham, 'The Funeral Liturgy', in M. F. Perham (ed.), *Towards Liturgy 2000* (London: Alcuin Club/SPCK, 1989).

4. Church of England texts by the Liturgical Commission not yet brought to the General Synod.

5. See E. Duffy, 'An apology for grief, fear and anger' and B. Harbert, 'Whose funeral is it?', in *Priests and People*, vol. 5, no. 11 (November, 1991); and J. Thewlis, 'The difficult funeral – sensitive issues in liturgy', *Theology*, January 1997.

6. Church of England texts by the Liturgical Commission not yet brought to the General Synod.

7. See the rubric at the beginning of the Prayer Book rite: 'Here is to be noted, that the Office ensuing is not to be used for any that die unbaptized, or excommunicate, or have laid violent hands upon themselves.'

References

The Alternative Service Book (ASB), (London: Hodder & Stoughton and other publishers, 1980).

D. Davies and A. Shaw, *Reusing Old Graves: A Report on Popular British Attitudes* (Crayford, Kent: Shaw and Sons, 1995).

R. C. D. Jasper and P. F. Bradshaw, *A Companion to the Alternative Service Book* (London: SPCK, 1986).

J. S. Lampard, 'Theology in ashes: the failure of the Churches to think theologically about cremation', in *Bereavement and Belief* (London: The Churches' Group on Funeral Services at Cemeteries and Crematoria, 1993).

D. A. Martin, *The Breaking of the Image* (Oxford: Blackwell, 1980).

Report of the Archbishops' Commission on Christian Doctrine, *Prayer and the Departed* (London: SPCK, 1971).

D. G. Rowell, *The Liturgy of Christian Burial* (London: Alcuin Club/SPCK, 1977).

J. V. Taylor, *The Primal Vision* (London: SCM Press, 1963).

J. A. Walter, *Funerals and How to Improve Them* (London: Hodder & Stoughton, 1990).

P. Wilcock, *Spiritual Care of Dying and Bereaved People* (especially Ch. 6) (London: SPCK, 1996).

A. Wilkinson, *The Church of England and the First World War* (London: SPCK, 1978, reprinted 1996).

14

Celebrating our journey into Christ: the Roman Catholic *Order of Christian Funerals*

Geoffrey Steel

In the decade following the Second Vatican Ecumenical Council, Latin editions of all the Roman ritual books were revised according to the principles laid down in the Council's Constitution on the Liturgy *Sacrosanctum Concilium* 1963 (hereafter SC).[1] Their translation into the vernacular was urgently required and promptly provided, but pastoral circumstances were changing rapidly and expanding, and the more people experienced the reformed Roman liturgy in English, the more their pastoral and ritual expectations of their liturgy increased. It soon became apparent that a second generation of English language liturgical books was needed. Away from the pressures of initial reform the normative Latin editions could be translated afresh, more original texts composed, and the material arranged in order better to suit diverse pastoral circumstances.[2] The *Order of Christian Funerals* (1990) (hereafter OCF) is the latest in this second generation, and seeks to implement further the Council's reform:

> The rite for the burial of the dead should evidence more clearly the paschal character of Christian death, and should correspond more clearly to the circumstances and traditions found in various regions. (SC, art. 81)

A resource

The OCF is the result of some twenty years' developing pastoral practice, reflection, and heightened appreciation of Christian ritual.[3] Much can be learned from the contents pages, not least that it is a resource rather than one rite to be performed in all circumstances. Rites for children (including infants, the stillborn and miscarried) are set out separately from those for adults and in full, to avoid having too many options in place and to facilitate sensitive and worthy celebration in very difficult pastoral circumstances. One of the richest sections of the OCF contains some 47 prayers for the deceased, addressing all sorts and conditions of person (e.g. a non-Christian married to a Catholic) and circumstance of death (e.g. suicide). There are also fifteen prayers for mourners, over half of them concerned with the death of a child or infant. The majority of these texts are new, composed in English to complement the rather sober tone of the Latin prayers and to supplement the pastoral provisions of the Latin *Ordo*.[4] The following (for a young person) could serve as an illustration:

> Lord God,
> source and destiny of our lives,
> in your loving providence
> you gave us *N.*
> to grow in wisdom, age, and grace.
> Now you have called him/her to yourself.
>
> As we grieve the loss of one so young,
> we seek to understand your purpose.
>
> Draw him/her to yourself
> and give him/her full stature in Christ.
> May he/she stand with all the angels and saints,
> who know your love and praise your saving will.
>
> We ask this through Christ our Lord.
> Amen.   (no. 28, p. 416)

An integral part of all second generation books is the general introduction and the notes prefacing individual rites. In the OCF these offer a rich theological statement of Christian death as a sharing in the paschal mystery of Jesus Christ; they indicate the aim and rationale of funeral rites; give a clear statement of liturgical principles, and apply these into specific areas. But fresh liturgical resources, no matter how well crafted and clearly labelled, also require a shared vision and sense of direction, at least a degree of collaboration, if they are to fulfil their function: worship, praise and thanksgiving to God the author of all life; intercession for the dead; affirmation of the communion of saints; hope and consolation for the living (nos 5–7).

The Second Vatican Council gave renewed value to the ministry of all the baptized. In liturgy, readers and ministers of communion are now evident; in pastoral care, lay people maintain the sick and housebound in communion by bringing them the sacrament of the eucharist, particularly from Sunday Mass. Increasingly, lay people are ministering alongside the priest in caring for someone who is no longer sick but dying, whether at home, in hospital or in a hospice. Pastoral care is needed also for the person's family and friends, and in response parishes are establishing bereavement support groups or training people to help families prepare a funeral.

Such developments provide a firm foundation for building the quality of ministry and participation encouraged throughout the OCF. Just as a parish's depth of commitment to initiating new members is a key indicator of the quality of parish life, the same can also be said for a parish's commitment to caring for its deceased and bereaved members: ' ... when a member of Christ's Body dies, the faithful are called to a ministry of consolation ... ' (no. 8).

In many places this is expressed in the supportive presence of parishioners, fostered by scheduling funeral rites at times that permit as many as possible to attend (no. 11). Within the liturgy, the potential for lay involvement is great and is already flourishing: ushers, readers, ministers of communion, even pallbearers, perhaps a musician and some people to support singing (no. 15). In some places lay people are now being called upon to lead prayers or more formal acts of worship, and the Bishops' Conference of England and Wales is preparing a resource book to assist this valuable ministry.[5]

Integrating ritual support, pastoral care and practical assistance is the over-arching vision of the OCF. This same dynamic runs through *Pastoral Care of the Sick*, where a person is accompanied through sickness to recovery, or through illness to dying and death.[6] The funeral of a Christian is not seen as a liturgy in isolation, but in continuity with the Church's care of the dying person and those surrounding them.

One of the main functions of funeral rites is to facilitate bereavement (nos 4–7), as several chapters in this book intend. This human experience often needs several moments of honouring, at different times and perhaps in different places. Accordingly, the paradigm presented in the OCF is the multi-phase or staged funeral, consisting of a vigil, the funeral liturgy and the committal (hence the title 'order' to indicate a sequence of separate but related rites). This model is based on the ancient Roman practice maintained in the 1969 *Ordo exsequiarum* (no. 42). But in comparison the OCF is less concerned with where rites and prayers are held (home, church, graveyard), and much more concerned with process and sequence. The experience of loss and bereavement is a genuine rite of passage which the multi-phase or staged funeral can truly enable. A key feature of any such passage is the sense of being dislocated from one's usual mode of living, of being at the margins. In this liminal experience, people are more than usually open to the power of rite and symbol; levels of perception and understanding are reached that verbal language alone cannot (no. 21). Liturgy offers people precious opportunities to engage with the whole mystery of human life and death.[7] For this reason, a phased and flexible funeral liturgy is encouraged wherever appropriate, always attentive to the needs of the family and adapted to local custom (no. 50 and *passim*).[8]

This chapter has already drawn attention to the parallel between death and initiation. The rich symbolism of the Roman funeral liturgy holds both together, and the OCF seeks to enhance the echoes of baptism and the mystery of our incorporation into Christ. When the coffin is received at the church door it is sprinkled with blessed or holy water; in church the large Easter candle stands next to it. Members of the family, friends, or parishioners may cover the coffin with a white pall, recalling the robe of baptism, and place on it a visible and real sign of the person's lived faith: a book of the word of God, for instance; their cross, or battered Sunday Missal. At the close of the funeral liturgy the coffin may be incensed (perhaps by the family) in an act of reverence for the body as a temple of the Holy Spirit (nos 35–8). Gestures of leave-taking can be particularly powerful, and opportunities are provided throughout the OCF: signing the forehead of the deceased, laying a hand on the coffin when leaving the church, throwing earth or sprinkling water into the grave. The memory of such actions and symbols will remain long after the minister's words are forgotten, yet the symbols must be truthful and the gestures authentic, lest family and friends be disaffected or further alienated by ritual dishonesty.

Planning and preparation is another valuable means of drawing the bereaved into the funeral and enabling their fuller participation in the liturgy (no. 17). Where they themselves have chosen the Scripture readings, they will not be hearing these in the liturgy as for the first time; where they have chosen among the differently focused prayers, they can feel that they have helped to create the liturgy. Choice of liturgical colour is also open to them, and it may be that the family would like different colours used in different rites:

> White expresses the hope of Easter, the fulfilment of baptism, and the wedding garment necessary for the kingdom. Violet recalls the eschatological expectation of Advent and the Lenten preparation for the paschal mystery. Black is used as a token of mourning, but, in our society, increasingly without the associations of Christian hope.[9]
> (no. 39)

While the funeral is a liturgy of the parish, not simply of the dead person's family and friends, mourners could be invited to undertake liturgical ministry (e.g. proclaiming Scripture, announcing intentions for prayer), bearing in mind that on the day they may be overwrought (no. 15).

Paradigm structure

Roman Catholic funeral practice varies considerably up and down the land. Formal reception of the body into church on the eve of the funeral is still common enough, but recent years have seen an increase in the single service held, not in church, but at the crematorium. In the face of this, the OCF directs attention to the human reality of the funeral as a journey: for the deceased, the mourners, the parish community, and above all as these participate in the Easter journey of Jesus Christ, through passion and death to resurrection and ascension (no. 1). The image is given clearer expression the more the paradigm structure of vigil, funeral and committal can appropriately be followed.

Vigil

This liturgy of the word and of common prayer is envisaged as the principal rite celebrated between the death and the funeral itself. As the first stage of the farewell journey, the mood of the vigil is gentle and supportive. Its focus is the life and lived faith of the one who has died, and its atmosphere one of keeping watch in prayer (nos 74, 82). A key function of this rite is to help the bereaved prepare for the final leave-taking. For this reason it may be held in the home of the deceased, the funeral home, or in another suitable place, for instance the chapel of a hospital or hospice. However, it may also be celebrated in church, possibly with the reception of the body, though this may also take place at the start of the funeral liturgy itself (nos 72–3). Where there is a delay between the death and the funeral, the vigil may be repeated as necessary and adapted to the circumstances (no. 85). It should be noted that ordained presidency is not required for the rites and prayers surrounding the funeral liturgy; the OCF uses 'priest', 'deacon', and 'minister' deliberately (no. 84, for example).

In the family home, the vigil will be intimate and less formal than in church. Family members and friends may feel more able to read scripture, to lead prayers or to take other parts in the service, perhaps reflecting in turn on the scriptures or sharing memories of the one who has died (no. 98).[10] They could arrange the room for prayer, with a Bible and a cross or icon of Christ, with photographs or other mementoes of the dead person, with candles, flowers, etc.; they could be involved in preparing the body of the deceased (no. 20). Neighbours might be invited to attend, especially any who supported the family during the period of sickness and the time of dying. Also, where parishioners exercise a pastoral ministry to the bereaved, one or two may be able to gather and by their prayerful presence show the parish's concern.

The vigil in church, particularly when it begins with the reception of the body, will be a fuller liturgy and can afford an occasion to gather for people who would otherwise be unable to attend the funeral. Such a vigil might also be appropriate when the deceased is very well known, for instance; or, where a high percentage of the congregation at a funeral Mass is likely to be non-communicating, some may prefer to attend a vigil in which they can take a full part. In addition, because it does not require the presence of the body, a vigil may still be held by a parish even when the family themselves do not wish to attend this (additional) service.

Funeral liturgy

This, the community's central ritual act for the deceased, is usually held in church (no. 137). Two forms are provided, a funeral Mass or a funeral liturgy outside Mass; these are accompanied by detailed notes on the rationale and celebration (nos 137–62, 188–93). The church setting and the gathering of the wider community around the family and friends of the dead person help distinguish the mood and atmosphere of the funeral liturgy from those of the vigil. Here, the primary focus shifts to the journey and *transitus* of Jesus Christ into which the deceased has now been drawn (no. 138). Not surprisingly, then, pride of place is given to the funeral Mass (no. 5).

In the eucharistic sacrifice, the Church's celebration of Christ's Passover from death to life, the faith of the baptised in the paschal mystery is renewed and nourished. Their union with Christ and with each other is strengthened: 'Because there is one bread, we who are many, are one body, for we all partake of the one bread.' (1 Corinthians 10.17) (no. 3)

At the same time the OCF acknowledges that, for various reasons, a Mass may not always be the best option (nos 189–90). This sensitive issue is taken up below.

The funeral liturgy begins with the reception of the body, if this has not already occurred. The liturgy of the word (and liturgy of the eucharist) follow the usual pattern and lead into the final commendation and farewell. This concluding element has a dual function. An act of respect by the members of the community for one of its members whom they entrust to God, it also: 'acknowledges the reality of separation and affirms that the community and the deceased, baptised into the one Body, share the same destiny, resurrection on the last day' (no. 155).

There is a distinct change of register at this point, especially following the eucharist. The final commendation, though a simple action like the reception, blends text, gesture, movement, silence, symbol and song (nos 154–8). Often a moment of heightened emotion for the mourners, how it is celebrated, is crucial.

Committal

This third stage of the funeral is the community's final act in caring for the body of its deceased member. The committal is a powerful and often stark expression of the separation of the mourners from the deceased, yet it also marks the transition to a new way of relating with the departed: one of remembrance, thanksgiving, and hope (no. 231). This is reflected in the gentleness of the prayers and comforting tone of the sample introductions. The full significance of the rite is expressed in the action of committal: 'Through this act the community of faith proclaims that the grave or place of interment, once a sign of futility and despair, has been transformed by means of Christ's own death and resurrection into a sign of hope and promise' (no. 224).

The OCF encourages the continued presence of the wider community of faith wherever practicable: 'By their presence and prayer members of the community signify their intention to continue to support the mourners in the time following the funeral' (no. 231). The committal may take place at the grave, the crematorium or at sea (no. 219). The British edition of the OCF provides three forms of the committal rite and each is adapted, to distinguish clearly cremation from burial and to make separate provision for children. In the paradigm pastoral and liturgical setting, the committal is a brief rite following a funeral liturgy in church (chapters 6 and 9 for adults, 16 and 19 for children). In a second, expanded form, the committal is combined with the final commendation to cater for a new gathering of people who were not present at the funeral liturgy itself, for instance where a funeral is held in one part of the country and the committal in another (chapters 7 and 10, 17 and 20). The third form of the committal is the fullest and is provided for the cemetery chapel or crematorium when this is the only funeral liturgy (chapters 8 and 11, 18 and 21). Here the rite comprises reception of the body, liturgy of the word, final commendation, and committal.

Roman Catholics in Britain have begun to opt increasingly for cremation over burial, and so special attention was given it when the British edition of the OCF was being prepared. Even when cremation follows a vigil and funeral Mass, the natural tensions around the committal are often compounded in the crematorium. Tight scheduling requires of the minister extra care and liturgical sensitivity; the building can lack the sense of being a familiar place of worship; the arrangement of the space and the furnishings can make the congregation passive spectators and the presiding minister the sole actor. The OCF addresses these issues and recommends that a simple (even simplified) rite be performed with grace and reverence, rather than a fuller liturgy be rushed in the restricted time allocated (nos 234–9).

As ritual, cremation can lack the opportunity for personal leave-taking naturally afforded by burial: the scattering of earth, the placing of flowers, lingering at the graveside. The OCF has sought to develop a parallel moment in the crematorium by indicating points in the liturgy where mourners could make a gesture of leave-taking, for instance sprinkling the coffin with blessed or holy water (see nos 226, 289, 294 and parallels). In addition, it provides a simple rite for the burial of ashes to help mark the end of business that otherwise might be felt to be unfinished (see Chapter 6, by Davies, and Chapter 17, by Walter).

Flexibility

The paradigm of vigil, funeral liturgy and committal is not invariable and rigid. Even without dropping one or other stage, many combinations of funeral rite are possible to help celebrate a person's journey into Christ. As already noted, the vigil is not tied to church and the reception of the body is not tied to the vigil. Reception can take place as part of the funeral liturgy itself, or the body may be brought to church in advance of the vigil or funeral liturgy.[11]

Three formats suggest themselves (a horizontal line indicates the following or a different day):

```
┌──────────────────────────────────┐
│ vigil                            │
│ ──────────────────────────       │
│ funeral with reception           │
│ committal                        │
└──────────────────────────────────┘

┌──────────────────────────────────┐
│ vigil with reception             │
│ ──────────────────────────       │
│ funeral                          │
│ committal                        │
└──────────────────────────────────┘

┌──────────────────────────────────┐
│ reception                        │
│ vigil                            │
│ ──────────────────────────       │
│ funeral                          │
│ committal                        │
└──────────────────────────────────┘
```

The funeral liturgy is not tied to a particular time of day, and it may be that most mourners are better able to attend an evening service, or that a priest is able to celebrate Mass only in the evening. The following day, a liturgy of the word will lead into the final commendation and rite of committal. A vigil is not precluded by this option, and the reception of the body may take place as above:

```
┌──────────────────────────────────┐
│ vigil                            │
│ ──────────────────────────       │
│ funeral                          │
│ ──────────────────────────       │
│ liturgy of the word              │
│ committal                        │
└──────────────────────────────────┘
```

Since the eucharist is the memorial celebration of Christ's own death and resurrection, a funeral Mass is encouraged. Nonetheless, for any number of sound reasons, it is not always the best option (nos 189–90). In such situations it can be helpful to reassure people that a service outside Mass is still a full Catholic liturgy, not something second rate.[12] A key pastoral and liturgical consideration is what percentage of the likely congregation will be able to take a reasonably full and active part in the eucharistic liturgy; another is that on certain key days of the Church's year a funeral Mass is precluded (no. 189). In addition, when a priest of the parish is not available, the family may prefer to have the funeral presided over by a parish deacon (or a lay leader) known to them, rather than import an unknown priest for the occasion. Nonetheless, when it is not possible or desirable to hold a funeral Mass, the OCF suggests inviting family and friends to a memorial Mass (no. 37). A further two options emerge and, as before, without prejudice to when the reception of the body takes place:

```
vigil
─────────────────

parish Mass
funeral
committal
```

```
vigil
─────────────────

funeral
committal
─────────────────

memorial Mass
```

Supplementary rites

In addition to the core rites of vigil, funeral liturgy and committal, other rites are offered to accompany the bereaved from the moment of death to the vigil. Again, ordained presidency is not required (nos 51–3).

Prayers after death

While the Church would like to accompany its members through all the stages of illness and dying, to be with them at the moment of death, and to support mourners in the period following, it is not unusual for the first contact with a family to be after someone has actually died. This can happen for a variety of reasons, whether sudden or accidental death, or because of the family's alienation from the Church. The OCF provides a model for this first expression of prayer and support for the mourners (chapter 1, p. 23).

Gathering in the presence of the body

Some places maintain the custom of family prayer in the presence of the body. The OCF seeks to encourage this whenever practicable, since it provides a supportive and prayerful setting in which the natural process of bereavement can begin (chapter 1, p. 31). The family's first gathering may happen in a variety of settings: hospital ward or residential care home, chapel of rest or home of the deceased. This model rite has also been found to be of great help when a family gathered before a life-support machine was switched off, and when people were called to a mortuary in the wake of an accident. It has been appreciated, too, by staff in a hospital or residential home who can become close to the person now dead. Emphasis is given to silence, and to gestures of touch and of sprinkling as signs of reverence for the body of the deceased (nos 63, 67, 71).

Gathering of the family and transfer of the body to the church or to the place of committal

This model, a little fuller than the rite previously described, is offered for use with the family and close friends on the day of the funeral, as they gather, perhaps for the first time since the death, and prepare to accompany the body to the church or to the place of committal (chapter 3, p. 71). It may take place, therefore, in the family home or at the funeral home, and is to be adapted to the circumstances. The transfer of the body can be an occasion of great emotion for the mourners: particularly when the procession will lead directly to the place of committal, it marks the beginning of their final separation from the deceased, all the more so if there is a formal closing of the coffin. They can feel a strong sense of support from the presence of one or two parishioners, especially any who have ministered to them or to the deceased, or who have assisted in preparing the funeral liturgy.

Beyond the funeral

The natural process of bereavement is not concluded with the closing of a liturgical book. It may require further moments of honouring over the weeks, months and even years following a funeral. Although the OCF ends with the rite of committal, it envisages maintaining the pastoral, ritual and practical continuum and sustaining the complementarity of lay and ordained ministry (no. 231). In addition to any private devotional practices of commemoration, public expression of ritual care could take one or other of the following forms:

(a) where a parishioner's funeral has taken place elsewhere, a parish could hold a memorial liturgy (perhaps modelled on the vigil);
(b) Evening Prayer for the departed could be held once a month, perhaps in a small chapel or meeting room; people could gather around the paschal candle; the names of those who have died over the intervening weeks could be recited;
(c) a parish could have a book on display listing the names of their dead, as a mark of honour and a visible encouragement to prayer;
(d) anniversaries may be marked with prayer in the home;[13]
(e) November affords an obvious opportunity for a liturgy of the word, memorial eucharist or other act of worship to commemorate all parishioners who have died over the previous year, those buried in a particular cemetery or perhaps all whose ashes are interred in a parish garden of remembrance.

The work of the people

The OCF is a rich resource, but for the liturgical reform of the Second Vatican Council truly to be implemented, more is required than publishing. The vision out of which it was created needs taking to heart; the implications for pastoral service and liturgical ministry need exploring; the flexibility and opportunities afforded by the OCF need presenting clearly and with enthusiasm. Prominent in our reflection must be the integrated weave of pastoral care, ritual support and practical assistance. In this context the rationale, structure and movement of the Church's funeral rites can be explored and brought to life: worship, praise and thanksgiving to God; intercession for the dead; affirmation of the communion of saints, hope and consolation for the living (nos 5–7).

A major challenge to the churches is to reclaim the dying and death of a Christian. People need to feel that ritual worship is theirs, personally and corporately. The more our parishes can accomplish in this area, the more the *Order of Christian Funerals* will help realize the great vision of the Second Vatican Council: funeral liturgy that will 'evidence more clearly the paschal character of Christian death' (SC, art. 81) and truly celebrate our journey into Christ.

Notes

1. See International Commission on English in the Liturgy (ICEL) (ed.) *Documents on the Liturgy 1963–1979: Conciliar, Papal, and Curial Texts* (Collegeville, MN: Liturgical Press, 1982).
2. In this case the normative Latin edition is *Ordo exsequiarum* (Vatican City, 1969).
3. ICEL and Bishops' Conference of England and Wales Liturgy Office (eds), *Order of Christian Funerals* (London: Geoffrey Chapman, 1990). All references in this essay are to this edition, authorized for use in England and Wales, and Scotland.
4. For a discussion of the original texts see Michael Hodgetts, 'Revising the Order of Christian Funerals', in Peter C. Finn and James M. Schellman (eds), *Shaping English Liturgy* (Washington DC: Pastoral Press, 1990), pp. 199–217.
5. *In Sure and Certain Hope: Rites and Prayers from the Order of Christian Funerals for the use of lay-leaders*, will combine the commendation of the dying from the official collection for the sick and the dying, *Pastoral Care of the Sick* (London: Geoffrey Chapman, 1982), with the opening chapters from the OCF. It will also include supplementary devotional material. An accompanying booklet will contain the Scripture readings for funerals together with the key presidential texts, and introductory notes will facilitate planning a funeral. (I am grateful to the Bishops' Conference Liturgy Office for allowing me to use here material I helped prepare for these publications.)
6. See *Pastoral Care of the Sick*, no. 33. The same model of process is displayed when an adult is brought step by step over a period of time into membership of the church, see *Order (Rite) of Christian Initiation of Adults* (London: Geoffrey Chapman, 1985). Something similar has been developed in the *Order of Christian Marriage*, now approved by the Bishops' Conference of England and Wales and, at the time of writing, awaiting the *approbatio* of the Holy See.
7. See, for instance, Roger Grainger, *The Language of the Rite* (London: Darton, Longman and Todd, 1974), and *The Message of the Rite: The Significance of Christian Rites of Passage* (Cambridge: Lutterworth, 1988). In this collection, see Paul Sheppy and John Heywood Thomas.
8. Within any one parish, of course, there could be more than one 'local custom': Irish and West Indian, for example.

9. Particularly when the person had suffered greatly before death, another option might be red, as used for the Good Friday celebration of the Lord's Passion.
10. Whether rites are held at home or in church, the OCF provides opportunities for someone to speak in remembrance of the dead person.
11. A simple rite of reception is given in the OCF, chapter 3, p. 63. Perhaps its most obvious use is to avoid undertakers working out of hours.
12. This very point is made by the bishops in their *Revised Directory on Mixed Marriages*, art. 9, p. 26 (London: Catholic Truth Society, 1990).
13. The Roman Catholic collection for the use of lay-leaders will include model forms of prayer to mark an anniversary.

15

Funeral liturgies of
the Free Churches

John Lampard

This chapter will examine recent funeral liturgies of the Baptist Union, Black Majority churches, the Methodist Church, the Salvation Army and the United Reformed Church. As there is not space to examine all the major issues which lie behind them,[1] I will concentrate on exploring in particular the shape of the liturgy, the language used, cremation rites and disposal of the ashes.

The Baptist Union

In 1991 the Baptist Union was the first Free Church to produce a service book containing a choice of two funeral services for adults.[2] The first is a 'Funeral service with committal followed later by a service of thanksgiving', while the second is a 'Funeral service ending with or followed by an act of committal'.

The first one reflects the recent discernible trend for funerals of active Christians to end with a church service of thanksgiving, rather than with the 'whimper' of a crematorium committal. However, it reflects the negative side of this trend as the committal is often 'private' for members of the family only, so the majority of mourners do not see the coffin, the stark reminder of the physical nature of death.

Both patterns (as they are called) offer a wide variety of prayer material, traditional, modern or new, to funeral services, such as the Celtic blessing:

Deep peace of the running wave to you:
Deep peace of the flowing air to you:
Deep peace of the quiet earth to you:
Deep peace of the shining stars to you:
Deep peace of the Son of Peace to you.

The liturgy also offers good thanksgiving material and resurrection imagery. The introduction does, however, indicate obliquely something of the problems faced by the Church in a secular age. It says that the material 'can be adapted for use in a variety of situations, including those where the minister feels that the person who has died has shown no discernible Christian faith'.

The order of the first pattern is, Welcome, Sentences, Prayer, Scripture Reading, Brief Address, Prayers and Act of Committal, followed by a fairly free order for a Service of Thanksgiving. Guidance for the sermon says that 'The emphasis will be on thanksgiving for the person's life and on a triumphant proclamation of the resurrection hope'. The service reflects a common shift in new funeral liturgies away from the language of sin and judgement and towards resurrection and thanksgiving. Both patterns encourage extempore prayer, although at all points they offer set prayers.

As far as prayers for the departed are concerned there are two interesting prayers worthy of comment. The second pattern contains the phrase 'And now we bless you that his/her sins are forgiven', which raises the question, at what point did this happen? Is the prayer suggesting that this might have happened after death, possibly as the result of prayers in this service?

The service also contains a truncated and amended version of 'Go forth upon your journey from this world, O Christian soul'. The service has omitted the second part with its references to Mary, the saints and archangels. It is interesting to note that the Baptists, who might be thought to be particularly strong in Reformed opposition to anything that smacks of 'prayers for the departed' can include material which contains both words addressed to the dead person and the imagery of journey, rather than the traditional Protestant emphasis on 'this day in Paradise'. Does this represent a groundswell of change among Baptists generally, or only among its liturgists?

The Baptists have also responded to the growing wish for an appropriate liturgy for disposal of the ashes, offering separate prayers for Interment and Scattering of Ashes. At the committal it is acknowledged that the body will be 'cremated' and, in view of the fact that the majority of funerals use cremation, this option is put first with burial as the second possibility.

Both the funeral services and the later service for the ashes use the word, 'commit', offering the dubious benefit of a double committal. The person who has died is commended to God and the mortal remains to the earth or elements. While it is possible to argue that remains can be committed in two stages (fire and then earth) is it theologically correct to commit to God more than once? It is an issue which awaits a more general theology of cremation which, to date, the Christian churches have failed to produce (Lampard, 1993), but which Davies seeks to stimulate in Chapter 6 above.

The Baptist material also includes helpful guidance and prayer material for use at a 'Memorial Service for a Public Tragedy', 'Sudden or Violent Death', with good material for use after a suicide and after violent death. Although there are suggested prayers, there are no full services for children or stillborn babies.

Black Majority Churches

Comment on the liturgies of Black Majority churches is limited by a lack of written material. Many of the churches are of pentecostal origin and use an extempore liturgy. From limited written material, and anecdotal experience, the following impressionistic summary can be offered.

Black Majority churches have inherited the funeral practices of their Afro-Caribbean origins. The practices associated with mourning contain a mixture of pre-Christian and Christian rites, although the language is fundamentally biblical. On the night before the funeral a wake is frequently held in the home of the principal mourners. In a usually packed room hymns are sung and prayers offered throughout the night. Sometimes the body is flown home to Africa or the West Indies, in which case a parallel wake can be held here, with a photograph of the deceased on a table, surrounded by flowers. Through the frequent use of the telephone the two parts of the same wake, in the two continents, can be kept in touch with each other.

Printed orders of service are frequently produced, with a photograph of the person who has died on the front cover. A typical order of service begins with a congregational song, such as:

Death has no terrors for the blood-bought one,
O glory hallelujah to the Lamb!
The boasted vict'ry of the grave is gone,
O glory hallelujah to the Lamb!

This is followed by the entry into church of the coffin, which is then opened, and an extempore prayer is offered. After Psalm and New Testament readings, eulogies are delivered by the minister and often by others in the congregation. An obituary is sometimes read, the text of which may also be printed in the order of service. One such obituary concludes with the words, 'Written and Read by his devoted daughter – the sentiments of the whole family.' After further singing by the congregation, all members file forward for the Viewing of the Deceased. Some people touch or kiss the body, others stand still for a moment of respect.

Once at the cemetery (cremation is not yet considered an option for members of Black Majority churches – nor for black members of white majority churches), large chunks of earth are thrown into the grave, landing with a loud thud on the coffin as the words of committal are said. After the official ceremony the mourners remain around the grave, singing hymns led by the women, while the sons of the deceased set to work to fill the grave. They may be assisted after a time in this backbreaking work by a local grave digger with a mechanical excavator. A hat is passed round to provide a gift for the grave diggers. The cellophane wrappers, covering displays of cut flowers donated by mourners, are torn off so that the flowers can be strewn on the bare earth, or 'planted' in it. Care is taken to see that no earth remains visible. Covering the earth with fresh flowers evokes a powerful sense of resurrection and a 'change' in the condition of the deceased.

The informal liturgies and rituals of Black Majority churches provide a powerful sense of raw contact with the fact of death, which is both healthy and realistic. They take much longer than their counterparts, the body is visible, it is literally buried, and the family play a physical part in the funeral activities. It will be interesting to observe, in the next generations, whether the Black Majority churches will succumb to the more privatized expressions of grief and mourning of their white neighbours. Or is it too much to hope that the reverse process might take place?

The Methodist Church

It is necessary to examine two sets of funeral liturgies for the Methodist Church, the 1975 Methodist Service Book (MSB)[3] and the 1994 provisional new Orders[4] which await approval in 1998 by the Methodist Conference, the final arbiter of official faith and liturgy. This section is thus a longer one.

The 1975 MSB service (which is now the oldest of the services reviewed in this chapter) reflected a more hopeful and resurrection-oriented approach to death than the earlier Methodist services which were, in the main, deeply influenced by Cranmer and the Church of England 1928 Prayer Book.

The structure of the service follows the Church of England 1928 service. The first section consists of biblical passages to be read during a procession into the church or chapel, a hymn and opening prayers. The remaining sections, which parallel the shape of the Sunday Preaching Service are: The Ministry of the Word; Thanksgiving; Commendation (marked out as a distinctive section for the first time); Committal.

One of the notable aspects of the service is that the basic structure provides opportunity for considerable flexibility. While earlier services have used the word 'may' in their rubrics, this service reflects a developing liturgical trend of offering a 'menu' from which a minister can pick and choose. This is another example of the current trend towards personalized funerals, instead of using the same Cranmerian wording for saint or sinner, old or young.

The chosen opening biblical sentences reflect a desire among the compilers to emphasize a positive approach to death, together with Christian hope and comfort. The opening prayer, adapted from the earlier Methodist 1936 order, skilfully combines pastoral and theological language:

Eternal God, the Lord of life, the conqueror of death, our help in every time of trouble, comfort us who mourn and give us grace, in the presence of death, to worship you, that we may have sure hope of eternal life and be enabled to put our whole trust in your goodness and mercy, through Jesus Christ our Lord. (MSB, 1975: f4)

The next innovation is the use of introductory words to The Ministry of the Word. This introduction is an example of the trend to personalize funerals, offering the opportunity to use the actual names of the person who has died, instead of simply calling him 'brother'. The introductory words set out the purpose of the service: 'We are met in this solemn moment to commend *N* into the hands of Almighty God our Father.'

On the other hand, there is no mention of giving thanks to God for the deceased or of expressing the mourners' grief or pain. The introductory words continue in a vein which can sound inappropriately triumphalist particularly if too much emphasis is put on the word 'Christians':

In the presence of death Christians have sure ground for hope and confidence and even for joy, because the Lord Jesus Christ, who shared our human life and death, was raised again triumphant and lives for evermore. In him his people find eternal life. Let us then in humble trust hear the words of Holy Scripture. (MSB, 1975: f5)

After the Bible reading a Sermon may be preached, and this is followed by a permissive recital of the Apostles' Creed. The next section is headed Thanksgiving, and offers a fine prayer of thanksgiving for Jesus Christ who conquered death and for the 'great company of the faithful whom Christ has brought through death to behold your face in glory, who join with us in worship, prayer and service' (MSB, 1975: f13).

The next prayer in this section is a thanksgiving for all faithful departed servants. It is couched in general terms, with no reference to the person who has died. Experience suggests that ministers may have personalized this prayer to include the names of the deceased and their immediate family. This prayer is followed, after a hymn, by the innovatory words of Commendation: 'Merciful God, you have made us all and given your Son for our redemption. We commend our *brother* (Baptismal name) to your perfect mercy and wisdom, for in you alone we put our trust' (MSB, 1975: f14).

The service then offers a choice of two Words of Committal, following the precedent set in the Anglican 1928 service. The first is an abbreviated form of 'Forasmuch as our *brother* has departed out of this life ... ', ending with the words, 'in sure and certain hope of the resurrection to eternal life through our Lord and Saviour Jesus Christ, to whom be glory for ever and ever' (MSB, 1975: f16).

The alternative Word of Committal is much less hopeful, as is the second one in the 1928 service. With no mention of resurrection it says, after 'dust to dust', 'trusting the infinite mercy of God, in Jesus Christ our Lord' (MSB, 1975: f16). Which should be used and when?

Neither Word of Committal uses either 'soul', which was in the 1936 service, or 'spirit', which was used in one of the prayers in that service. By limiting the biblical imagery about what happens after death, which is a difficult area of belief anyway, the compilers appear to have reduced the options or categories within which mourners can operate, requiring every-one to fit into one theological viewpoint. Thus the service, whilst espousing greater choice of material, limits metaphors for life after death.

Whichever Word of Committal is used, the next prayer asks, 'that when we depart this life we may with this our *brother* be found acceptable to you' (MSB, 1975: f16). Although the congregation may not have asked that the brother might be found acceptable, linking him with its prayer for its members suggests the hope that he is.

This skilful theological fudging has been used since at least 1662. The next, optional, prayer for the departed comes from the 1928 order, 'Father of all we pray for those whom we love'. When the inclusion of this prayer was first proposed in 1971 it was opposed in the Methodist Conference by a leading Conservative Evangelical. He set out the traditional Reformation arguments against prayers for the departed. However, he received little support from the floor of Conference and his amendment to delete the prayer was overwhelmingly defeated.

The service has no liturgy for the disposal of the ashes, whether they are buried or scattered. Indeed General Direction 9 indicated that such a service was really not appropriate:

> When the Words of Committal have already been said, it is not usual to conduct a further service at the time of the disposal of cremated ashes; but there are circumstances in which the minister may consider that such a service is appropriate. On such an occasion a psalm or lesson or both may be read, the ashes deposited or scattered, and prayers said. (MSB, 1975: f2)

There is no indication here that such a service might be pastorally valuable; that it is of Christian or liturgical importance; or that a family might be asked if this is its wish. It is surprising that the question of the disposal of ashes figures so low in the funeral agenda of the church. In her survey among ministers in Sheffield, Jenny Hockey did not raise the matter with them nor, apparently, did they in their interviews with her (Hockey, 1992).

Final, but brief, mention should be made of the burial or cremation of a child. As General Direction 6 makes clear:

> As a matter of principle the same basic form is provided for all occasions. The special variations for the Burial of a Child will be adapted at the minister's discretion according to the child's age and circumstances, bearing in mind the need for the whole service to be comparatively brief. (MSB, 1975: f1)

The service thus offers one additional reading (Mark 10.13–16), and an alternative Committal, which steers a strange route between the alternative words of the two Committals in the adult service: 'Forasmuch as this child is in the care of Almighty God, we therefore ... in sure and certain hope of eternal life, through our Lord Jesus Christ' (MSB, 1975: f20).

The 1994 experimental orders make a radical break from traditional Methodist tradition. They owe more to the Roman Catholic *Order of Christian Funerals*[5] in their shape and contents than they do to traditional Methodist liturgy. There are eight services for use; Prayers in the Home or Hospital after Death; an Office of Commendation; a Vigil; Funeral Service followed by a Thanksgiving Service; Church Service followed by a Committal; Funeral Service for a Child; Service for a Stillborn Child; and a Service of Scattering or Burial of Ashes.

The fact that a number of the services are new to some Methodists means that there may be opposition to some of the innovations. For example, the services suggest the use of a white funeral pall and contain prayers which some will interpret as 'prayers for the dead'. The Office of Commendation is strongly influenced by the service in *Celebrating Common Prayer.*[6] The services cover a wider 'spread' of liturgical material than previous services, and offer material that may supplement what is already offered in an extempore manner by individual ministers. While the main influence has certainly been the Liturgical Movement, the growing number of Afro-Caribbean Methodists may well have influenced the inclusion of the Vigil and formal Prayers in the Home.

But while the format may at first sight look very 'Catholic' the actual words of the services are strongly biblical, in keeping with a Methodist emphasis on scriptural holiness. The two chief funeral services differ in the main by offering a choice of either a committal-thanksgiving service or the more traditional service-committal.

The final service offers a liturgy for the disposal of cremated remains. The introduction reminds mourners that in some Christian traditions (mainly Orthodox) a post-funeral service is held forty days after the death, reflecting the symbolism of death-resurrection-ascension. The fact that Methodists are not alone in introducing a service for the disposal of ashes suggests that there is a developing awareness that cremation by itself does not provide an adequate final disposal.

The experimental services are currently in the process of being revised, in the light of comments received.

The Salvation Army

The funeral service material of the Salvation Army contains three sections. The first and longest section is not a liturgy but general guidance for the officer conducting the service, from which a free order may be created. It states that a Salvationist is 'promoted to Glory' so the ethos should be one of the triumph of faith over sorrow. The evangelical nature of the Salvation Army is emphasized by the direction, 'Every funeral should be regarded as an occasion to challenge the unconverted'. This overt emphasis also challenges the practice of many other Nonconformists who would judge that mourners, in a secular age, should not be 'got at' by a blatant Gospel appeal.

The section also offers sensitive guidance on pastoral relationships with the bereaved, the need to discuss special arrangements and requests and plans for a memorial service. 'The funeral service should seek to combine the formality required by the occasion with the personal touch, spontaneity, freedom and warmth which are the hallmarks of a Salvation Army meeting' (*Salvation Army Ceremonies*, 1989, p. 23). The only liturgical guidance is that the service should include songs, prayer, Scripture, a brief message and may include tributes and musical items.

A distinctive aspect of the funeral is that the coffin should be draped with a Salvation Army flag, with the deceased's cap or bonnet placed on top. White streamers may be attached to another flag which is paraded, but it should not be lowered or placed at half-mast, the traditional secular sign of mourning. The person has, after all, been 'promoted to Glory'.

The second section contains a variety of words of committal, the officer conducting the service making the appropriate choice. They include, 'As God our eternal Father has promoted our brother/sister ... to the home prepared' or 'has received ... unto himself' with concluding words 'in the certainty of the resurrection to eternal life through our Lord Jesus Christ'. The third option, 'allowed to be taken from us', ends with the less certain 'in the certainty of the resurrection and of the eternal wisdom and mercy of God'. In each case the traditional 'earth to earth' is used for burials and 'to the elements' for cremations.

The final section contains prayers and guidance for the funeral of a child (including stillborn and newborn babies) and of a suicide. The prayers are sound, both theologically and pastorally. In the case of a child, the words of committal are 'As this dear child (baby) is now in the loving care of God his/her heavenly Father'. For a suicide a more muted note is sounded, 'As our brother/sister ... has departed this life we now commit ... '. In neither of these cases is there prayer for the person who has died, there are only pastoral prayers for the bereaved.

The final note of guidance has nothing to say about the disposal of the ashes, only that the promotion to Glory of an officer should be notified to headquarters, without delay!

The United Reformed Church

The sub-title of the United Reformed Church (URC) Funeral Service,[8] 'A Service of Witness to the Resurrection' is another example of the way in which modern funeral services are moving away from an emphasis on sorrow and death to one of resurrection hope. Directions in the service include phrases such as 'Sermon on the Christian Hope' rather than the more familiar 'An address may be given', etc. and 'Hymn of Confident Hope'. There is no choice of Commendation, the text assumes that the deceased 'lives for ever in (God's) love and care'.

The prayers draw on the work of other denominations (there are at least two of Janet Morley's prayers and one from the United Methodist Church of the USA among others). This reflects the universal trend of borrowing what is considered to be the best of other churches' traditions, and is not to be condemned.

The service reflects a measure of confusion over the role and nature of Commendation and Committal. Section 8 (entitled 'Prayers of Confident Faith' in the opening synopsis, but only 'Prayers' in the actual section) offers three sub-sections, which are not indicated as different options although the material in them overlaps. They are called 'Commendation of the Departed', 'Thanksgiving, Commendation, and Petition', and 'Commendation, Petition and Intercession'. In fact neither of these latter two sections actually uses the word 'commendation' in the text, while both of them use the word 'commit'. The confusion is compounded by the next section entitled 'The Committal'.

While a dead person can be commended to God a number of times (see the Methodist 'Service of Commendation' for use before a funeral) can there be more than one final committal? This is not a problem when there is a final committal to a grave, but what is the position with a cremation? Although most people go along with the fiction that the final committal takes place in the crematorium chapel, what should then be said over the ashes, if there is a separate service?

The service commits the body to be buried/cremated. The 'Prayer at The Burial or Scattering of Ashes' (contained in the Appendix, there being no separate service for the burial of ashes) commits the ashes 'to the ground' (to their final resting place). While giving thanks 'for all that *A* . . . still means to us', the prayer offers no pastoral prayer for the bereaved as they continue to mourn, and surprisingly makes no further mention of the resurrection hope!

There is no separate service for the funerals of children or stillborn babies, but there are appropriate prayers in the Appendix. The person conducting the funeral has to weave together suitable material from different parts of the service. There is no separate form of Commendation for a child, but there is a separate prayer, which is pastorally sensitive, for a death in 'Particularly Distressing Circumstances'.

The URC services are sensitive to many of the issues that have been discussed in the examination of the liturgies of the other churches. It has been successful in solving some of the problems, but like all the other liturgies examined it has failed to solve others. No one has analysed all the questions, let alone found all the answers.

Conclusion

All the services show the ways in which the Free Churches are engaging with many of the same issues as other denominations. In particular all the services attempt to offer a more 'personal' service, which the minister can adapt and alter, often using a 'menu' of prayers. Several of the services are happy to use prayer material which some would regard as being 'prayers for the departed' and thus traditionally outlawed from the Free Church liturgy. They indicate a marked retreat from the classic Protestant position.

Many of the services introduce specific material for the disposal of ashes, which is a liturgical innovation in the second half of this century. All the services illustrate the struggle going on to interpret death in a way suitable for the age in which they are written. They reflect a general shift from an emphasis on sinfulness, sorrow and judgement, to one of Christian resurrection, hope and thanksgiving. However, this theologically commendable change only highlights a new problem. Increasingly, funerals are for people who have little or no Christian faith, so the gap between the liturgy and the community for which it should speak, is ever wider. No church has yet found a way to speak of sacred things to a secular society which has difficulty in relating to the sacred.

Notes

1. Many of them are picked up by Michael Perham in Chapter 12.
2. Baptist Union of Great Britain, *Patterns and Prayers for Christian Worship: A Guidebook for Worship Leaders* (Oxford: Oxford University Press, 1991).
3. *The Methodist Service Book* (Peterborough: Methodist Publishing House, 1975).
4. *Funeral and Related Services* (Peterborough: Methodist Publishing House, 1994).
5. *Order of Christian Funerals* (London: Geoffrey Chapman, 1990).
6. *Celebrating Common Prayer: A Version of the Daily Office SSF* (London: Mowbray, 1992).
7. *Salvation Army Ceremonies* (London: International Headquarters of the Salvation Army, 1989).
8. *Service Book, The United Reformed Church in the United Kingdom* (Oxford: Oxford University Press, 1989).

References

J. Hockey, *Making the Most of a Funeral* (Richmond-upon-Thames: Cruse-Bereavement Care, 1992).

J. S. Lampard, 'Theology in ashes – the failure of the churches to think theologically about cremation', in *Bereavement and Belief* (London: The Churches' Group on Funeral Services at Cemeteries and Crematoria, 1993).

16

Singing the Lord's song in a strange land

Paul Denyer

Not long ago, I was asked by a local undertaker to officiate at the funeral of a sixteen-year-old joyrider who had died violently when the stolen car in which he was travelling collided head-on with a builder's skip. The boy's mother wanted her son's body to lie in state, in an open coffin in the front room, while the parish priest said prayers, after which the funeral service (no expenses spared) was to be held in church. When I visited the house, great deference was accorded to my ministrations. At the same time, I was informed that, at the church service, there was to be 'none of that f****** God-music'.

This anecdote reveals the arena in which the parish priest can perform today and the way in which funerals are perceived and have to be negotiated by mourners, clergy and undertakers. Divergent beliefs will be encountered by the Christian minister and the choice of music is an area where negotiation and divergence are frequently manifest.

In recent years, an unapologetically consumerist attitude has become apparent amongst the public. If they are paying for the funeral, they are entitled to call the tune. This trend is aided and abetted by the variety and availability of recorded music, which can be reproduced to a high quality on modern, electronic equipment. The result is that, at some funerals, the organ becomes marginalized. While the organ will often 'top and tail' the service, and accompany at least one traditional hymn, there has been an increase in the number of recorded items. As Ruth Gledhill reported in *The Times* (9 April 1996), 'a survey in one local newspaper showed that almost a third of funeral services now include a pop tune, up from only two percent ten years ago'. The *Independent* (27 March 1996) reported that the local council in Hull has employed an extra technician in the city's crematorium to cope with requests for popular music. According to Mr LeNepveu, then Assistant Director of Leisure Services: 'It has created a lot of work, making sure the tapes are set up correctly.' Favourites include Kylie Minogue's 'I should be so lucky', 'Simply the best' by Tina Turner, and – perhaps unwittingly appropriate – 'Smoke gets in your eyes' by the Platters, and Frank Sinatra's highly individualist 'I did it my way', containing the reference to facing 'the final curtain'.

The fragmentation of popular culture has resulted in an almost infinite choice which a minister of even the most catholic taste is likely to find bewildering. As *The Times* leader bluntly put it (9 April 1996): 'There are no real rules, except that the deceased be dead. Requiem Masses by classical composers are but a matter of musical preference.' If the funeral is, for example, of a young person, he or she is likely to be a devotee of a particular musical style, reflected in clothes and hair-styles, which their friends would consider it sacrilegious to ignore or get wrong. Older people may have a favourite, 'classical' tune, but played in a manner and on instruments not considered orthodox by the purist. People identify strongly with music and the way in which it is presented. The local minister, in helping to make choices at a funeral, comes up against not only wide musical variety and loyalties, but also his or her own innate preferences and dislikes.

Before long a minister will become aware of assumptions about 'God-music'. For a significant portion of the non-church-going public, God-music is perceived to be slow, lugubrious, dull and unrhythmic. Lyrics are couched in an antiquated language which may seem alien and irrelevant to the person who has died. It would be wrong, however, to assume that music chosen from a secular source will always be devoid of 'religious' content. The music will often have been chosen with an instinctive feeling for what is suitable to the occasion. Whilst human love is the theme of many popular songs, the lyrics invariably contain reference to eternal themes, such as the power of love to survive and overcome death. People with faith and no faith want and expect the funeral to place their loved one in a more significant and abiding context than the here and now. The finality of death, while it challenges the believer, challenges the unbeliever too. The possibility of eternity stirs in the hearts of every human being, and secular music, no less than sacred music, reflects that possibility. While the priest or minister may not like the choice of music and have doubts about the lyrics, there is usually some aspect that can be taken up and used, even if it is in order to contrast the Church's view with the sentiments expressed in the song.

Undertakers will usually ask the family what hymns, and entrance and exit music, they would like. Where families have little idea what is suitable and expected, the funeral director's office is a safe, unthreatening environment in which to confess their ignorance and seek advice. They may not feel the same about the minister's study. The undertaker will also indicate the reception and range of choice the family can expect if they choose a particular minister.

When the family meet the minister, further signals as to what is considered appropriate and allowable will be given and received. There are issues which the minister and family need to start resolving. What are their respective backgrounds and beliefs? Where these diverge, can each party be trusted to respect and work with the other; or are there going to be misunderstandings and an atmosphere of conflict? Can compromise and agreement be reached over what the funeral is intended to express? The family may want the main focus to be the deceased's life – for the funeral to express a 'retrospective fulfilment of identity'; whereas the minister may want the main focus to be a 'prospective fulfilment of identity in God's good time' (Davies, 1995). Is the hope of everlasting life and the judgement that precedes it to be given unwelcome prominence, whether the family like it or not, or will they be slipped in quietly between admiring references to Bill's runner beans and Mary's crochet work? And is the music to be strictly Wesley and Watts, or will Presley and Pink Floyd be permitted? It is instructive to note that, as recently as the 1930s, church hymnbooks had large sections for use at funerals which reflected the view that the life to come was infinitely preferable to life on earth (Lysons, 1996).

Another practical consideration affects the final choice of music. If there is to be congregational singing, the minister bears in mind that nowadays, many funerals are sparsely attended by mourners whose knowledge of hymnody is limited. It is no good choosing something which nobody knows or can sing. Every minister has experienced the funeral at which five verses of a hymn have been played, each verse at a slightly different volume and tempo, but with no audible accompaniment by the human voice. Crimond, 'The Old Rugged Cross' and 'All Things Bright and Beautiful' may not (in the minister's opinion) be the high ground of religious poetry, but they do have the merit of being well known. There can be as much comfort derived from singing 'The Lord's My Shepherd' as there can be from reciting the traditional words of the Lord's Prayer. It feels 'right' and there is a strong sense that the same words were sung to the same tune at the grand- and great-grandparents' funerals.

About 65 per cent of funerals nowadays are held entirely at the local authority's crematorium, with no preceding church service; even though, as Douglas Davies points out, in their use of stained glass, altars, crosses and candles, most crematoria attempt a church-like sanctity in their design (Davies, 1996). But, however well designed and looked-after the crematorium is (and many are excellent), they can seem alien, non-community centres whose exclusive business is death. For the minister, the environment is familiar. He or she can be seen smiling and casually passing the time of day with the staff. But mourners entering this environment need time to adjust and become acclimatized. A hymn, near the beginning of the ceremony, has the purpose of giving people time to settle and focus on the coffin, the minister and the purpose of their visit. The choice of familiar and undemanding music at this point is a kindness. It will help the rest of the funeral to flow.

Hymns and songs fulfil other, important psychological and social purposes that may, but do not necessarily, have to do with the actual words and melody. The passage of a hymn gives mourners the opportunity to revive their own memories of the deceased and their own thoughts about mortality. Hymns provide welcome spaces within the ceremony where the mourners are not assailed by the spoken word. Music, in its many forms and for all kinds of reasons, can reach the aching void within. It can touch inner sensibilities that are too deep, too inchoate and too painful to be expressed in words. Hymn-singing is a communal activity, with everyone standing up to sing the hymn as one body. Even if some are holding their hymnbooks before expressionless eyes and motionless lips, there is solidarity in the action. 'The Lord's my Shepherd' and 'Guide me, O Thou great Redeemer', sung shoulder to shoulder become anthems of a common humanity and a shared mortality. Music has the power to rouse dormant and helpful feelings which awaken the possibility of optimism and renewal.

When all these considerations have been taken into account and given due weight, the Christian minister may nevertheless feel justified in protesting that he or she is not a cipher, carrying out the wishes of the family and acquiescing to pressure from the undertaker. The minister must be allowed to be proactive. He or she is a Christian. If their ministry is asked for, the public must expect and get a Christian interpretation of the meaning and significance of death in words and music. It is here that serious difficulties can be experienced, especially by the clergy of the Church of England.

Because of their established position, their services are the prerogative of all citizens, whatever their faith or lack of it (see Wilcock in Chapter 12). This link with the unchurched is highly valued by most parish priests; but, in our more demandingly consumerist society, it raises tensions for the minister of tender conscience. Every minister has to draw his or her line. The line will waver, depending on the circumstances of the death and the nature of the mourners; but a line there will almost certainly be, even if more of a guideline than a fixed rubric.

Where does this leave Christian ministry? How are we to 'sing the Lord's song in a strange land'? How are demands that the funeral ceremony be focused on the life of the deceased to be reconciled with the Christian imperative to preach the resurrection Gospel? Even a cursory study reveals a situation of widely divergent belief and expectation as between clergy, family and funeral director. As time goes on, the choice of hymns, songs and recorded music becomes less and less the result of the minister's choice or subject to the minister's veto.

One option is to cut loose from a society that does not respect Christian belief and ministry. If the family want a worldly, sentimental, 'I did it my way' type of funeral, they must seek it elsewhere; but such an attitude alienates, in their hour of need, the very people whom the minister is called to serve. A minister unable to cope with the confusion of thought and feeling which afflicts and characterizes the human condition will end up ministering to no-one. For many clergy, a funeral provides an opportunity not for confrontation, but for the encouragement of the tentative to advance further in their faith.

There is, however, an alternative model, based on the medieval church, in which the nave belonged to the people and the sanctuary to God. The church is one building; but within its walls, two worlds meet. The simplicity and power of this model is that it reflects the contrast but contiguity to be found in every human being's relationship with God. For relationship there is – professed or denied – and that relationship, like all worthwhile relationships, is a struggle. The grieving mother of the joyrider, who opened this chapter, said she had no belief in God; but she was not simply an atheist. She was angry and confused. We all bring our inadequate and broken selves to the altar. As we climb the chancel step we feel, sometimes acutely, the change in altitude – the contrast but contiguity between our terrestrial shabbiness and the heavenly Father who loves and greets us. When a parishioner approaches us as their minister at a time of grief, they bring with them, into the nave, all sorts of worldly baggage. The baggage is a lifetime's accumulation of experience and culture. The musical content of the baggage will often appear banal and unworthy of God's house; but, as I have tried to show, even in the most banal and unworthy offering, there will be intimations of immortality.

It is the Christ-like and redemptive work of the minister to receive that person in the nave and help them towards the sanctuary – the sanctuary where, as St Augustine said, they will find the rest for which their hearts are ever restless. Christian ministry is not to indulge every whim and demand of the grieving family, any more than it is to lay down the law about style and content. The minister's job is more difficult, more creative, more rewarding. In the choice of music there is a profound and particular opportunity to discover the significance of the deceased, their family and the society to which they belonged. The music holds valuable clues about the situation with which we are dealing. The minister is there to pick up the clues, to take musical requests seriously and, where appropriate and possible, to affect and effect choice. The progress is educative: it starts in the nave and leads towards the sanctuary. Occasionally, progress from one to the other will be striking and obvious; frequently it will be imperceptible; sometimes it won't happen. Nevertheless, all human beings are the children of God. They are entitled to enter the nave at the very least, even if they refuse to approach the sanctuary.

The choice of music at funerals has never been greater, more various or so fragmented. It reflects the width, variety and fragmentation of musical styles and presentation in society. The church, with its organ, its Ancient and Modern hymnbook and its robed clergy, has an important, helpful and traditional way of laying the dead to rest and showing the living the doorway to eternal life. For many people – not all of them from the older generation – this continues to be the helpful and acceptable way. But where the choice of music is more idiosyncratic and has a different cultural reference, it is not right or Christian that the first reaction should be shock and disapproval. Many of the tunes attributed to the devil are to be redeemed as God-music.

References

D. Davies, 'The theology of cremation', in P. C. Jupp (ed.) *Clergy and Cremation Today* (London: The Churches' Group on Funeral Services at Cemeteries and Crematoria/The National Funerals College, 1995).
D. Davies, 'The sacred crematorium', *Mortality*, vol. 1, no. 1, 1996.
K. Lysons, 'More on hymns for the funeral', *Funeral Service Journal*, July 1996.

17

Committal in the crematorium: theology, death and architecture

Tony Walter

This book is devoted largely to the spiritual and emotional aspects of death and bereavement. But death is defined by the physical, by a body ceasing to function; and funerals are defined by the need to dispose of that body – no body, no funeral. This chapter looks at some physical aspects of the funeral, especially in the British crematorium. This has been explored before by Bond (1970) and also in Part 4 of my *Funerals – and how to improve them* (1990b); what follows are some reflections since writing that book.[1]

The last farewell

Toward the end of the movie *Out of Africa*, Karen Blixen's lover Dennis unexpectedly dies in a plane crash. The penultimate scene of the movie is his burial, on a hillside in the Kenyan bush. A score or two of people stand around the grave as Blixen womanfully struggles through reading a poem to her dead lover; one wonders how she will get through each verse without breaking down, but she does. She then picks up a handful of dust to be the first to throw it on the grave – but that is the one thing she cannot do. Clutching the dirt, she walks off into the bush, leaving the others to bury Dennis.

This scene reminds us that, whatever else it is, a funeral must dispose of the body. The thud of earth on the coffin, the closing of the crematorium curtains, this is what mourners have come to witness. This moment is the turning point, the moment mourners dread yet are relieved to be over and done with. Afterwards, they must somehow get on with life without the physical presence of the one who has died. It is what a funeral – in contrast to a memorial service, a *Jahrzeit*, a wake, or a requiem mass, a letter of condolence or any other post-death ritual – is about. It is this moment that ends what Turner (1974) has called the liminal period – that betwixt-and-between time during which the deceased is no longer alive but not yet buried.

This moment is never easy. It is the subject of many of the comments people in Britain make about crematorium funerals. 'I can't stand the way the curtains close – it gives me the creeps', 'There's this grinding noise as the coffin slides out of sight', 'It was weird. The last funeral I went to, they just left the coffin there and walked out.' Though nobody enjoys the final moments of a burial, they are not the subject of such widely reported unease as are the final moments in a British crematorium.

For those unfamiliar with British crematoria, there are four main ways in which mourners and coffin part company, depending on the particular crematorium. (Frequency figures come from Davies (1995, p. 20) and refer to 1990. The figures do not total 100 per cent because some crematoria reported more than one form of removal process.):

1. curtains are drawn, or less often a gate is closed, so that the coffin is no longer, or only partly, visible (75 per cent);
2. the coffin descends out of view, in an unconvincing imitation of burial (21 per cent);
3. the coffin itself moves on a system of rollers horizontally out of view (6 per cent);
4. the coffin is left in full view as the congregation files out – typically without passing by the coffin, which is likely to be out of reach and/or nowhere near the way out (17 per cent).

The first three methods are effected automatically, following the minister or officiant pressing a button hidden to the congregation. Possibly because of the mechanical anonymity of these procedures, possibly because of uncertainty as to what happens to the coffin after it has disappeared, an increasing number of mourners are asking for the fourth option.

A glance at practice in continental Europe quickly reveals the missing option. Mechanical removal of the coffin from view seems to be a British innovation, its dissemination confined to Britain and its former colonies. In the crematorium chapels I have observed in the Netherlands, Finland and the USA, the physical layout is similar to a church, with the coffin on a low plinth just in front of the front row of seats. In that position, it is possible – as in a church – for mourners to file past it on their way in and out, which is likely to be by the same door. On their way past, they may touch it for a moment, or several moments, or just pause by it or place flowers or mementoes on it. The final exit is not of the coffin from the mourners but of the mourners from the coffin.

One effect of this was described to me in 1992 by a funeral director from New Zealand who had installed a cremator in his premises and built his own chapel. He specifically rejected the British assumption that the coffin has to disappear from the congregation and modelled his chapel on the American/ European layout. As he explained to me: 'The curtain tells mourners when to leave, but in my chapel they spend as long or as little as they like, and *they* decide.' He has had no problems with mourners clinging to the coffin and refusing to leave; if anything, this is more likely to occur in the British crematorium where a mourner feels that everything is out of his or her hands and their beloved is being removed by soulless machinery.

Burial includes both kinds of removal, of the coffin from the mourners and of the mourners from the coffin. First the coffin begins to disappear as earth and flowers are thrown in and then the mourners move off. As in the New Zealand cremation chapel, the mourners can leave as and when they are ready, not as and when technology dictates. They can pause a while to reflect, to hug fellow mourners, to drop in their own flower after the others have left.

So what is the source of the British automation which dictates exactly when the coffin disappears and exactly when mourners should leave the chapel? I do not know the history of our curtains, gates and rollers, but they are consistent with the secularity of British cremation. All but one of Finland's crematoria were commissioned by and are operated by the Lutheran Church; much the same occurs throughout Scandinavia. Such crematoria were presumably therefore designed by architects who used the church funeral as their basic guide. In the UK, by contrast, some of the early crematoria were private ventures, while the vast majority of the massive post-1945 expansion were local authority initiatives whose motives were practical and financial (Jupp, 1990). The public took to the new crematoria – death now usually occurred in hospital rather than at home and so increasing numbers of people were unaccustomed to dealing with dying, let alone dead, bodies, and increasing numbers wanted much simpler mourning practices than the Victorian excesses with which their parents had been brought up. Crematoria which denied mourners the chance to say their goodbyes were what were built, and to an extent were what people wanted. The addition of a cross to the decor did little to resacralize what is an inherently secular and death-denying interior.[2]

Given the existence of these buildings, what can crematorium managers, funeral directors and clergy do? Firstly, they can explore together how the continental option can be provided within their current chapel. This may simply be a matter of providing a low bier that can be placed at the front of the seating. This may necessitate the removal of a few seats. More problematically, it may entail redesigning the way out at the end of the service.

Secondly, it should become established good practice that when a family ask that 'the coffin just be left there', the funeral director or minister suggest the possibility of filing past the coffin on the way out. I consider it unprofessional if this option is not proffered, indicating a basic lack of understanding of what a funeral is. Either the coffin must depart from the people or the people must depart from the coffin. Is it really in the mourners' interest that it is just be left there while they turn their backs on it and go away?

Flowers

Jupp (1995, p. 86) has argued that acting as though the coffin does not exist is a very Protestant sentiment. He cites the difference in England between Catholic and Anglican practices and reports a Catholic funeral he witnessed in Burgundy: 'Each member of the congregation was encouraged to stand up, walk around the corpse, take the sprinkler and scatter holy water ... Whoever was in that coffin, he was certainly the centre of attention.' I have made similar observations myself. And yet I think something more than Protestantism versus Catholicism is involved here. I say this because Protestant mourners interact much more with the coffin in Scandinavia than they do in Britain, and because the British found little difficulty in interacting with the coffin a few generations ago and – with a little encouragement – find little difficulty today. This may be illustrated by the use of flowers.

In a funeral service I attended in Finland in 1990, there were about a hundred mourners. Each group of family, friends and colleagues came with their floral tribute and, on entering, placed this on a stand. At a particular point in the service, each member of the close family got up in turn, took their flowers and placed them on the coffin. Then a representative from each group of mourners got up and took their flowers and stood facing the family from across the coffin. He or she spoke a few words of tribute (if nervous, reading from a card) and then laid the flowers and card at the side of the coffin. The tribute was thus addressed to both corpse and family. The placing of all the flowers took about fifteen minutes and formed the central part of the ritual.

The Finns, like the British, are a reserved and Protestant people who do not show their emotions freely. The emotional tone of the service was very similar to a British funeral, yet the rather formal giving of the floral tributes provided a way of interacting with the coffin and giving support to the family without in any way threatening the emotional composure of the mourners.

The contrast with the British use of funeral flowers (Walter 1990a, 1996) could not be more stark. The British mourner orders the flowers from the florist, who makes them up and sends them to the funeral director, who places them in the hearse. Often only the family's flowers are taken into the crematorium chapel, the others being put by the funeral director on the patio outside for mourners to look at after the funeral. The British love flowers and love giving flowers. They may take great care in tending the flowers on the graves they are responsible for. Well-wishers throng to place flowers at the scene of a disaster. Yet at funerals the British arrange for their flowers to be given to a stranger who then puts them on the floor! Unlike the Finns, they never actually hand the flowers to the intended recipient – whether this be the corpse or the family. Is it any surprise that more and more Britons, offended by the commercialism and impersonality, put a notice in the paper 'No flowers. Donations to St Luke's Hospital.'

I am not necessarily suggesting that we adopt the Finnish approach – one nation cannot usually adopt another nation's traditions. But readers have responded warmly to one suggestion in *Funerals* (Walter 1990b, pp. 144–6). I gave an example of an English funeral in which the family requested each mourner, or group of mourners, to bring a particular flower that meant a lot to the deceased and at a particular point in the service to come and place it on the coffin. In doing this, they acknowledged the coffin and what it meant; and the giving of a flower says 'I love you'. No speeches, no fancy florists' sprays, no great show of emotion, no religious mumbo-jumbo that only initiates understand. Understated, English, powerful.

The coffin

Why in this book on Christian theology do I emphasize the importance of acknowledging the significance of the coffin and its disposal? Firstly, a funeral that acknowledges the spirit and that acknowledges grief and emotion but that fails to acknowledge the awful reality of the dead body – a body that has hugged its children, made love to its spouse and been nursed through illness – will fail spiritually and emotionally. No matter how perfect the sermon, no matter how sympathetic the minister, nobody will hear the message or feel the sympathy if the entire service is pervaded by a lack of physical reality. If Parkes (1986) is right that the early days of bereavement are often marked by numbness and denial, and Worden (1991) that an important first task of grieving is to accept the reality of the loss, then the dreadful reality of the coffin must be apparent if mourners are to be freed to begin grieving.

Secondly, clergy who preach the resurrection of the body must in their actions make clear that the body has died, for a body that has not died cannot be resurrected (see the chapters by Sheppy and Davies above). Davies (1990, p. 33) suggests that the British crematorium with its denial of the body speaks not of bodily resurrection but of an immortal soul: 'The only hope that many can read into the cremation service is the hope of a surviving soul' – this being the most common British belief about the afterlife (Davies in Chapter 11 above; Walter 1995, pp. 109–12). This belief may underlie the popularity of cremation in Britain; in turn, the crematorium, by ignoring the body and highlighting memory, legitimates the belief. Effective preaching of resurrection must therefore challenge the architectural order of the British crematorium.

Even if the family do not want any of the options I have suggested – still less Orthodox and Caribbean open coffins (see Lampard's chapter above) – the minister can still create a sense of physical reality. Even if no-one in the congregation wants to touch the coffin, the minister can. Simply touching the coffin while reading the committal prayer – having previously arranged for a crematorium official to start the exit sequence – can transform a funeral. The minister is effectively saying: 'You may find it hard acknowledging the physical reality of what has happened. I will do it for you.' That is perfectly in order – remember the grieving Karen Blixen who was better able to handle social and emotional reality than physical reality.

Church, crematorium and crumpets: getting it together

So far, I have looked at the physical layout of British crematorium chapels and how to overcome the problems this causes for anyone wishing the funeral to express certain understandings of death and resurrection. I now will look at problems of space and time caused by the relationship of the crematorium service to other components of the funeral.

If asked to think of a traditional funeral, many English people think of a service in the parish church, followed by a procession to the surrounding churchyard where the burial takes place. I have myself attended two such funerals as a mourner and, though each followed a particularly tragic loss, they had great integrity. Such funerals, however, are far from typical nowadays. First, in the 1850s the Church of England was absolved from responsibility for the dead by Burial Acts which moved urban burials from overcrowded but local churchyards to new edge-of-town cemeteries. Most new urban churches were subsequently built without burial grounds. Second, the 1950s and 1960s saw local authorities building out-of-town crematoria – even less likely to be local than municipal cemeteries. Third, churches in Britain have long since given up reusing old graves, so that even in the countryside the churchyards are full and local residents have to travel to be buried – a situation very different from the rest of Europe where recycling of graves is widely practised and local burial the norm (Walter, 1990b, ch.18; 1995).

I want here to look at the most common situation in Britain, namely cremation. What are the possibilities?

(1) Probably more than half[3] of British (and especially English) cremations involve no other service than that held in the crematorium chapel. That leaves just twenty minutes or so in an unfortunately designed building; it is perhaps not surprising if such ceremonies all too often fail adequately to mark the passing of a human life. Moreover, if, as is likely, the crematorium is not near the home, mourners from out of town may experience considerable strain in finding the building and getting there on time.

(2) Most other cremations[4] in the UK entail a funeral service in a church (or temple or synagogue), followed by a short 'committal' service in the crematorium attended by close family. This pattern is more common in the more religious parts of the UK such as Scotland and Northern Ireland. This can be more satisfactory, since the church is not a special 'death building' but one that is part of everyday life, in which weddings, baptisms and the ongoing worship of God take place. The coffin is accessible to the congregation. If there are graves in the churchyard, the procession in and out reminds mourners that although this death is special to them, death is the universal lot of humankind.

However, linking the two services, church and crematorium, can be problematic. Apart from the liturgical nonsense of two committals, one in church and one in the crematorium (Lampard, 1993), there is the practical question of how to occupy the other mourners while the family is at the crematorium? In my experience in my home city (Bath), the mourners go to the family home for refreshments, only to find that the chief actors, the close family, are not there. For an hour or so we talk to each other, and are just about ready to leave when the family return to an emptying house. It is less than satisfactory. In rural settings where the crematorium may be an hour's journey away, a post funeral reception for everyone is simply impossible.

(3) This impasse has been overcome in the Netherlands, Australia and elsewhere by crematoria that provide refreshments. The entire party can go to the crematorium for the funeral and stay on after for refreshments. This of course requires considerable investment by crematoria in extra facilities, an investment that few if any British crematoria have made. Golders Green, London, has refreshment facilities, but, unlike Amsterdam crematorium, insufficient to enable two or three large parties to be refreshed simultaneously. (Since the refreshments take two or three times longer than the cremation service, two or three reception areas may be needed.) Whether some of the newly privatized British crematoria will go down this route remains to be seen.

(4) Given that this option is not yet routinely available in Britain, what alternatives are there? One is to hold a private cremation the day after the public ceremony, but it might feel strange to have the refreshments before the cremation – like holding the wedding reception before the couple were married! On the other hand, a somewhat similar practice is common in the USA. Inspired perhaps by the Irish wake, a day or two before the funeral the family hold open house in the funeral parlour, offering refreshments to the considerable number who come view the body in the open casket. It would be interesting to know whether the American company, Service Corporation International, is thinking of introducing this facility into its UK operations.

(5) Less radical is an option which is also not uncommon in the USA. This is to hold the private committal one day, to be followed next day by a public memorial service and full reception. I would welcome this being tried more often in the UK to see how both public and professionals respond. Given that all but a few mourners will not have attended the funeral, the focal point of the memorial service should be the casket.

At present, not all funeral directors are prepared for this. I was informed just the other day about someone who died abroad and who for practical reasons was cremated before being returned to England for the funeral. My correspondent wrote:

> I then discovered – I had never thought about it before – that people are never cremated before their funeral services. The undertakers were unable to offer anything even remotely decent in the way of a casket – just grotty little plywood boxes. Luckily, being a skilled woodworker, I was able to make one myself in a very short time, but this option is not open to most people.

Not only would such a service require a decent casket, it would also require a tailor-made liturgy, which as far as I am aware is not yet available in the Church of England.

(6) Another possibility is to eschew the crematorium altogether. Given that (a) the placing of the coffin into the cremator may post-date the committal in the crematorium chapel by several hours; (b) most crematorium chapels are not designed for a proper farewell to the body; and (c) most churches are designed for such a farewell – why not hold the entire service in the church? Afterwards, the entire party may then proceed to the home or a hotel for refreshments. This can work very well, so long as at the end of the church service there is a ritualized exit of the coffin from the mourners and/or of the mourners from the coffin that meets the criteria outlined earlier in this chapter. It must avoid charges of 'committal into the hearse'. In my book (1990b, p. 127) I give an example of a funeral that did this very well, in fact much better than most funerals I have attended in crematorium chapels. Since many churches are designed for ritual procession, this may often be done very effectively.

The objection usually made to this option is that, though it is true mourners are not present when the coffin goes into the cremator, the very fact that the committal takes place in the crematorium is very important. Not to go there is to collude in denial. I can only from my own experience disagree. Whether this option is taken would depend on time constraints, how far the crematorium is from the home, the unpredictability of traffic congestion en route, if and where the family would like refreshments after the service, and so forth. One may respond to the 'denial' charge by providing a post-cremation local service for the local burial of ashes.

(7) Though churches are well suited to funeral services, one other possibility is to use an entirely secular building for the funeral ceremony and for the refreshments. The comparison with weddings is instructive. Approximately half the funerals in Britain consist solely of a few minutes in a bland municipal building – the crematorium. Approximately half the weddings in Britain consist solely of a few minutes in a bland municipal building – the registry office. Many who get married in a registry office would wish for rather more style, but for various reasons either do not want or cannot have a church wedding. A couple of years ago, therefore, the law was amended to enable other places to apply for wedding licences: one may now get married in a hotel, stately home or castle. I do not see why the same option cannot be available for funerals as well.

As far as secular law is concerned, this option has long been available. It is the ecclesiastical law of the Church of England that prohibits the saying of the Anglican funeral service in an unauthorized place. I cannot see why the Church should authorize a thoroughly secular crematorium but not the hotel in which the deceased had his wedding reception twenty years before. There are of course practical arrangements that the hotel or other venue would have to make, such as ensuring that the coffin be kept out of view of regular customers. Other possible venues could be a hospice, or the old people's home in which the deceased spent the last years of their life, or similar institution.

Conclusion

In so far as British funerals are often less than satisfactory it is often because the various elements do not cohere. At a time when mourners desperately need to make sense of things, they are faced with disintegration. The chief players – crematorium staff, undertakers and clergy – may have different agendas and less than excellent working relationships with one another (Naylor, 1991). In this chapter, I have looked at the disintegration that can result not so much from the personnel as from the physical space in which the funeral takes place – the crematorium. Creating a funeral that is Christian, that has a sense of reality and that enables family and other mourners to support one another over food and drink is by no means easy when the crematorium is physically distant from the community in which the family live and worship and when its interior design hides the bodily reality of the event that has occurred. I hope in this chapter to have demonstrated both the importance of these issues, and the various options that can begin to resolve them. Needless to say, such options are possible only when clergy, funeral directors and crematorium staff agree they are desirable and in the interests of those they seek to serve.

Notes

1. This chapter discusses rituals concerning the disposal of the body in the crematorium. A fuller discussion, which space here prevents, would link this with final disposal of the ashes; this would require consideration of anthropological work on the 'double funeral' (Davies, 1990), along with practical (Friar, 1982) and liturgical options.
2. Davies (1996), by contrast, suggests that the more people attend crematoria, the more they invest them with sacred meaning – people have always sacralized places associated with the dead.
3. Two-thirds in a 1993 survey at York Crematorium.
4. One-third in the York survey.

References

P. Bond, 'Architecture for mourning', in G. Cope (ed.) *Dying, Death and Disposal* (London: SPCK, 1970).

D. Davies, *Cremation Today and Tomorrow* (Nottingham: Alcuin/GROW Books, 1990).

D. Davies, *British Crematoria in Public Profile* (Maidstone: Cremation Society of Great Britain, 1995).

D. Davies, 'The sacred crematorium', *Mortality*, vol. 1, no. 1, pp. 83–94, 1996.

D. Davies and A. Shaw, *Reusing Old Graves: A Report on Popular British Attitudes* (Crayford, Kent: Shaw & Sons, 1995).

B. Friar, 'The disposal of cremation ashes', *Journal of the Institute of Burial and Cremation Administration*, vol. 50, no. 2, pp. 43–50, 1982.

P. C. Jupp, *From Dust to Ashes: the Replacement of Burial by Cremation in England 1840–1967* (London: The Congregational Memorial Hall Trust, 1990).

P. C. Jupp, 'Whose funeral is it anyway?', in K. A. G. Elliott (ed.) *Report of the Joint Conference of the Burial and Cremation Authorities* (Swansea: 1995).

J. S. Lampard, 'Theology in ashes: the failure of the churches to think theologically about cremation', in *Bereavement and Belief*. Report of the day conference held at Church House, Westminster on 12 October 1993 (London: The Churches' Group on Funeral Services at Cemeteries and Crematoria, 1993).

M. Naylor, 'Crossed wires, frustrations and conflict in crematoria funerals', in *The Role of a Minister at a Funeral*. Report of the day conference held at Carrs Lane Church Centre, Birmingham, on 20 October 1991 (London: The Churches' Group on Funeral Services at Cemeteries and Crematoria, 1991).

C. M. Parkes, *Bereavement: Studies of Grief in Adult Life* (London: Tavistock, 1986).

V. Turner, *The Ritual Process* (London: Penguin, 1974).

T. Walter (1990a), 'Floral tributes', *Funeral Service Journal*, November, pp. 47–55, 1990.

T. Walter (1990b), *Funerals – and How to Improve Them* (London: Hodder Headline, 1990).

T. Walter, *The Eclipse of Eternity: A Sociology of the Afterlife* (Basingstoke: Macmillan, 1995).

T. Walter, 'Funeral flowers – a response to Drury', *Folklore* 107, pp. 106–7, 1996.

J. W. Worden, *Grief Counselling and Grief Therapy*, 2nd edition (London: Routledge, 1991).

Index

Milton, J.   58
Miscarriage Association, the   147
Moltmann, J.   75, 123, 127–8
mourning wear   6
multicultural society   92–4, 99–100
music   ch.16
Mystery of Salvation   27–8

National Association of Bereavement
    Services   4, 117
National Funerals College   11
neonatal *see* death, peri-natal
New Zealand   205
Niebuhr, R.   61
Nonconformists *see* Free Churches
Nouwen, H.   116

Order of Christian Funerals, The (OCF)   27,
    ch.14 *passim*, 192
Origen   37
Out of Africa (film)   203–4

Pastoral Care of the Sick   173
Pearce, J.   12
penance   21, 165–6
penitence   58
1 Peter   28, 48
population structure, changes in   5
prayer *see* dead, prayers for; funerals, prayers
predestination   24
Prior, L.   70–1
Psalms, Book of   17, 42, 122
punishment, eternal   24–6, 37
purgatory   ch.2 *passim*, 32, 37

Rahner, K.   45–6, 59, 61, 68
Reformation (Protestant)   4, 13, 22–4
reincarnation *see* resurrection, returning as
    another
relationships and identity   79
release   49–50
religious experience   31
resurrection
    of the body   65, 78, 208, ch.11; *see also* body
    hope   ch.2 *passim*, ch.6 *passim*
    of Jesus   115
    returning as another   136–7
revival
    Catholic   25–6
    Evangelical/Methodist   25
rites
    of passage   30–1; *see also* Van Gennep
    purpose of   36, ch.8 *passim*
    staged   168–9, ch.14
ritual   32–3
    and death   33
    flexibility in   178–80
    and funerals   88, ch.8
    and the grief process   88–9
Road Peace   5

sacrament   69, 105, 117–18, 176–80

death and initiation   167–9, 174
    see also Viaticum
Sacrosanctum Concilium (SC)   ch.14
Sadducees   18
2 Samuel   120–1
secularization
    of death   4, 7, 9
    of grace   57
self, the   57–8
separation, rites of   102–4, 144, 166–9
Service Corporation International (SCI)   10
sin   58–9
    sinfulness of man   61
Society for Psychical Research   26
soul   ch.6, ch.11
    belief in   133–4
    and body   70–1
    immortality of   23–5, ch.6, 64–5, 208
    journey of   18–19
Stillbirth and Neonatal Deaths Society
    (SANDS)   5, 147
Support After Termination for Abnormality
    (SATFA)   147
Swinburne, R. W.   43

Taylor, J. V.   127, 160
Teilhard de Chardin, P.   77
Temple, W.   26, 74
theology
    of burial   ch.6
    of cremation   ch.6
Thomas, K.   13
Tillich, I.   60–2, 73ff
Times, The   197–8
transition
    for the bereaved   105–7
    for the deceased   104–5
    rites of   104–7

undertakers *see* funeral directors

Van Gennep   ch.3 *passim*, 48, ch.8 *passim*
Vatican Council, Second   114, 115, 171ff
Viaticum   19
vigil   175–6, 187
violence to corpse   78, 80–1

wake *see* vigil
Wakefield, W. Yorks.   35, 36, 38–9
war *see* First World War
Wheeler, M.   26
Wiesel, E.   123, 128
Winnington Ingram, Bishop A. F.   26
Wittgenstein, L.   63
worship *see* liturgy; rites of passage

Yeats, W. B.   30
Young, M.   7

zoë   44–6

KING ALFRED'S COLLEGE
LIBRARY